What Kids Need

What Kids Need

Today's Best Ideas for Nurturing,
Teaching, and Protecting
Young Children

A CARNEGIE CORPORATION INITIATIVE
*A Decade of Progress
in Early Education*

BEACON PRESS | BOSTON

Beacon Press
25 Beacon Street
Boston, Massachusetts 02108-2892
www.beacon.org

Beacon Press books
are published under the auspices of
the Unitarian Universalist Association of Congregations.

Printed in the United States of America

06 05 04 03 02   8 7 6 5 4 3 2 1

This book is printed on acid-free paper that meets the uncoated
paper ANSI/NISO specifications for permanence as revised in 1992.

Composition by Wilsted & Taylor Publishing Services

Library of Congress Cataloging-in-Publication Data
Shore, Rima.
    What kids need : today's best ideas for nurturing, teaching, and
protecting young children.
        p. cm.
"A Carnegie Corporation initiative: A Decade of Progress in
Early Education."
Includes bibliographical references and index.
    ISBN 0-8070-4128-9 (cloth : alk. paper)
    1. Child development—United States. 2. Child welfare—United States.
3. Parenting—United States. 4. Early childhood education—United
States. 5. Family services—United States. I. Title.
HQ 792.U5 S536 2002
649'.1—dc21

                                                              2002006202

CONTENTS

For centuries, humankind has asked the philosophical question, *What does it mean to be an educated person?* In different eras, it may have seemed that there were different answers to that question, but over time, I think we can say that the concept of an educated person has come to include some steadfast and enduring qualities. An educated individual is surely someone with a sharp intellect and sound judgment; someone who can pierce the darkness of confused and conflicting facts and theories with the light of deft analysis. And surely he or she is someone who understands the lessons of history and the stories it has to tell of society's hunger for power and thirst for dignity and of its condemnation to repeat an eternity of mistakes if the examples of the past are not heeded and absorbed.

I would suggest that today, there are other wellsprings of knowledge that an educated person must be acquainted with: the philosophical yearnings of the Greeks and Romans, for example, as well as the profound beliefs of the world's great religions, including Islam and Hinduism. This person must be someone who has read the scribes of old and the novelists who are reconstructing and deconstructing the language of tomorrow. And this individual must be aware of the divine music composed in the seventeenth century but perhaps equally at home with the popular music streaming out from the clubs in New York City or the pubs of Dublin or the streets of Soweto. As we move through this new century with its complex challenges, some of them thrilling, some of them fraught with danger, and many of them still unknown to us, the age-old question of what it means to be *educated* takes on new layers of possibility along with a growing urgency.

Andrew Carnegie, the founder of Carnegie Corporation of New York, believed deeply in the ability of individuals to lift themselves to heights above the accidental social, economic, and even geographic circumstances of birth and upbringing. His undying faith in the ability of society to improve, to learn, to change, to grow wise, and to use that wisdom well was expressed in the very words he used to describe this ascension, calling it the "sweetness and light" that elevates the conditions of one's life. And Carnegie, who lived out his own version of that American dream-come-to-pass, rising from the position of bobbin boy in a Scottish textile mill to being a multimillionaire living in a New York City mansion, put the great wealth he amassed through his own vision and effort into the service of his beliefs, using his money to found universities, research centers, and institutions of science that would help his fellow humans reach out and grasp a new and better world.

Carnegie also spent a large part of his fortune to help establish libraries throughout the United States, not only to provide resources that would enable people to improve their lot in life, but also, simply, to offer them a chance to learn, to educate themselves. "All knowledge," he said, "is useful," and he believed that with every fiber of his being. To Carnegie, the greatest evil in the world was ignorance. The way to combat it was through knowledge and understanding, and he devoted a great deal of his time and energy, as well as his money, to convey that message to everyone he could, from kings and presidents to workers in factories and on farms.

At Carnegie Corporation of New York, we continue to carry out the work that Andrew Carnegie began, pursuing it in all its forms, through all its dimensions and complexities. Since the Corporation was founded in 1911 with Carnegie himself as the first president, supporting and improving education has been the consistent theme that has informed all the foundation's activities and strategies. And it is perhaps an even more pressing concern today as we consider what it means to be an educated person—what it takes to help a child *become* an educated person—in the multidimensional and increasingly interdependent world of the twenty-first century. There is so much information in this information age, so much to analyze and to master, that clearly, the process of introducing a child to learning and knowledge must begin in the earliest years. And it does, even before we as adults start to help the process along. Education—not as a series of rote lessons but as an extraordinary lifelong journey of understanding—is an experience that belongs even to the smallest infants as they learn to identify their mother's smiling face or the special touch that means the presence of their father's strong hand.

Years of research have awakened us to the fact that babies' brains are not simply a tangled mass of neurons waiting for months, even years to go by before they coalesce into something that human beings call *the mind*. Instead, we must acknowledge that from the moment they are born, babies are equipped with the capacity to absorb information from the world around them— even if at first, it is only tiny bit by tiny bit. And if that is the case, then we also have to acknowledge that education can take place anywhere, at any time, not just in the isolated realm of the academy or in the ivy-covered halls of colleges and universities. Instead, education must be available in all kinds of settings and as early in life as possible because the different stimuli that an infant is exposed to, the way a toddler is nurtured or how a three-year-old's curiosity is challenged, may all contribute to what kind of an educated person that child grows up to be.

For the past decade, Carnegie Corporation of New York has been at the forefront of efforts to understand how children learn. Research, scholarship, and study about how children's early development is affected by their educational experiences are a critical part of our education agenda. We began our quest for this kind of understanding with the belief that first and foremost, children need to be loved and cared for, and that the nurturing they receive long before they are exposed to any kind of formal or even informal schooling will have a significant effect on their ability to perform well in an educational environment. What we learned was even more of a revelation than we had expected. Science, and in particular, neurological studies, have uncovered the fact that infants' brain waves appear to be as active—perhaps even more so—as during any other phase of human development and that even small children are indeed tremendously receptive to all kinds of learning that the developing mind and personality can later build on and enhance. This is critically important because as new thinking and greater skills are required to become a successful participant in an increasingly complex and demanding world, then clearly, the early years of life are an integral component of the learning process and represent time and potential that cannot be wasted.

Research that the Corporation has supported demonstrates how much knowledge can be given and how much can be gained in the early stages of a youngster's life. What we now call emotional intelligence, for example, born in the give-and-take between parents and child, is an important contributor to the balanced development of a mature adult. And the loving *goo goos* and baby talk that an infant hears murmured above the rails of its crib are, in fact, the essential building blocks of language that children later learn to transform into the magic of words and sentences. And we have learned so much more, as well: that early exposure to those loving parental coos and "nonsense" syllables, for instance, can and should be extended to all children in a systemic way so that they are acquainted with the wonders of language long before they even know what it is. In yet another example—that programs aimed at helping all children arrive for their first day of school prepared to learn can make a lifelong difference in their ability to achieve.

And we are still learning, because there is so much more we need to know. Perhaps we are only beginning to get the first real clues we need to fully answer the question of how a child becomes an educated person, but there are some things we are deeply certain of: that what kids need are parents who love and nurture them, teachers who are prepared to challenge and guide them, a society that keeps them safe and secure, and an educational system that offers flexibility and opportunity and welcomes all children from all backgrounds and levels of ability. Additionally, what we know without a doubt is that how well we care for and educate the youngest and most vulnerable among us is the true indictor of how far we humans can advance and what we and our civilization will become in the years ahead.

The writer Graham Greene once said, "There is always one moment in childhood when the door opens and lets the future in." At Carnegie Corporation, we believe that moment comes when life itself begins, and that we must open the door for all America's children. The book you are about to read was written with deep faith in that belief and with hope for the future of every child in our nation. We have science to draw on, research to learn from, and stories to tell of success and achievement—the only thing that may be missing is a national will to create an early childhood education system that is as good as our children deserve. It is my profound wish that, in reading these pages, you will become one of the people who helps to create that will, one of the voices raised in support of early education and early opportunity for all. All our children are depending on that. They are depending on you.

Vartan Gregorian
President, Carnegie Corporation
of New York

We Start with Gifts

W*hat Kids Need* makes the case that young children's well-being and learning should be raised high on our national agenda. The plea that parents hear daily from young children—lift me up—is one we ought to take seriously. The reason is simple: "we start with gifts." These words, taken from poet Jean Toomer, offer the most powerful rationale for public policies and private actions that honor and foster the promise of America's young children.

Young children produce virtually none of our gross domestic product. They do not run multinational corporations or shape foreign policy. They represent 0 percent of legislators and 0 percent of voters. But they are 100 percent of our future—our gross domestic promise.

Starting now, we can do more to fulfill that promise, building on what has been learned and accomplished over the last decade. Today, at the outset of a new century, more is known than ever before about how children acquire the skills and concepts needed for school readiness and achievement, how families and communities can support their healthy development, and how our institutions, both public and private, can better support the people who nurture, teach, and protect young children.

This book describes the findings of the latest research on how kids develop as well as promising strategies for improving children's lives and prospects. Interspersed in the text are stories from reporters across the nation about people and programs that are making good things happen for kids.

In the realm of private life, there is one recurring theme: parents and families matter. Many factors influence children's well-being and life prospects, but none is more important than the family.

And in the public arena, there is one overarching message: investment and policy can and do affect both the daily lives and the long-term prospects of millions of young children. Policies and laws can seem remote from the day-to-day realities of children. Trying to fathom their impact on daily life is often like trying to feel the influence of the moon as you ride the waves in the ocean. But the effects can be just as powerful.

Other industrialized countries provide examples. We know that when ordinary people and their leaders make early childhood services a high national priority, as Sweden has done, children thrive and parents have greater peace of mind. We also know that when the social fabric frays and public investments in children shrink, the results can be devastating. Russia provides a tragic counterpoint: the dislocations and policy zigzags of the last decade have resulted in a sharp rise in infant mortality, a dramatic decline in immunization rates, and shorter life expectancy for people in every age group.

In the past, efforts to bring home the power of policy have relied on examples from other countries. But now, since so much of the action in the early childhood field takes place at the state and local levels, comparisons are possible within our nation's borders. Many of the policies are too new to allow firm judgments. But early returns suggest that at the state level, investments in early childhood make a demonstrable difference in children's lives.[1] At the federal level, a steady focus on early childhood is needed to level the playing field as different states and localities offer unequal opportunities to their youngest residents.

Children's well-being is affected not only by policy in spheres directly related to their care and education, but also by policy in other areas, including health, employment, elementary through higher education, welfare, housing, and justice. Efforts by private and nongovernmental organizations, including employers, unions, faith organizations, community organizations, and foundations, can powerfully influence children's prospects as well.

Today's best ideas for nurturing, teaching, and protecting young children build upon years of research and practice, focusing on families, infants and toddlers, preschoolers, and communities. Across the nation, individuals and organizations have come up with inventive responses to pressing issues. In North Carolina, Smart Start partnerships have galvanized communities around young children's needs, boosting school readiness. In states that are home to many migrant workers, Head Start moves with the kids as seasons change and families relocate. In New Haven, Connecticut, social workers and psychologists trained in child development accompany police to crime scenes where kids are involved. In Maine, the Kmihqitahasultipon Program uses videophone technology to offer mental health assessments for children in rural communities. In Vermont, every family with a new baby can have a home visitor help them learn about newborn care and adjust to the huge changes in their lives. In many states, community-based programs are helping struggling fathers confront the barriers that stand between them and responsible, rewarding parenthood. In

California, Pennsylvania, and Kentucky, statewide campaigns are making videos and guides about healthy development available to new parents.

Policymakers have come up with powerful strategies for improving children's well-being and school readiness. In states around the nation, safe haven laws prevent abandonment by allowing parents who cannot cope with a newborn to entrust the baby to a responsible institution, such as a church or hospital.[2] In Rhode Island, groundbreaking legislation made many child care workers eligible for state funded health insurance for themselves and their dependents, whether they work in a center or care for kids in their own homes. All over the nation, there are new efforts to include young children with a wide range of disabilities and special needs in early education programs that were once closed to them.

Victories have been won at the polls and in the courtroom. In California, voters have instituted a new tobacco tax to support school readiness efforts, and in Georgia, voters supported a lottery that funded the nation's first universal prekindergarten program. In New Jersey, citing equity concerns and a troubling achievement gap, a court decision mandated high-quality preschool programs for three- and four-year-olds in thirty school districts.

Each program or policy has its own story, its own movers and shakers, and its own dynamics. What all share is the conviction that in the long run, our society's strength will hinge not only on the way we raise our own children but on the commitments we make to each other's children.

Beyond the Quiet Crisis

Almost a decade has passed since Carnegie Corporation released *Starting Points*, a report from its Task Force on Meeting the

Needs of Young Children that drew attention to a "quiet crisis"—the existence of significant, unacknowledged risks facing millions of the youngest Americans. It was followed by *Years of Promise,* a report by another Carnegie task force focusing on the years from three to ten.

In the years since these reports were published, there have been significant efforts across the nation to address the well-being of young children and strengthen supports for families.[3] New initiatives have sprung up in nearly every state of the union and in thousands of communities across the nation; at the same time, many existing organizations have expanded their missions to include a focus on young children and their families.

Progress has been made toward each of the four *Starting Points* goals:

- *Promote responsible parenthood.* Over the last decade, public education efforts have raised awareness of young children's needs.[4] There is, across the nation, greater recognition that children grow and learn in the context of families and that efforts designed to help children without taking their families into account cannot fully succeed. More than half of the states now fund one or more family support or child development programs for infants and toddlers.[5] Many family support and parent education programs are moving beyond the stand-alone model to meet families' multiple needs, addressing not only parenting and child development issues but also adult literacy and employment. Many now focus on fathers' contributions as nurturers and providers.[6]

- *Ensure good health and protection.* Today, most of our nation's young children have some form of health insurance, but we have yet to make the same commitment to insuring the youngest Americans that we have to covering the oldest.[7] Public health officials report significant improvements in some areas. More women are avoiding smoking during pregnancy, lowering their risks of having low birth weight babies. Immunization rates are up. The "Back to Sleep" campaign, an effort to make parents aware of the importance of putting babies to sleep on their backs, has been associated with a stunning 40 percent drop in the rate of sudden infant death syndrome (SIDS). Child abuse and neglect rates, while still unacceptably high, have improved. To be sure, these problems persist, and sustained effort is needed in all of these areas. At the same time, it appears that public and private investments are showing some results.

- *Guarantee quality child care choices.* Long strides have been made in the realm of early childhood education. On the federal level, the expansion of Head Start and the funding of Early Head Start programs for infants and toddlers were major milestones of the last decade. The vast majority of states have passed legislation related to early care and education and are making efforts to coordinate family and children's services at the state and local levels.[8] About 60 percent of the states are investing in programs for infants and toddlers and about 80 percent in programs for preschoolers.[9] Several states are moving toward universal, voluntary preschool. Despite this progress, the United States continues to lag behind our peer nations in the realm of early learning.[10] The quality of early care and education remains, on the whole, mediocre to poor, and access remains limited, especially for low-income families. Improving infant and toddler care is especially urgent.

- *Mobilize communities to support young children and their families.* Community mobilization efforts have come a long way over the decade. More than half of the states report community mobilization strategies linked with state-level efforts to promote systemic change on behalf of children. Some states—such as Colorado, Hawaii, California, and North Carolina—are focusing intensively on very young children and families.[11] Some, including Massachusetts and Ohio, have launched community-driven initiatives that coordinate subsidized child care, Head Start, and state prekindergarten programs.[12]

The progress is substantial, but it is uneven. If our nation had an Early Childhood Situation Room, its map would be covered with thousands of pulsing lights, marking efforts across the nation to meet the needs of young children and strengthen their families. However, those lights would be densely clustered in some places and sparse in others. In many places, children remain a low priority; in some, programs exist for children of some age groups but not others or for children in some communities but not others. Different places have always offered different resources and opportunities to children. But today, the variation is extreme. As researchers from the National Center for Children in Poverty (NCCP) put it: "What a difference a state makes!"[13]

Looking ahead, the problems are imposing. Despite the last decade's strong economy and record employment, many families with young children are not earning enough to raise their families out of poverty. In March 2002, the NCCP reported that 4 million children under the age of six live in poverty. An economic slowdown now further jeopardizes these families.

Many parents are concerned about their children's safety in their neighborhoods and schools. Too many children are spending their days in settings that do not come close to meeting their health and educational needs. Elementary school teachers are finding that many of the children who come to them at age five or six have missed out on some of the experiences needed to help them adjust to school and keep up with its demands.

Reauthorization of the 1996 welfare legislation is a major challenge for those concerned about young children. The crisis described in *Starting Points* was called "quiet" because young kids do not ordinarily attract a great deal of attention or inspire headlines. They neither win prizes nor join gangs; they do not publish books or shred documents. However, there is one thing that young children do—in great numbers—that has turned the spotlight on them in recent years: they receive welfare. In fact, most recipients of public assistance are children. And yet, the provisions of welfare legislation focus primarily on adults. Subsidizing child care is primarily a way to support welfare-to-work efforts. While funding is sufficiently flexible to allow quality incentives for providers of subsidized care, the welfare law is silent on children's developmental needs and sets no goals that relate to early education or school readiness.

These are immense problems that will not respond readily to piecemeal solutions. They will take large-scale, coordinated, multifaceted efforts. Many policymakers are beginning to think in terms of building systems of care. According to Columbia University researchers who track progress in the early childhood field, in the year 2000, thirty states have reported some level of early childhood systems-building efforts—nearly double the number that reported such efforts two years earlier. But only eleven states say that they are dedicating public dollars to these efforts.[14]

In the realm of early childhood policy, our nation has a long way to go. We have not a single model on the home front to look to for inspiration as an effective, integrated approach to early childhood development and learning—one that transcends the barriers of race and income. No state has yet achieved a seamless system of early childhood services. None has made sufficient investments to build the strong framework needed to ensure that programs and services for young children and their families are of high quality. The number and scope of early childhood initiatives now underway across the country are unprecedented, but the hardest, most important work lies ahead.

Building early learning systems will take large-scale, sustained public investment, and that is not possible without significant efforts to rally political will.[15] In this realm as well, the last decade has seen significant progress. Increasingly, child advocates are working together to develop powerful messages about the benefits of investing in the early years. Many have grounded their efforts in research, drawing upon scholarship in numerous fields, including education, developmental psychology, cognitive science, and neuroscience. Scientists have gotten in on the act, infusing into public discourse on children's issues not only the tools and insights but also the prestige of science.

Public officials have responded. Both Democratic and Republican administrations have convened White House conferences on early childhood learning. Early education now figures frequently in state of the union and state of the state addresses.[16] Discussions once consigned to pediatricians' waiting rooms, nursery school parking lots, or employee lunchrooms are now taking place in legislative forums all over the country. State legislators and local officials are becoming conversant with policy issues such as family child care, school readiness, and parental leave.

Organizations outside of government have responded as well. Public-private partnerships have come together to shape policies and programs aimed at improving young children's life prospects.[17] Higher education, faith communities, and labor unions are contributing resources and strategies. Businesses are getting involved in child care initiatives; at the same time, many are rethinking human resource policy, with a view toward attracting and retaining employees with young children.[18]

The word is out: investments in the early years can make a dif-

ference for children, their families, and the nation they will inherit. People in all walks of life have turned up the volume, making their voices heard in the White House and Congress; in state
houses and legislatures all over the country; on news programs and
talk shows; at town meetings and local school gatherings; around
water coolers at work and on welfare office lines. Stories about
child care sometimes migrate from the women's pages to the front
pages of leading newspapers. And candidates for public office, including the highest office in the land, now include in their stump
speeches proposals aimed at combating child poverty and expanding access to high-quality early education and care.

The "quiet crisis" is no longer quiet. In fact, sometimes the dec-
ibel level is turned up so high that all that comes through is political static. In the last presidential election, some commentators
complained that children were mentioned incessantly but, for the
most part, emblematically, resulting in the "dumbing down of
American politics."[19] There is a strong need to modulate the rhetoric, documenting what we know about the well-being of young
children and highlighting the most effective strategies for improving their life chances in terms that neither sentimentalize children,
on the one hand, nor treat them as units of economic productivity,
on the other.

Neither greeting cards nor spreadsheets can capture the complexity of parents' needs as they try to support and raise their families. Nor can they capture children's needs as they meet the many
developmental tasks of the early years. This book focuses on the realities of children's lives and highlights today's best ideas for making them better.

Looking back over the last decade, it is clear that long strides
have been made. They are all the more remarkable in view of
Americans' bent for seeing issues related to raising young children
as highly private and beyond the range of public policy. Looking

ahead, it is clear that shaping a coherent national agenda will not be easy in a diverse nation with a mind-boggling array of religious beliefs and value systems. At times, it is even difficult to agree on language for describing what young kids need: Child care? Early learning? Developmentally appropriate care? An early care and education system?

Whatever we call it, we can be sure that most families want and need it. And if quality is high, young kids stand to benefit. There is growing consensus that efforts to strengthen achievement cannot wait until children reach age five or six. And there is stronger agreement that the public has an interest in young children's safety, health, and school readiness.

In the wake of the 11 September 2001 terrorist attacks, there is also heightened concern about children's emotional and social development and the impact of world and local events on children's well-being. And there is stronger conviction that, in addition to reading readiness and number skills, children need to master civic literacy—the capacity to feel part of and make positive contributions to the various groups that constitute their world, including families and extended families, schools, affinity groups (such as clubs, teams, or congregations), and communities.

War overseas, security concerns at home, and recession have also intensified economic pressures and raised new policy challenges. Will resources diverted to these problems derail the progress our nation has begun to make in the realm of children's well-being and school readiness? As national priorities shift, it is important to document that progress, acknowledge its limitations, and press on with efforts to lift our children up.

Today, the values and beliefs that underlie day-to-day child-rearing remain squarely within the realm of the personal. But as concern about educational achievement persists, as the reauthorization of welfare and Head Start legislation draws attention to young children, and as world events sharpen the focus on kids' well-being, there is a greater sense than ever before that the chronicle of domestic life—punctuated as always with private jokes, spats, giggles, and tantrums; filled as always with private troubles and triumphs—can and must figure in the sweeping story of public life and public responsibility in twenty-first-century America.

CHAPTER I

What Families Need

Brooklyn, New York: It is still the old neighborhood, but the longer you walk around, the more change you notice. The Laundromat has a sign taped to its door announcing round-the-clock hours, the candy store promises to send your faxes to anywhere in the world, and the supermarket offers sales in Russian. Down the street, the library still presides; a woman is steering a big pushcart, specially outfitted to seat six preschoolers, up the long sidewalk towards the entrance. It is story time on Ocean Parkway.

East Dallas, Texas: At ten past one, a young woman pushes two kids in a stroller hurriedly past the Bryan Street playground—the one right next to the police storefront. They want to stop and play. She tells them, as she does every day, that she only has twenty minutes to get them from preschool to Mrs. Lopez before it is time to punch back in at work at the Fiesta Store. As usual, they are unimpressed by her sense of urgency.

Virginia Beach, Virginia: A man parks his pickup in front of the Haygood United Methodist Church and waves a little shyly to three women who are just leaving. He needs to get some errands done before reporting for the noon-to-eight shift, so he is dropping his eight-month-old at "Mother's Morning Out."

Pine Ridge Reservation, South Dakota: After driving for forty minutes, a gray-haired woman with a car full of young children pulls into the parking lot of the Porcupine Clinic and glances at the rearview mirror to check on the shrieking bundle in the car seat behind her. Two of the toddlers are grandchildren who live with her, and three others are kids she watches while their parents work. When one of them gets sick, everyone goes to the doctor.

Marietta, Georgia: In the strip mall parking lot, a man answers his cell phone as he wheels a shopping cart containing one toddler and nine bags of groceries to his van. He stoops to retrieve a box of diapers that has slid to the ground from the mountain of groceries and barely manages to restrain his daughter—who has leaned way over to watch it fall down.

For families with young children, this is where the rubber meets the road—the real world, where policies, programs, and polls meet up with kids' needs, parents' pressures, and families' schedules. This is the landscape of day to day, where families and communities come together (or unravel); where commitments deepen (or dissolve); where paychecks stretch (or run out); where work instills pride and optimism (or frustration); and where promise is fulfilled (or lost). This book is about the world that young children and their families inhabit at the outset of a new century and about the forces that can help the great majority of them secure more hopeful, interesting lives.

Children are our present. As we so often hear, they are also our future. They will build tomorrow's institutions, protect tomorrow's planet, and conceive and chronicle tomorrow's boldest ideas. But for parents—and the other adults who provide nurture—young children are here and now. Their flashes of brilliance, or humor, or rage are front and center. Their diapers must be changed, their coughs attended to, their questions considered, their missteps corrected, and their favorite stories retold. They are counting on us to love, to teach, to protect and guide them, and to provide for them.

If parents do all these things, and do them well, most children will thrive and their prospects will improve. For most Americans, this is a dazzling glimpse of the obvious; as a nation, however, we do not always act on this conviction. Many policymakers lack first-hand experience of today's most effective programs, and the clear-cut evidence they seek cannot always be marshaled. As a result, policy is sometimes shaped as if children can flourish while families struggle and parents despair. How do parents matter? How can efforts aimed at parents and families improve children's well-being and their readiness to succeed?

At the Crossroads

At-home dad. Soccer mom. Teen mother. Custodial father. Working mother. Deadbeat dad. Welfare mom. Over the last decade, terms like these turned up with increasing frequency in headlines, journals, opinion polls, and public debate. On the map of American experience, they became signposts, marking the intersection between parenthood—an intensely private realm where personal conviction and individual accountability prevail, and politics—the public sphere where popular opinion and social responsibility hold sway. It is at this crossroads that some of today's most pressing policy issues are now being sorted out.

That intersection has been the site of many collisions. A widespread preference for keeping young children in their own parents' care has conflicted with economic and social realities. A tradition of public concern for children's welfare has clashed with the conviction that parents should take personal responsibility for their own sons and daughters. A desire to come to the aid of needy children has clashed with a reluctance to help parents who are thought to be undeserving. A respect for the privacy of family life has collided with a widespread perception that too many parents are raising or tolerating out-of-control kids.

A broad set of issues involving parents' roles, families' responsibilities, and children's well-being continue to spark controversy: How are young children affected when mothers go to work? What should be done when parents hold down jobs but still cannot meet their families' needs? What constitutes responsible fatherhood—beyond the provision of child support? When parents choose to care for their own children at home, should they receive economic breaks? Can parents be held accountable when children commit antisocial acts? And does it take a village, as Hillary Clinton put it in her best-selling book—a community as well as parents—to raise a child? Or should the village mind its own business?

How Parents Matter

Today, parenthood has come of age as a focus of societal concern, research, and public policy. Existing solutions are imperfect. The good news is the American public's willingness to address the realities of family life with more realism, compassion, and insight than ever before. The knowledge base has become more solid; policy options are more clearly articulated; proven programs aimed at strengthening families and promoting responsible parenthood are being expanded and replicated; and public debate appears to be more reasoned and better informed. Americans have always had diverse views about the kinds of parenting or family life children need; what is new is the precision with which we disagree. The hazardous intersection still exists, but now bright street lamps illuminate the terrain.

On the subject of parenthood, passions run high, and no subject is closer to home. For many Americans, having or adopting a child becomes, for better or for worse, a powerful driving force for the rest of their lives. Most Americans worry that they are not doing enough for their young children. They want to raise "good kids," but lack the time, knowledge, or economic resources to be the kind of parents they want to be. For working parents with very young children, the strain of balancing work and family can be especially stressful. Leaving babies with strangers is a stomach-wrenching experience.

Parents are not the only ones who are concerned about how our children are turning out. Many Americans believe that parents are not doing enough to guide and to regulate children. Others say parents are doing too much, creating households and communities that are too child-centered and that cater to children's every whim.[1] According to Public Agenda, in dozens of focus groups conducted in recent years, Americans (with and without children of their own) lament problems of unruly children, stressed-out parents, and a general decline in civility and moral values.[2]

Kids have opinions too. According to a recent study, those with employed parents accept the idea that their mothers and fathers go to work, but they are worried about their parents' high stress levels at home. They are concerned that their parents are—as one youngster put it—"too wired."[3]

In the nineties, as the focus on family life sharpened, theoretical issues once confined to professional conferences and journals came into public view. A number of books and the media coverage they generated threw into question many assumptions as old as the scriptures, including the notion that parents influence their children through action and example (and not simply by means of heredity). *The Bell Curve,* a controversial 1995 book, claimed that achievement hinges largely on genetic endowment—on nature, not nurture. In 1998, a *Newsweek* cover story entitled "Do Parents Matter?" reported the claim of another book, *The Nurture Assumption,* that when it comes to shaping children's destinies, parents matter less than most people think and peers matter more. On its heels, a 1999 book called *The Myth of the First Three Years* asserted that researchers and child advocates had exaggerated the importance of early experience and, by extension, of parents' roles in shaping the future of their young children.

In the media, the debates lost a great deal in translation. Few experts doubt that parents influence children; they have only to consult their own experience. As pediatrician Perri Klass has written, in reflecting on our own life stories, adults "understand that we are shaped by our parents, siblings, homes, heredity, culture, schools, friends, teachers—and by their remarkably complex and elaborate interplays. We are shaped by what we are told to be and do, but also by good luck and bad, by the times in which we happen to live and by the place."[4]

To be sure, many factors shape children's lives and the paths they take as they move into adulthood. Children are the products of the historical moment into which they are born, the traditions they absorb, the ideas they breathe in, and the social conventions and political movements they experience.[5] Some influences that are not obvious can turn out to have a strong influence on children's economic prospects, such as the number of children born in the same year with them.[6] Other influences are more obvious, but may still be underestimated. But no influence has greater impact than that of families and parents. According to the lead researchers, that was among the most important findings of the National Research Council panel that recently reviewed the science of early childhood development.[7]

But *how* do parents matter? What are the pathways by which that influence occurs? And are current research methods sufficiently rigorous or powerful to capture the full range of factors that shape children's development and socialization? There are some things parents cannot control. This is the first—and the hardest —lesson that newborns teach their mothers and fathers. Parents' best-laid plans often go awry. Furthermore, the same parenting techniques, applied to two children, often have different results. It is easy to understand why even the most confident parents may sometimes doubt their own importance and influence.

An infant's capacity to gain a sense of security and competence hinges on many things, including the child's own temperament, that is, the repertoire of traits with which each child is born, which helps to determine how individuals react to the world around them.[8] The intensity with which children respond to events or express emotion is often a matter of temperament. Researchers have observed that there is often continuity in a person's temperament throughout life, but how that temperament is expressed, how it "plays out," can be affected by life experience, including early interactions with parents and other caregivers. For example, a highly reactive infant may express strong emotion in response to a fairly routine event, like having her hair washed. Her cries may be loud and long. And that may reflect her temperament. But how a parent responds to those cries can affect the baby's growing ability to regulate her emotions.[9] Over time, parents can help a high-strung child become calmer, or a shy child become bolder, and these traits can affect children's learning and adjustment to school. In short, while some traits appear to be inborn, parents can certainly influence them, fostering healthy development and learning.[10]

Of course, peers also help to shape children's attitudes and behavior. Young children learn a great deal during play with siblings and other children. Some experts report that the single best predictor of how children will function as adults is not their IQ or academic achievement, but rather their ability to make a place for themselves in the peer culture.[11] Lagging behind in reading places an elementary school child at heightened risk of becoming a school dropout, but so does eating lunch alone.[12]

That in no way diminishes parents' importance. In fact, most experts say that it is early relationships with parents that lay the groundwork on which social competence is built. The benefits of secure early attachments have been reported in many studies. As developmental psychologists have shown, in the first months of life, parents' warm, responsive care facilitates infants' secure attachments. And a secure attachment, in turn, predicts social competence throughout childhood.[13]

Moreover, the style of parenting experienced by a child early in life can, in some cases, affect school readiness and adjustment in the early grades. The ways that parents and other important adults arrange children's environments and the ways that they frame their behavior and language can ease or impede children's learning. For example, studies have linked intrusive parenting, observed during mother-child feeding and play at six months, with learning and behavior problems in first and second grade.[14] They also have associated ineffective parenting (characterized by an absence of warmth and structure) with shy behavior and learning difficulties in kindergarten.[15]

In contrast, highly nurturing parenting can help to foster school achievement, as measured at age six by math and reading achievement, conversation, vocabulary skill, and block design. Parents who provide this kind of care adjust their own behavior in accordance with their developing child's needs.[16] They interact with children affectionately; show consideration for their feelings, desires, and needs; express interest in their daily activities; respect their viewpoints; express pride in their accomplishments; and provide encouragement and support during times of stress.[17]

All things being equal, children who receive warm, responsive care, consistent guidance, and appropriate stimulation will do well. But when it comes to raising children, all things are rarely equal. Even within the same family, some children bring more challenge than others—and "challenge" will sound decidedly euphemistic to parents who struggle just to get through the day.

Young children can experience behavioral or emotional difficulties for many reasons. Undiagnosed health problems or biological risk factors can contribute to erratic or difficult behavior. Many children will gain greater capacity for self-regulation as they grow and mature. Some will respond well to common strategies, such as behavior modification or highly structured early care and education settings.[18]

When, despite families' best efforts, young children are unusually aggressive or withdrawn, sad or frustrated, listless or frenetic, parents may conclude that their efforts are futile. In fact, when problems arise, families—and the way they relate to their young children—can matter a great deal. Mental health professionals can make progress by addressing children's overall health issues and working directly with the children, but they say that an effective way to help is often to change the ways that parents and other family members or caregivers relate to the children. High-quality child care, offering nurturance and appropriate stimulation, can be especially crucial for these children.[19]

Becoming an Expectant Parent

Nurturing a child begins even before conception. A newborn's health and birth weight are affected by the choices a woman makes even before she knows she is pregnant—such as practicing safe sex, eating and exercising sensibly, and taking a multivitamin with folic acid. They are also influenced by the decisions women make about smoking, drinking, using drugs, and taking medications.

Access to information, both through school curricula and health services, is therefore crucial for women of childbearing age.

Once they are expecting, mothers can care for their babies (and themselves) by seeking early prenatal care, paying attention to diet and exercise, and avoiding substances that can harm their child's growth and development. Fathers play a role by supporting these behaviors, participating in childbirth preparation classes, and understanding that for pregnant women, a significant weight gain—of twenty-five to thirty-five pounds—is recommended by most health care providers and benefits the baby.

Positive choices and attitudes cannot guarantee an easy delivery or healthy baby, but they do raise the odds that the baby's birth and birth weight will be normal. A normal birth weight is important, because low birth weight (LBW) babies—especially those born at very low birth weights—may face serious health problems as newborns and are at increased risk of long-term developmental delays and impairments.

Scientists know some, but not all, of the reasons that babies are born too soon, too small, or both. They do know a great deal about the kinds of settings and supports that bolster their chances for healthy development. Preterm babies in neonatal intensive care units designed to meet their need for soothing environments, to protect them from sensory overloads, and to allow close contact with parents have been found to fare better and leave the hospital sooner. Other newborns with low birth weights and multiple medical complications also benefit from intensive, individualized developmental care.[20] Sustained follow-up, including family support and home visitation, can be particularly important for these babies.

Prevention efforts are relatively inexpensive but can yield significant savings in the long run. According to a 1998 study published in *Pediatrics,* every averted LBW birth saves $59,700 in the first year of care. Furthermore, interventions that simply shift very low birth weight infants into higher weight categories can improve outcomes and result in substantial savings.[21] Prevention strategies now focus on three factors known to contribute to LBW:

- *Smoking.* Cigarette smoking during pregnancy is the single most important known cause of LBW. Many women stop smoking when they learn they are pregnant, but about 13 percent of expectant mothers smoke throughout pregnancy.[22] Epidemiologists estimate that as much as 25 percent of LBW cases could be prevented if pregnant women did not smoke.[23] Research consistently shows that, even after controlling for other factors, smokers are about twice as likely to deliver a low birth weight baby as nonsmokers.[24] According to a report by the surgeon general, women who quit cigarette smoking at almost any point during pregnancy can lower their risk of having a LBW baby.[25]

- *Nutrition.* There is strong evidence that a mother's nutrition has a crucial impact on her child's later health. Research shows that a baby's weight at birth is affected both by the mother's pre-pregnancy weight and by her weight gain during pregnancy.[26] Programs that offer nutritional support to low-income expectant mothers and infants are very important. The WIC program (the Special Supplemental Food Program for Women, Infants and Children), designed for low-income families at nutritional risk, combines nutritional education with vouchers for certain foods. Most studies of the WIC program show positive effects on birth outcomes.[27] Food stamps also can help to ensure that low-income women and infants are well nourished, but today, many people who leave the welfare rolls but remain eligible for food stamps are not making use of them.[28] Barriers to participation include lack of information about eligibility, administrative problems, or lack of funding. Nutrition programs also have an educational function. Expectant mothers need to know what to avoid—especially alcohol. Alcohol abuse is associated with a range of birth defects; indeed, heavy alcohol consumption is the leading preventable cause of mental retardation worldwide.[29]

- *Medical care.* Researchers have found that women who have access to adequate health services before, during, and after childbirth have better pregnancy outcomes and healthier babies.[30] It is not just the number of prenatal visits that counts, but also the timing and content of those visits. For example, the Los Angeles Preterm Birth Prevention Program has been credited with a 19 percent reduction in the preterm birth rate among program participants at a time when rates were increasing in Los Angeles and nationwide. Geared to expectant mothers at high risk of poor pregnancy outcomes, the program focused on behavior modification (i.e., smoking cessation, nutrition, and appropriate weight gain), stress reduction, and recognition of the signs and symptoms of preterm labor.[31] In particular, it is important to ensure that all eligible individuals receive Medicaid and SCHIP services, including eligible families who have recently left the welfare rolls.[32] In short, good prenatal care is crucial—but not sufficient. Prenatal care alone has had a limited impact on reducing the number of low-weight and preterm births. However, intensive, multicomponent programs can help to achieve this goal.[33] A broader strategy is needed—one that addresses medical, social, and psychological needs.[34]

Becoming Someone's World

A distinguishing characteristic of our species is that human children are totally dependent on their parents or other caregivers.

For a significant stretch of time, becoming a parent means becoming someone's world. It is hard to imagine a more demanding role.

When women and men are prepared for the opportunities of parenthood, they are more likely to provide the care and create the conditions that promote healthy development. The kind of knowledge that can help parents give their children a good start in life does not come naturally nor is it always available from relatives and neighbors. And compared with previous generations, today's young people spend less time caring for younger children in their families or communities. As David A. Hamburg has written, "by and large, young people moving toward parenthood today are far less experienced in the care of children than were their grand-parents."[35]

Preparation for becoming someone's world must therefore start even before parenthood is a biological possibility. It begins with experiences that model for children the pleasures and responsibilities associated with providing nurture and care. As children move into adolescence, it encompasses a wide range of experiences that promote good decision-making. A focus on decision-making is crucial because so many births in the United States are unintended. Excluding miscarriages, half of all pregnancies—and three-quarters of teen pregnancies—are unintended.[36]

Today, nearly one-third of children in the United States do not live with two parents. This statistic reflects both a sharp increase in births to unmarried parents in recent decades and a high divorce rate.[37] To be sure, single or divorced parents can do a wonderful job raising families, and many have sturdy support systems. One surprising finding that came to light in the late nineties is the high percentage of unmarried parents who have ongoing relationships and co-parent their children. Recent studies show that the great majority of unmarried fathers are strongly attached to their families, at least at the outset, and that many unmarried mothers live with or have ongoing relationships with the father of their children.

Efforts to support fragile families and to involve both men and women in children's lives can make a real difference. According to researchers, most unmarried fathers want to help raise their child, and most mothers are eager to have help. However, many unmarried fathers are unprepared to support their new families. Nearly half lack a high school degree and only one-fifth have education beyond high school. Those who work may earn very low wages. Efforts to improve the prospects of men with low skills and education can make a difference—especially at the time a new baby arrives, when motivation is very high.[38]

While children can thrive in many kinds of families, they certainly benefit emotionally and materially from having two nurturing parents. Moreover, the trend away from marriage in recent decades has increased child poverty.[39] To encourage two-parent families, policymakers have pursued several avenues.

- *Discourage teen births.* The nation has made substantial progress in this effort. The 1990s witnessed a steady decline in both the teenage birthrate and the teenage pregnancy rate. This decline has been attributed to a wide range of factors: broad societal factors, such as fear of HIV, changing attitudes about sexuality, and the availability of new contraceptive methods; a strong economy with its promise of improved career opportunities for young people; and new requirements for public assistance recipients. Effective initiatives combating teen pregnancy have also helped.[40] Today, many experts favor a broad, positive approach to reducing the number of young, single mothers. They stress the value of addressing young men as well as young women, encouraging a broad range of healthy behaviors, fostering sound decision-making, and providing incentives for young people to postpone parenthood, stay in school, pursue career goals, and form positive, stable relationships.[41] Many states are making use of freed-up welfare dollars to develop or to expand youth development programs. Additionally, prenatal and infancy home visitation programs by nurses have been shown to help delay subsequent pregnancies.[42] Some prevention efforts are starting to come to grips with the reality that many teen pregnancies result from coercive sex.

• *Encourage family formation.* Because marriage entails a personal commitment and has, for many Americans, a religious aspect as well, public policies related to marriage and divorce are often controversial. There is some evidence suggesting that removing or reversing economic disincentives can increase marriage rates.[43] Government agencies can identify and root out laws, policies, regulations, and procedures that in effect penalize people for forming stable relationships.[44] Some policy analysts believe that employment and job training initiatives can encourage family formation, since, as one researcher has written, "stable employment is the sine qua non of establishing lifelong family commitments and reestablishing marriage as an important building block in the kinship system."[45]

• *Help families stay together.* In recent years, however, concern about a high divorce rate has moved some communities and states to take measures to increase couples' chances of staying together, especially when children are involved. Some states, such as Florida, are incorporating premarital education into high school curricula. Other states have introduced incentives, such as shorter waits or lower fees for marriage licenses, to couples who take part in premarital education programs. A variety of program models exist.

- *Ensure that children receive support from both parents.* In recent years, most states have introduced stronger measures to enforce child support as part of welfare reform.[46] Child support legislation reflects the widespread conviction that all fathers, including those with low incomes, can make some contribution to their children's care. Moreover, it reflects a recent effort to shift more of the burden of raising children from the state to parents and from mothers to fathers. Proponents of tougher enforcement cite evidence that increasing nonresident fathers' financial investments in children may increase their motivation to spend time with them and take part in important decisions about their lives. However, researchers have concluded that tougher child support enforcement, by itself, will not change children's economic status. Most nonresident fathers who do not pay child support have very low incomes. Harsher treatment of low-income fathers makes no sense in the absence of efforts to help them qualify for, find, and keep jobs.[47]

- *Provide parent support and parent education.* States can use dollars that are freed up when welfare rolls decline to support parent education and family support programs, especially those that help both mothers and fathers become better nurturers as well as better economic providers.[48]

. . . .

Fathers Stand and Deliver in Baltimore

By Peter Novobatzky

THIRTY AFRICAN AMERICAN MEN of different ages sit facing one another in a circle in a sparsely furnished meeting room. Some wear suits and ties, others loose-fitting street clothes, a few wear blue-collar work uniforms. One by one the men talk about life on the streets, about crime and drugs and jail time, and about hitting rock bottom and awakening with a desire for change. The stories are matter-of-fact, heartfelt, powerful, and real. All attention is riveted on the teller of each tale.

One man says he first became involved in crime "for the recognition." After being homeless for five years, he decided to change his life. Now he owns a home. He passes around a credit card offer he just received for a card with a twenty-thousand-dollar spending limit. *"Look at what they're sending me now."*

This is the Baltimore-based Center for Fathers, Families, and Workforce Development (CFWD). The men, all fathers, hail from the city's poorest neighborhoods. Along with a few counselors, they are talking honestly about what it takes to make a difference in a man's life and in the life of a child.

Helping low-income noncustodial fathers become emotionally and financially responsible for their children is CFWD's purpose. Tonight's meeting aims to introduce clients to graduates of Support and Training Result in Valuable Employees (STRIVE), CFWD's employment program.

What impresses the outsider is the men's candor as they discuss their past and the strong, positive atmosphere of support. They are here because they want to step up and make a difference in the lives of their children. Succeeding will require all of their own inner resources, as well as help from programs like CFWD and from each other.

Joseph T. Jones Jr., founder and CEO of CFWD, was working with mothers in Baltimore's Healthy Start program in 1993 when he recognized the need to engage men in promoting the health and well-being of children. Over time, he developed Men's Services to provide support for men who wanted to become responsible fathers but who were not prepared for the job.

Two beliefs became central to the CFWD approach: that men want to be emotionally and financially responsible for their children and that poverty can hamper involvement and support. In 1999, Jones moved Men's Services out of Healthy Start and under the aegis of the newly-formed CFWD and added related programs such as STRIVE. Now Healthy Start contracts out to CFWD for programs geared toward men.

Toward Responsible Parenthood

The year-long, three-trimester Men's Services program, which has served some 450 participants to date, focuses on case management, parenting education, and life skills development. "First come the barriers, then come the goals," says Johnny Rice II, director of Men's Services.

The average participant is in his mid-twenties, unemployed, and poor. Many have histories of criminal activity and drug abuse. They lack education, may have mental health problems, and live in neighborhoods where they are vulnerable to relapses into crime, drugs, and the underground lifestyle. Few have custody of their children, and most have outstanding arrearages with the Child Support Enforcement Administration. And since most have never had active fathers in their own lives, the challenges are many. Counselors speak of having to contend with participants' anguish and hopelessness, as well as an "incarceration mentality."

Two things enable CFWD to make progress with such men, despite the challenges: the efforts of their talented and dedicated staff and the participants' strong desire to assume responsibility for their children.

Men's Services concentrates on small goals at first: the "One Man Plan" sets up milestones for individual participants, such as getting necessary forms of ID together, getting a GED, or establishing visitation rights to a child.

Program participants attend two mandatory group meetings per week: one is a peer support group and the other is instructional and follows the CFWD curriculum. In the former, fathers deal with issues, challenges, and problems affecting their lives, whatever they may be.

One man's brother moved in with him off the street, but he is still using drugs and stole the VCR. Another man is worried that he will be fired if his employer finds out he injured his back on the job.

Virtually all of CFWD's participants are African American, and the program's Afro-centric perspective challenges them to think critically about such topics as their identity and values, about black stereotypes and male-female relations, and about their health, goals, and strategies. Through it all, participants are urged to be responsible and accountable and to recognize their duty and obligation to their children.

"They have to acknowledge that they have a responsibility to their child, emotionally and financially, even if they're not with their significant other," says Rice.

In practice, this entails paying child support consistently. By the end of the third trimester, participants are expected to make their monthly payments and to either be employed or actively looking for a job.

Employment Services

To provide a crash course in what it takes to obtain and retain a job, CFWD has STRIVE, an intensive three-week program that has been described as "part boot camp, part group therapy." Based on the successful East Harlem program of the same name, it has been operating in Baltimore since 1998.

STRIVE simulates a nine-to-five job. Participants, both men and women, are expected to dress properly, arrive on time, follow instructions, and complete assignments during the day. They are held accountable; if a person shows up late, a counselor may nominate someone to assume the role of a supervisor, with consequences analogous to those one could expect on the job.

Says Moses Hammett, Director of Workforce Development for STRIVE: "We not only provide a person with the soft skills they need to procure employment, but we also try to address some of the emotional barriers, too. Starting from the initial orientation, we challenge participants on their thinking and belief systems, and on behaviors that prevent them from securing and retaining employment."

Initially, participants are assessed. What is their educational level? What are their "hard" (specific work-related) skills and "soft" (communication, presentation, and work ethic) skills? Do they have problems that require outside referral, such as illiteracy? The participants perform exercises designed to help them better navigate the social maze of the workplace. A high point of the first week is the "stand and deliver" speech, which requires them to talk about themselves for five minutes in front of the room. In the second week, participants receive computer literacy training, learn how to put together a resume, how to market themselves, and how to behave in a job interview. The third week is a full-fledged job search.

There are always dropouts, but the majority of those who complete the program are placed in jobs. Graduates also gain a real sense of accomplishment; for many of them, it is the first time they have completed any educational program. But STRIVE involvement does not end with job placement. There are follow-up groups, and graduates are invited back to talk to new classes. "It doesn't stop," says Moses.

Outreach Is Essential

"CFWD works with the father to empower the family," says Jones. "By not giving up on them, we develop trust. Then we can move forward and teach and counsel." Working out of Healthy Start offices in East and West Baltimore and from their own headquarters on Druid Park Drive, CFWD performs outreach services to pull fathers from the streets into the programs.

"In any viable men's program you need outreach," says Edward Pitchford, forty-two, senior counselor for CFWD Men's Services. "You can't sit behind a desk."

Today, this means he and counselor Christopher Banks, twenty-eight, are driving the CFWD van through the Sandtown neighborhood in Baltimore, picking up program participants for the evening meeting. After the meeting they will drive the men home. It is a sunny afternoon in early fall, and the streets are alive with residents. The pair make numerous calls, zipping from address to address, knocking on doors, stopping and talking to men they recognize on the street, and trying to locate participants.

"For any program to be successful, you need to get staff from that community," says Pitchford. "I come from the streets of East Baltimore. That's how I'm able to relate to a lot of the guys."

"Outreach means caring for people and caring for what you're doing," he says. "Whether it's knocking on someone's door and waiting 20 minutes for them to come down so you can take them to group, or whatever it takes to keep them involved: telephone calls, letters, functions, outings, even jail visits. It's not a nine-to-five job."

"It's anything you would do for your own family," says Banks. "You have to go out and engage guys to get them to come into the program. Sometimes it goes over to the weekends or evenings. When we go home, we leave our pagers on. You have to genuinely care about what you're doing."

"The trust factor comes from consistent commitment," says Pitchford. "We tell guys we'll be coming by, but when we actually show up, you should see some of their faces. It's like—wow, I know you said you were coming, but I didn't *believe* it."

It is also important to follow up on the men, says Banks: "Once they're out there working, there's a tendency for them to disconnect from the program. We try to keep in contact with them, to keep them focused."

New Directions

CFWD is expanding its menu of programs. Targeting men who have completed the Men's Services curriculum, Team Parenting aims to promote child well-being through the participation of both parents, regardless of the status of their relationship. And a pilot program is being developed to provide a way for men who make consistent child support payments to incrementally wipe away their back debt with the Child Services Administration.

Says Joe Jones: "We're trying to get fathers to do the right thing, but the system has got to be flexible enough to tell the difference between dead *beat* dads and dead *broke* dads. Otherwise, the incentive is for guys to remain underground, and Child Services will never see any money from them. From a policy standpoint, if the debt-leveraging program increases child support collection, it will have been a success."

Times have changed since the early days of Men's Services, says Jones. "The research has started to justify the need for services for this group of fathers," he says. "I don't think we're going to go back to the days when fatherhood was not included in discussions on social policy." However, he notes a need to move programs such as CFWD to more secure funding from private philanthropies. "We've got to find public funding streams to support this work," he says. "That's the challenge."

. . . .

Becoming a Child's First Teacher

Parents also exert their influence by instructing their children. In recent years much has been made of the fact that young children are biologically primed for certain kinds of learning. But there is less appreciation of the fact that adults seem to be primed for certain kinds of teaching. Indeed, humans are the only species whose parents actively and intentionally teach their young—and we do it very well. In fact, as psychologist Jerome Bruner has written, "Parents seem to know a very great deal more than they know that they know."[49] For example, many mothers and fathers speak "parentese"—the slow, melodic language babies respond to—without instruction and without realizing how crucial it is for modeling the prosody and sound structures of a language.[50]

A father sitting with a baby and a pile of toys will help his child focus on one or two objects, retrieve items that have been pushed out of reach, turn toys so they can be more easily manipulated, or demonstrate how they work, all the while adjusting his body as his baby needs physical support or easier access to the toys.[51] As they do things together, parents (and other caregivers) stimulate young children's learning by organizing new tasks, regulating their difficulty, and modeling mature performance.

Babies are also remarkably adept at these interactions. As Bruner has written, "There is no other species whose young point to things and bring them to an adult's attention. These are miracles that parents take for granted."

Children are born ready and eager to learn. They are naturally curious. But no crib is an island. Infants' solitary activities are complemented by interactions with adults who gradually involve them in activities valued in the culture they share. These joint activities are not extracurricular, but rather they build competency in the core subjects that babies need to master.

By scaffolding young children's learning, adults allow them to climb to dizzying heights. Another miracle that parents take for granted: within a mere three years, children born with no discernable language become competent communicators and storytellers. A variety of literacy experiences help children master these complex tasks. When parents explore picture books with young children, helping them "read"—or relate—the stories and tying them to their own shared experiences, they are fostering language development and helping children become independent readers. Parents have always suspected that this kind of joint activity promoted children's literacy skills; now researchers have confirmed its value.[52]

Becoming a Guide

Different societies and different communities conceive of parenthood in different ways. But for all, becoming a parent does not just mean reproducing and sustaining the species. It also means reproducing and sustaining a culture. Parents are not only children's first teachers but also their guides—helping them learn about rules and moral precepts (and the difference between them).

Today, many Americans are concerned about children's moral development. As difficult as it is to provide for small children, looking after their physical well-being and their health, most Americans believe that it is even harder these days to raise children who behave appropriately and demonstrate good values.[53] They care about children's school readiness and achievement, but they are also concerned that, as the writer Walker Percy put it, it is possible to "get all A's and flunk life."[54]

Psychologists believe that like other kinds of learning, moral learning begins from a newborn's earliest days, as children and parents respond to each other's "feeling states." In this way, emotions constitute the native language in which parents and children first converse. Infants respond to their parents' facial expressions and vocal tones. In turn, parents "read" and react to their infants' moods and signals. To do this well, parents have to keep in mind both the baby's viewpoint and their own, like an accomplished pianist simultaneously reading two lines of music, each with its own rhythm and register.

These early parent-child interactions affect young children's moods and behavior. A facial expression can spur a toddler to venture out on his own or stay close to Mom to comply willingly with a request or just say no. With practice, parents and children develop clear expectations about each other's actions, aims, and meanings, and more fully coordinate their activities.[55]

These interactions also play an important role in determining whether toddlers will react with empathy to someone else's distress.[56] From an early age, young children engage in cooperative play—sharing toys and food with others and taking account of other people's feelings. They gradually gain social understanding. In the process, they begin to develop a sense of ethics.[57] They react when expected kindness, sharing, or cooperation is withheld, and come to realize that someone who has been pushed or had a toy grabbed away will be upset.

In fact, from a very early age, small children can distinguish between what they are expected to do (based on rules and conventions) and what they should do (based on a moral framework). Even before the age of three, children have been shown to grasp that behavior that breaks a rule, like talking loud in the library, would not be wrong in the absence of the rule, but that moral violations, like biting the librarian, should not happen whether or not there is a rule. They understand that moral transgressions—such as hitting, biting, lying, or stealing—are more serious than actions that simply break rules or violate conventions.[58]

A key point is that they learn these lessons through interactions, and most child development experts believe that such lessons can be taught. Psychologist Urie Bronfenbrenner has long advocated what he calls "a curriculum for caring," beginning in preschool. He stresses that concern for other people is learned in the family but can be reinforced by other institutions.[59]

Today, many parents concerned about their children's moral development are looking for methods of discipline that they can live with. Studies suggest that "authoritative" parenting is best— a style that is very nurturing but leaves no doubt about who is in charge.[60] This kind of parenting occupies the middle ground between a more permissive style and a more authoritarian style and it is not easy. It calls upon parents to be kind and understanding but at the same time firm, and it requires both negotiation and confrontation.[61] But abstractions and broad guidelines do not always help the parent who is trying to get a thrashing three-year-old into his car seat, or struggling to convince a four-year-old that yanking her baby sister's hair is unacceptable behavior.

Many parents remain ambivalent or confused about spanking and other forms of physical discipline. It is little wonder, the messages they receive are wildly mixed. In many parts of the country, corporal punishment is condoned in public schools: twenty-three states permit paddling.[62] Schools continue to paddle children despite the fact that numerous prestigious institutions, as well as legions of respected pediatricians, authors of child-rearing manuals, and child advocates, have taken forceful positions against physical punishment. In August 2000, for example, the American Academy of Pediatrics (AAP) recommended that corporal punishment in schools be abolished in all states by law and that alternative forms of student behavior management be used.[63]

Two years earlier, in 1998, the AAP had recommended that physicians counsel parents to develop alternatives to spanking, such as "time out" and removal of privileges. In making this recommendation, the AAP noted that parents are much more likely to resort to physical punishment when they are tired, irritable, or depressed. It argued that spanking teaches children that aggressive behavior is a solution to conflict and has been associated with increased aggression in preschool and school-age children. It also asserted that the use of spanking and threats of spanking can alter the parent-child relationship, which makes discipline substantially more difficult when physical punishment is no longer an option (such as in adolescence). Finally, the AAP cited research showing that while spanking may immediately reduce or stop an undesired behavior, its effectiveness decreases with repeated use.[64]

Becoming a Protector

In addition to their other roles, parents keep children out of harm's way. The last century has witnessed enormous progress in medical care and sanitation, resulting in dramatic declines in child mortality.[65] Today, scientific breakthroughs continue to save lives, but an urgent challenge is to prevent deaths from accidents and violence, which play a larger role in child mortality than a hundred years ago.

Public education campaigns can have a dramatic impact on parents' ability to safeguard their children. Case in point: the effective "Back to Sleep" campaign to prevent sudden death syndrome (SIDS) by encouraging parents and other caregivers to put healthy babies to sleep on their backs.[66] However, changing parental practices takes time. African American, American Indian, and Alaska Native mothers, for instance, are more likely than white mothers to put their babies to sleep on their stomach.[67] This has drawn the attention of public health experts, since babies born to these mothers are more likely to die of SIDS than white babies. Since this finding came out in 1998, the U.S. Department of Health and Human Services has intensified public information efforts in minority communities.

Once children reach the age of one, unintentional injury presents the greatest threat to their survival.[68] Parents play a crucial role in keeping children out of harm's way, but public policy has a role to play as well. Safety experts believe that with strong educational and legislative efforts, as many as 90 percent of unintentional injuries could be prevented.[69] The need to improve prevention is especially urgent in four areas:

- *Motor vehicle safety.* Motor vehicle accidents are a leading cause of death for young children. Parents can keep children safe by ensuring that they have the appropriate restraints for their size and age. As things stand, 40 percent of children under the age of five ride unrestrained, doubling their chances of death in an accident. Even those with car seats may not be safe, since most children who are placed in child safety seats are improperly restrained. All fifty states have child occupant protection laws; however, these laws vary widely in their age requirements, exemptions, enforcement procedures, and penalties. Safety studies have shown that in states where officers may stop and ticket drivers for seat-belt violations, there are lower fatality and injury rates.[70] A promising approach is to include car seat checks as part of every state's motor vehicle inspection process.

- *Fire safety.* Child deaths from fire and flame injury have declined in recent years. However, when home fires do occur, young children continue to be at the highest risk of death and injury.[71] The chances of dying in a residential fire are cut in half when a smoke alarm is present. Most homes in the United States have at least one smoke alarm, but in one large study, almost three-quarters of the smoke detectors did not work, usually due to run-down batteries.[72] States are not doing enough. Currently, thirty-two states and the District of Columbia require smoke alarms in both new and existing dwellings.

- *Firearm safety.* Children as young as age three are strong enough to pull the trigger of many of the handguns available in the United States. Many child advocates therefore fervently support gun control. About one-third of states hold gun owners criminally liable if children use their loaded weapons to harm themselves or others. Research shows that such laws decrease the rate of child death due to firearm accidents.[73]

- *Drowning prevention.* Among children between the ages of one and five, drowning is the leading cause of unintentional injury-related death.[74] Young children can drown in very little water, and many accidents involve bathtubs or buckets. But most drownings and near-drownings of young children occur in residential swimming pools. A few states and many communities nationwide have passed laws requiring fencing around residential swimming pools; many others have not yet taken this precaution.

Becoming a Provider

Today, the family is often viewed by educators as a powerful learning system—a context for intellectual development that is so effective that many early childhood programs and elementary schools are trying to replicate its main features. The important adults in children's lives provide scaffolds for their efforts—interesting children in learning activities; simplifying problems; motivating, directing, and critiquing their efforts; helping them control frustration; and modeling performance.[75]

But beyond this textbook view lies the real world where "environments" hold last night's dinner dishes, vast quantities of laundry, and piles of Legos; "scaffolds" are likely to be planks surrounding run-down apartment buildings; and the most consistent learning system may be the television. The realities of that world—including the economic and policy contexts in which families live—constrain many families' capacity to nurture, teach, and protect their young children. Many factors influence parents' ability to do a good job: not just whether they are working but also the kinds of jobs they hold; not just whether they qualify for benefits such as food stamps or child care subsidies but whether they can access those benefits; not just whether they are familiar with good parenting practices but whether they have the time, energy, and peace of mind to apply them.

Large economic trends may seem remote from Legos and dinner dishes, but they can decisively shape the experience of children and families. Economists say that when it comes to affecting the quality of day-to-day life, programs barely make a dent compared with the sledgehammer of the economy.[76] And in fact, in the nineties, an expanding economy and tight labor market benefited most families, increasing income for most and boosting the number of children who had working parents. Many believe that the robust economy of the nineties also muted the adverse effects of welfare reform on the well-being of young children. They are concerned about the impact of recession in the early years of the new century.

Today, work does not necessarily lift families out of poverty, and the income gap between the richest and poorest Americans remains very wide. Globalization and technological advance have intensified the need for employees who can meet the demands of a fast-paced, computer-driven workplace, leaving behind those with less education and fewer skills. New jobs are likely to be in the service sector, where wages are generally low, benefits are few, and hours tend to be long and irregular. Many of the workers who are leaving the welfare rolls to take such jobs are shifting from the ranks of the poor to the ranks of the working poor. Indeed, one-fifth of poor children today live in families with incomes below the official poverty threshold despite the fact that the head of household works full time all year round.[77]

Some progress has been made in ensuring that families have a steady stream of income. Increases in employment rates and wages, along with expansion of Earned Income Tax Credit (EITC), have reduced child poverty. However, household income still does not cover basic expenses for many families. Moreover, several major safety net programs have contracted substantially and now reduce child poverty less than in the past. The percentage of poor families with children receiving cash assistance and food stamp benefits has fallen sharply. So while the strong economy of recent years reduced the number of children living in official poverty, those who remain below the poverty line are, on average, poorer now than they were in 1997.[78]

Today, 17 percent of our nation's under-six population—about 4 million young children—live in families with incomes under the federal poverty line. These children live in every kind of community. From the midseventies to the midnineties, the rate of growth of the young child poverty rate was much higher in the suburbs (50 percent) than in the cities (31 percent). The rate of growth was also much higher among whites (25 percent) than African Americans (18 percent).

And the 4 million figure counts only young children living in *official* poverty. Most experts agree that this measure underestimates the actual number of families who face economic hardship.[79] Many more families live in "near poverty"—under 185 percent of the poverty line, a figure used to determine eligibility for many programs serving at-risk families. According to the National Center for Children in Poverty, in fourteen states, more than half of all children under the age of six live in poverty or near poverty.

Financial worries weigh heavily even on parents whose income exceeds twice the official poverty level. In a Commonwealth Fund survey of families with children from birth to age three, one-third of families with incomes under forty thousand dollars reported some difficulty in paying for such basic child supplies as formula, food, diapers, clothes, and shoes; nearly one-quarter say that they have difficulty paying for their child's medical expenses. The need for child care further strains family budgets.[80]

Both poor and near-poor children are subject to the well-documented effects of economic hardship, including health problems and developmental delays. Studies that control for other family characteristics have found that the effect of family income on intelligence and verbal test scores at ages two, three, and five years are quite large. Other studies show that mothers in families whose income fails to cover basic needs are more likely to report behavior problems for five-year-olds, including aggression, tantrums, anxiety, and moodiness.[81]

Moreover, children in poor or near-poor families may suffer from undernourishment. Food insecurity is widespread and affects millions of children. In 1999, the most comprehensive health examination survey in the United States found that 10 million Americans, including 4 million children, suffer from hunger.[82] Hunger among children in the United States does not take the form of mass starvation, as it does in some poorer nations. The effects are less obvious and more difficult to measure: fatigue, irritability, dizziness, frequent headaches, frequent colds and infections, and difficulty concentrating.[83] Scientists believe that malnutrition compromises many different aspects of a child's development through a complex interplay of factors such as increased illness, delayed physical growth, and increased lethargy and withdrawal.[84]

In the lives of families on both sides of the poverty line, work plays an immense role. Today, most mothers and fathers have to go to work. Many are working harder—putting in longer hours as well as expending more physical and emotional energy. And many more Americans are working unpredictable or nonstandard schedules, making household management and child care arrangements much more difficult.[85]

Family time is an especially important factor, because the amount of time and the kind of time parents have available to spend with children demonstrably affect children's health and development.[86] Yet today it is the one resource that virtually every family finds in short supply. Once the exception, two-earner families are now the rule. Most women with children under the age of six hold jobs outside of their homes, and most of them—nearly seven million mothers with young children—hold full-time jobs.[87] Parents are not only going to work in greater numbers; they are also spending more time working.[88]

The global service economy operates around the clock. Its expansion has compelled more workers to accept evening, night, or weekend work, rotating shifts, and unpredictable schedules. One study has found that more than a quarter of low-income working mothers now work nontraditional hours, mostly at night.[89] In addition, more than 7 million Americans hold down more than one job (nearly half women).[90]

While all parents need time to meet their children's needs, it is particularly critical for low-income parents. Their children are more likely to have health problems, developmental delays, or learning issues that require attention and care.[91] Low-wage earners can seldom get time off from their jobs to meet responsibilities like caring for a sick child at home, taking children to medical appointments, or having children with learning difficulties evaluated.[92] Low-income workers, even those who work full-time, are less likely than higher-wage earners to have paid leave, and most cannot afford to take unpaid leave.[93]

The problem is most severe when children get sick. In one out of every four families, children's illnesses require parental (or back-up) care for three or more weeks each year.[94] This can mean upheaval for all working parents, but low-wage earners have less flexibility than other workers. Research shows that children recover more quickly from illnesses and injuries when their parents are present and involved in their care. Parents' active involvement has been shown to cut hospital stays by nearly one-third.[95]

Becoming a "Shield"

In the aftermath of 11 September 2001 many parents found themselves wondering how their world had changed and how to convey those changes to their children. Soon after the attacks, a conference at Columbia University brought together several experts on child development to address the impact of stress and trauma on young children and their families. One speaker offered historical perspective, recalling a classic 1944 study by Dorothy Burlingham and Anna Freud of children evacuated from London during World War II. This study found that children were actually less traumatized by the dangers of the bombing than by evacuation and separation from their families.[96]

Experts say that in times of stress, children need loving, responsive care more than ever. Parents need to listen carefully to how children express their concerns, keeping in mind that children of different ages will express their anxieties in very different ways. How children respond to trauma reflects their perception of how effectively their parents deal with external dangers. Parents serve as a protective shield, and children need this shield most in times of stress—but that is exactly when parents may find it most difficult to keep it in place.[97]

Researchers also say that responses to stress and trauma (whether in the world or in the home) can be transmitted across the generations. They are learning more about how post-traumatic stress syndrome and other serious psychologically based conditions (such as depression or anxiety disorder) can affect adults' responsiveness to young children, which in turn influences children's development. Parents who are able to see the world from their children's viewpoint and to reflect on their children's experiences are better able to promote children's resilience and help them recover from trauma.[98]

What can parents do to help their children thrive in challenging times? Much of the expert advice boils down to these "Four
R's":

- *Reassurance.* Parents may need to express their feelings but
  should stay as calm as possible because children are keenly attuned to adults' emotions. Parents should answer children's
  questions as simply and directly as possible; limit their exposure to disturbing images on television; and let them know that
  they will do everything possible to keep their family safe.

- *Routine.* As much as possible, parents should maintain their
  regular schedule, keeping mealtime, homework time, and bed-
  time consistent. Playtime may be especially important. Relief
  organizations around the world have found that games, stories,
  and imaginative play can help children bounce back from many
  kinds of adversity.

- *Ritual.* Families can do something special to respond to difficult or upsetting events. They can hold a family "meeting" to
  talk about the events, attend a worship service, take part in a
  special community activity, help raise or earn money to donate
  to relief efforts, or—if tragedy strikes—write to victims' families to express sorrow or to rescuers to express thanks.

- *Reading.* Reading and storytelling—always important—can
  take on greater significance in the aftermath of trauma. Jerome
  Bruner has written that narratives are among a culture's main
  resources for helping people deal with "an exception to the ordinary." The function of the story is to make "comprehensible a
  deviation from a cultural pattern."[99] According to Bruner, great
  stories "reopen [reality] for new questioning. That's why ty-
  rants put the novelists and poets in jail first. That's why I want
  them in democratic classrooms—to help us see again, fresh."[100]

It is not just the content, but also the form of stories that can help in trying times. Stories that have familiar elements (in form or content) can be very comforting for children and adults alike.[101] Many psychologists have also stressed the importance of children's creative expression through art, music, and poetry in times of stress.

Helping individual parents to meet their children's needs during periods of stress is important, but not sufficient. Intensifying public education and expanding supports for families are also crucial. What has become clear since the attacks on New York and Washington is that how parents, physicians, teachers, and other caregivers nurture children in the face of stress and trauma is a major public health issue. At the same time, it is important to consider that millions of children were growing up in stressful or even traumatic circumstances even before 11 September. When parents have insight into their children's feelings and thoughts and can reflect upon them, when they spend time with their children and engage in reading and storytelling with them, children are more likely to thrive. To do these things effectively in difficult times, many parents need support—from peers and professionals.

The Case for Parent Education and Family Support

Even in less trying times, new parents often experience shortages of vital resources, including time, energy, sleep, and money. Most also experience an information deficit. According to a survey by the organization Zero to Three, many say that they find it hard to understand their babies' feelings and needs and do not know how to handle difficult situations with their young children.[102]

Compared to ten years ago, parents have many more sources of information, including countless internet sites. More communities have child care resource and referral agencies that provide a wide range of information, and books and videos are available on a wide range of topics of interest to parents with young children. Many of these materials, and the messages they carry, need to be translated into other languages and made relevant to diverse cultures.

The preponderance of evidence confirms that parents are vital both because of the experiences they provide directly and those they arrange for children to have. The debate about parents' influence has not overturned this widespread conviction, but it has been helpful in a number of ways.

First, it pointed to some problems with the way researchers have tried to document parents' influence on their children. Many socialization studies have relied on superficial measures, such as checklists of behaviors or beliefs.[103] Researchers need a more complex, multidisciplinary approach that draws together research in diverse arenas, including anthropology and psychology, to detect the impact of nurture.

Second, the debate has raised the possibility that some parents may feel anxious about the recent stress on parenthood. Recent debates about the importance of the early years and, in particular, parents' impact on early brain development, have put moms and dads in the spotlight. As pediatrician T. Berry Brazelton has observed, "Many parents may be uncomfortable there." According to Brazelton, "Parents may be looking for ways not to feel so important. Perhaps it comes from the stress of having so many responsibilities."[104]

Many go to bed at night convinced that they have not spent enough good time with their children. More than half of today's parents believe that they are not doing as good a job at child-rearing as their own parents did.[105] In 1997, a survey by Zero to Three found that few first-time parents felt fully prepared for their new role. Those who are the youngest and have the lowest income and those who are going it alone as single parents feel particularly unprepared.

Most parents say they have a pretty good idea what to look for in terms of their babies' physical development but need more help recognizing social and emotional milestones. They are perplexed by recent findings about the importance of the early years. They know they need to stimulate their children, but how? And how much? And how can they be sure that the other adults who care for their children will give them what they need?

Family support programs first appeared in the early seventies and have spread across the country. They began as small, grass-roots efforts but have grown rapidly in number, size, and complexity. According to Family Support America (formerly the Family Resource Coalition), half of the states in the union now have formal family support networks linking community-based programs.

Family support has two key aims: first, creating programs of services aimed at strengthening effective family functioning and fostering a sense of family self-sufficiency and empowerment; and second, ensuring that families' strengths and needs are factored into all policies and programs related to children's well-being.

Over the last decade, hundreds of family support programs have sprung up in diverse communities and settings. Many are free-standing, nonprofit agencies, and others are sponsored by churches, hospitals, schools, day-care centers, or colleges and universities. What they have in common is commitment to a set of assumptions, including these:

- *Families have primary responsibility for their children's development and well-being.* They need resources and supports that will enable them to fulfill that responsibility effectively. They should take part in planning and improving early childhood services.

- *Families operate as part of a total system.* Children cannot be viewed as separate from their families, nor can families be viewed separately from their communities, their cultural heritage, or the society at large. Decisions made on behalf of children must consider the ways in which these various systems are interconnected.

- *The systems and institutions upon which families rely for support must assist families' efforts to effectively raise their children.* They must adjust and coordinate their services so as not to hinder families' abilities to maintain positive environments for their children.[106]

Family support programs may include information and referral services; life skills for parents; parent education classes and support groups; parent-child groups and family activities; drop-in time for children and their caregivers; crisis intervention and family counseling; and auxiliary support services (such as clothing exchanges, emergency food, and transportation). Some offer education and second-language instruction.

Family support programs flourish in all kinds of communities but can be especially valuable in rural areas where isolation can be a difficult fact of life for families with small children. In West Virginia, beginning in 1996, a Starting Points grant from Carnegie Corporation allowed nine counties to develop Starting Points Early Childhood Centers, serving families with young children. These centers bring together, in a single location, a wide range of existing services such as child care and parent education, health and nutrition services, and home-based outreach. The Governor's Cabinet on Children and Families took the lead in developing and implementing the Starting Point Centers, forging an important and new type of partnership between state government and local communities.

Family literacy programs are another form of family support. Parents play a crucial role in laying a foundation for literacy by reading aloud to their children, familiarizing them with the format of books, and helping them grasp the relationship between sound and print. For many parents, these are easy, natural activities, but for others, they are very difficult.

Today, tens of millions of adults across the nation cannot read, write, or perform basic math problems well enough to find and keep decent jobs, support their children's education, and participate actively in civic life. According to the National Adult Literacy Survey (NALS), more than one-fifth of the adult population (some 44 million people) is functionally illiterate. Many are immigrants and most did not complete high school. Another quarter of the adult population (44–50 million people) have somewhat stronger literacy skills, but still lack a sufficient foundation of basic skills to function successfully in our society.[107]

These numbers are worrisome, in view of evidence that children's achievement is closely tied to parents' educational level and the literacy environment of the home. Family literacy programs seek to change intergenerational educational patterns, connecting early education for children and adult literacy instruction for parents. At least seventy-five thousand parents in adult education programs participate in family literacy services each year. State evaluations show that both parents and children participating in family literacy programs make educational progress, and parents become more involved in helping their children learn.[108]

Family literacy programs can be home-based, or they can meet at family resource centers, schools, libraries, or workplaces. They generally include activities for children and for adults, as well as family support. They are also intergenerational, reaching out to children's immediate or extended family members of all ages.

Even Start is the nation's largest family literacy program, serving about eight hundred sites across the nation and serving approximately 1 million parents and children under the age of eight. The program focuses on the educational needs of low-income families with young children, with the goal of helping to break the cycle of poverty and illiteracy. To reach this goal, all Even Start projects build on existing community resources to integrate adult basic education, parenting education, and early childhood education services into a unified program.

Since its inception in 1989, the Even Start program has grown significantly. The program has helped many adults attain a GED. According to national evaluations, the program appears to support children's language development and school readiness—especially for those who remain in the program for more than one year. More sustained, rigorous evaluation is needed to gauge the program's long-term effects.[109]

Home Visitation

The arrival of a new baby can overwhelm even the calmest new parents and can disrupt even the most smoothly running household. Relationships are altered; old schedules, routines, and expectations no longer work; and new responsibilities and skills must be internalized. At the same time new parents must cope with more mundane concerns: getting the right supplies, creating an environment that is safe and healthy for a newborn, buying or borrowing new furnishings and equipment, and finding help with child care, medical care, and day-to-day tasks. For more than a century, organizations dedicated to giving babies a good start in life have made visits to new or expectant parents, to help them cope with all of these challenges.[110]

Programs vary widely: some focus on the new baby and others try to help the whole family adjust. Some focus on mothers and fathers in their role as parents, while others try to help them improve their own lives. One key to children's healthy development is parents' ability to read and respond to their baby's signals. Helping parents become more responsive caregivers is an important aim of most home visitation programs. Some programs begin before a child is born, seeking to improve the outcomes of pregnancy, the quality of care that parents provide to their children, and families' economic self-sufficiency.

Home visitation programs also differ in terms of the frequency of visits, the content of those visits, and the staffing. The visitor can be a professional with a degree in nursing, social work or education, or can be an experienced parent or layperson who knows a great deal about raising young children.

A recent survey showed that most states have home visitation programs, and many have made substantial commitments to them.[111] These programs may be administered by a State Department of Health, Department of Human Services, or Department of Education. State Maternal and Child Health programs are frequently involved. These programs may support or complement local, community-based programs. Most use a combination of state and federal dollars, and a few use private funds. Some states provide staff time for training, coordinating, or evaluating local efforts but provide no public funds to directly support home visitation. The majority of state-based home visiting programs use preexisting program designs and about half are part of a broader initiative or larger intervention strategy.[112]

Nearly half of state-based home visitation efforts are tied to legislative mandates, such as comprehensive state children's initiatives, welfare reform, or maternity care access. Early hospital discharge legislation is particularly influential. Today, the federal government and more than half of the states have legislation regarding early hospital discharge, and most of these new laws require private insurers to cover one or more home visits when mothers and newborns have had very brief hospital stays. Some laws specify the minimum content and timing of such visits. However, little is known about the extent to which such laws are being carried out.[113]

According to the organization Healthy Families America, effective home visitation programs do the following:

1. Initiate services before or at the time of birth.

2. Use a standardized assessment process or guidelines to identify families in need.

3. Offer services voluntarily and in a positive manner to build family trust.

4. Offer services intensively (at least one per week) with well-defined criteria for varying the level of intensity for a period of three to five years.

5. Offer culturally competent services.

6. Focus services on supporting parents and supporting parent-child interaction and child development.

7. Link families to a health care provider at least, to ensure timely immunization and well-child care, and link to additional services as necessary.

8. Limit staff caseloads (typically no more than 15 families per visitor).

9. Select staff who have appropriate personal characteristics, willingness to work in culturally diverse communities, and skills to do the job.

10. Select staff whose education and experience enable them to manage

the range of issues they may encounter working with at-risk families.

11. Provide staff with intensive training specific to their roles.

12. Ensure ongoing supervision so that staff are able to develop realistic plans, work effectively with families, and solve problems.[114]

Home visitation programs can be comforting for families and can help to connect parents with a range of community resources. But do they actually improve children's outcomes or prospects? An early proponent of home visitation programs, Florence Nightingale, insisted in 1894 that "results shown are the only test."[115] But it has often been difficult to judge effectiveness, because programs have not been designed in ways that allowed a sharp focus on results.[116]

However, based on a fifteen-year study of one prenatal and home visiting program serving low-income, unmarried teen mothers and their children, there is now strong evidence that such programs can indeed produce positive effects for children and parents alike—but it is not easy.

The Prenatal/Early Infancy Project began in Elmira, New York, as a home visitation program for low-income mothers having their first babies. Most were unmarried and many were teens. Visiting nurses worked with mothers and families in their homes during pregnancy and throughout the first two years of the child's life to accomplish three goals: improving pregnancy outcomes; improving the child's health and development by helping parents provide more responsible and competent care; and improving families' economic self-sufficiency.

A fifteen-year follow-up to the original Elmira participants found that the program had long-term benefits for the mothers, resulting in fewer state-verified reports of child abuse and neglect; fewer maternal behavioral problems due to alcohol and drug use;

and fewer arrests. Some observers believe that the program had such a strong impact on the life-course development of participating mothers because it focused intensively on the choices they make early in their personal development as parents.

Among the children born to participating mothers, who were fifteen years old at the time of the follow-up study, researchers found fewer arrests and convictions; fewer sexual partners; and less smoking and drinking. An economic evaluation of the Elmira program concluded that when the program focused on low-income families in which the mother was unmarried, it saved four dollars for every one dollar invested.

In Elmira, the program served a primarily white population. The model was later replicated in Memphis and Denver, where the challenge was to adapt to the cultural beliefs of the African Americans and Mexican American families that it increasingly served. The program succeeded by continuing to include other family members and friends in the program and by engaging racially and ethnically diverse teams of visitors and supervisors.

Based on these positive results, the program has been replicated in many communities. A major concern is maintaining program quality as the initiative is scaled up, because there is strong evidence that to make a difference, home visitation programs have to get the implementation right.[117]

The Prenatal/Early Infancy Project is but one of many home visitation models. In 1999, an issue of the *Future of Children* reviewed the results of six of the largest initiatives. The six models differed in many ways but shared a common focus on prevention and a commitment to helping parents learn skills and behaviors that are known to improve children's health and development.

A key finding was that results vary dramatically depending on how the programs were implemented. It appeared that better, more consistent implementation would have produced better results. For example, across all of the programs, most families received about half of the visits that they were scheduled to receive, and in many programs, a small subset of families received many more than the expected number of visits. Across most programs, many—if not most—families left the program early. And so did the home visitors: staff turnover was as high as 50 percent in some programs.

The evaluations suggested that most of these shortcomings can be remedied. A key to the program's effectiveness is the home visitor's ability to establish a rapport with families, to recognize and to respond to special situations (such as parental depression or substance abuse), and to present the program's curriculum with conviction. Appropriate compensation and good training and supervision are therefore crucial. Home visitation programs need to set clear goals, to align the content of visits as well as training and supervision with those goals, and to build in quality assessment and monitoring components from the outset.[118]

Some projects now offer home visitation on a universal, voluntary basis. The state of Vermont offers a home visit to every family with a newborn.[119] However, most home visitation programs, like the Prenatal/Early Infancy Program, focus on low-income parents or teen parents.

Some programs, like Healthy Families America (HFA), are designed to help prevent child abuse. Developed by the National Committee to Prevent Child Abuse as an adaptation of Hawaii's Healthy Start Program, HFA now has 270 programs in thirty-eight states and the District of Columbia. Sites have considerable flexibility in implementing HFA, and programs vary significantly from place to place. However, all programs are committed to key principles including a commitment to serving families at high risk for child abuse, to strong collaboration with existing service systems, and to rigorous staff training and supervision. Two evaluations in

Arizona found that twice as many families in comparison groups (similar families who did not take part in the program) were reported for abuse or neglect during a two-year period as HFA participant families.[120]

If our nation is to improve results for young children, no challenge is more important than strengthening the capacity of families to nurture, to protect, and to teach their sons and daughters. But no challenge is more difficult. As they cope with multiple roles and responsibilities, all parents can benefit from wider access to information and resources. For our nation's more vulnerable families, this access can be especially critical.

In the years since *Starting Points* and *Years of Promise* appeared, efforts aimed at promoting responsible parenthood have expanded dramatically. No single approach has succeeded at meeting the complex needs of vulnerable families or of addressing the multiple risk factors many children face. However, some useful strategies have been identified and strengthened, including resource and referral services, public awareness campaigns, family support initiatives, parent education, home visitation, and family literacy programs. The next steps are to strengthen and expand today's best strategies and to adapt them to the diverse ethnicities, language groups, and cultures represented by today's families. Because deciding which programs have the best chance of working is not an easy task, new approaches to evaluation are a critical challenge.

CHAPTER 2

Infants and Toddlers

A blooming, buzzing confusion"—that is how pioneering American psychologist William James described the inner world of an infant more than a century ago. His vivid phrase was meant to convey infants' helpless response to the onrush of myriad unfamiliar sensations.

As is often the case, the phrase outlived the theory. A century of observation and study has yielded new insight into early development. A convergence of knowledge from many fields has focused attention on children's needs during the first three years of life.

- *Neuroscientists* have shown that the brains of young children are biologically primed for certain kinds of learning, and that experience has a direct influence on how the brain is "wired." They have found that in the early years, children's capabilities grow very rapidly, and that early experiences lay a foundation for later learning.

- *Biochemists* have studied brain chemistry, shedding light on issues like mood and attention. They have shown how parents' smoking, drinking, or drug use can affect children before and after birth.

- *Developmental scientists* have shown that secure attachments to loving, responsive adults are crucial as children learn to regulate their own emotions and behaviors.

- *Language experts* have shown that even very young babies are attuned to subtle differences in sounds, and that very small children can master the fundamental grammatical system of their native language. They have illuminated connections between language learning and other kinds of development.

- *Early childhood educators* have shown that school readiness involves many aspects of development. They have found that early literacy experiences (such as looking at picture books or being read to) help children learn to read.

- *Social scientists and biomedical scientists*, working together, have clarified the links between children's experiences in their homes and communities and their chances for healthy development.

These new understandings about child development have led to greater public awareness of opportunities to promote healthy development and learning in the early years. They have helped to build support for new or expanded early childhood services, such as Early Head Start. They have inspired efforts to improve the quality of early education and care received by the millions of infants and toddlers who spend their days in nonparental care.[1]

The research, as translated for the public by child advocates, has also sparked debate. If the first years are said to be very important, are other developmental periods necessarily diminished?

How can we, as a society, strengthen services for young children without depriving their older brothers and sisters? Will public statements about the effects of early deprivation needlessly frighten parents or mislead policymakers?

Today, it is the academics and advocates who are abuzz, and understandably, onlookers are more than occasionally confused. The children, meanwhile, do not wait for controversies to abate. They continue to grow and learn. This chapter presents some of today's best ideas for meeting the needs of our youngest children— in whatever setting they happen to be.

Late Bloomers

We humans are late bloomers. We come into the world in a relatively unfinished state. Compared with other primates, more of our development takes place after birth, in contact with the external environment—the touches, sights, sounds, and other sensations of childhood.

But what bloomers! From the very beginning, we are learning and changing, and these processes never stop. We are fitted with a unique ability to adjust to many settings and situations and to recover from adversity. Anthropologists tell us that much of what it means to be human—the extraordinary cultural variability so unique to our species—relates to the fact that so much of our development takes place in the world.[2]

Children are eager, active learners from the start. On the first day of life, newborns can search the room with their eyes, visually trace the edges of a triangle, and look intently into their mothers' eyes during a feeding.[3] By the fourth feeding, infants already anticipate events. As soon as they are held close to their mothers' bodies, they begin to show the clinging, sucking behavior they associate with being fed. They quickly learn the sound of their mothers' voices, turning to look for them.[4]

In the first three years of life, children make breathtaking developmental leaps, acquiring not only words, but also a grasp of abstract linguistic structure; not only the ability to move about on their own, but also an impressive understanding of their surroundings; not only basic social skills, but also the beginnings of empathy and moral reasoning; not only an awareness of emotion, but also a capacity for self-regulation; not only an aptitude for analyzing their own situations, but also a propensity to ponder other people's perspectives.[5]

Cognitive scientists have invented innovative ways to ask babies what they know and when they know it. For example, by attaching a nipple to a pressure switch that controls a film projector lens, they have found that five- to twelve-week-old infants can adjust their sucking in order to bring a blurry image into focus. Using similar methods, they have found that babies as young as five months old can count up to three. Babies learn quickly about the physical world as well. For example, they understand that objects need support to keep them from falling. When three-month-old babies are shown an event that contradicts basic laws of nature (the object doesn't fall when support is withdrawn), they look at it longer than they look at more ordinary events. Before their first birthdays, infants grasp that inanimate objects cannot move themselves but need to be propelled into action.[6]

How do newborns transform so quickly into beings with such remarkable human capacities? Scientists have found that child development is an exceedingly complex process, shaped by a dynamic, ongoing interaction between heredity and experience. Some aspects of early development seem to be inborn. For example, infants seem to have, from birth, a powerful drive to try to master new behaviors and skills. But the kind of care they receive and the settings they experience can facilitate—or impede—this tendency.[7]

A key insight of recent decades is that experience can have a significant influence on early brain development. Many kinds of experience can affect how brain cells form neural pathways and how those pathways are streamlined and strengthened. Experience can also affect the brain's biochemistry, blood supply, and cellular support systems. The impact of experience on brain development has been observed in every stage of life but can be especially dramatic in the early years.

In recent years, the National Research Council reviewed the immense body of literature on early development in a study entitled *From Neurons to Neighborhoods: The Science of Early Childhood Development*, which drew upon research in many disciplines. Concerned that some popular accounts of early brain development may give the impression that the developmental die is cast by age three, the scientists who contributed to this study looked very carefully at the issue of timing. They stressed that while "the timing of early experiences can matter," more often than not, "the developing child remains vulnerable to risks and open to protective influences throughout the early years of life and into adulthood."[8]

From Neurons to Neighborhoods identified this idea as a core concept of early development: "The course of development can be altered in early childhood by effective interventions that change the balance between risk and protection, thereby shifting the odds in favor of more adaptive outcomes."[9] In other words, young children are resilient and many thrive even in difficult circumstances. When they grow up with many risk factors, such as poor nutrition or a stressful home life, they can be influenced as well by protective factors, such as good health care or a strong bond with a loving adult. When children receive timely help that tips the scales in favor of protection, they can succeed against heavy odds.

While stressing children's resilience, *From Neurons to Neighborhoods* also confirmed that the early years pose special risks. Severe stress or trauma can affect people of any age, but adversity in the first years of life can have an especially powerful impact. Studies of children who have grown up in desolate institutional settings have provided insight into the impact of early deprivation. Given very little social or intellectual stimulation, these children tend to become unresponsive, and the longer they remain in these circumstances, the more their development suffers. The good news is that children can make dramatic progress when they are adopted by loving, stable families, especially if this takes place early in the preschool years.[10] Even those who lag behind a year or more, in terms of behavior and physical development, can make up for lost time. A number of studies have followed children who experienced severe social deprivation in orphanages in eastern European countries before adoption by families from other countries. According to researcher Megan Gunnar, "A few children appear to bear most of the cost of their early adverse rearing while the majority appear to do quite well."[11]

However, not all children who suffer severe early deprivation bounce back. Despite the loving care of adoptive families, some continue to have serious problems that affect their achievement and behavior.[12] While most children can recover from early adversity, in some cases, the effects can be difficult to reverse.

Health Care for Young Children

Good health care, including preventive services, is so crucial to children's healthy development that the American Academy of

Pediatrics has called for universal access to comprehensive health care benefits for all children, youth, and pregnant women.[13]

Today, many young children lack coverage. According to the U.S. Census Bureau, 2.6 million children under the age of six (more than 11 percent) had no health insurance coverage during the entire year of 2000.[14] Having an employed parent does not assure children adequate health care. In fact, poor children whose parents are meeting the work standards established by the 1996 welfare legislation are less likely to be covered by health insurance than those whose parents are unemployed.[15]

In recent years, the nation has made some progress in extending health care coverage to more kids. Two programs provide public health insurance for many low-income children: Medicaid and the State Children's Health Insurance Plan (SCHIP).

Medicaid covers the costs of medically necessary health care for eligible adults and children, including all children with family income below the federal poverty line. Since its creation, Medicaid has been tied to the welfare system; in 1996, the two programs were delinked. As a result, Medicaid has contracted significantly and now reduces child poverty less than in the past. Many uninsured children under the age of six are eligible for Medicaid but are not enrolled.[16]

The second public insurance program is SCHIP. Enacted in 1997, SCHIP was designed to expand health insurance coverage to working families who earn too much for traditional Medicaid, yet not enough to afford private health insurance. The program provides federal dollars to states to fund affordable health insurance coverage for uninsured children in lower-income families. States design their own SCHIP programs by expanding their Medicaid programs, setting up separate SCHIP plans, or combining the two. Under the program, children may be eligible for physician visits, prescription medications, and hospitalizations at little or no cost.

Parents and other household members do not have to give information about their immigration status to qualify for the program.

States have found that simply establishing a SCHIP program is not enough. Nationwide, one-third of the children who qualify for SCHIP remain without coverage. Enrollment rates vary by states, and low-income children's access to health insurance depends, in part, on where they happen to live.[17] Immigrant children are particularly vulnerable. Compared with the children of U.S.-born parents, first-generation immigrant children are three times as likely, and second-generation immigrant children twice as likely, to lack health insurance.[18]

The American Academy of Pediatrics has launched an effort to increase enrollment of eligible children in Medicaid and SCHIP. Reaching Children: Building Systems of Care is a three-year initiative funded by Health Resources and Services Administration's Maternal and Child Health Bureau. The effort informs pediatricians and other health providers about SCHIP eligibility, and supports outreach efforts by local community networks.

States are focusing on outreach as well, and Congress now allows states with unspent SCHIP funds to use up to 10 percent of the money for this purpose. Those states with the most innovative efforts have been most successful at raising SCHIP enrollment. In New Mexico, SCHIP works with the Immigration and Naturalization Service to reassure immigrant families that when they apply for SCHIP coverage for their children, they will not be asked about their immigration status. A California outreach program to the Islamic community is designed to be responsive to the community's unique cultural values. In New York, an "in-reach" program focuses on child care centers and other worksites where employees' children are likely to be eligible for SCHIP.[19]

Of course, lack of coverage is not the only obstacle to good health care for young children. For families living in rural areas, distance and isolation can be steep barriers. Rural communities may have too few people to support critical services. Culture and language are also key factors. Some families avoid health care because they cannot find providers who speak their language. Others do not feel welcome at sites that are insensitive to their cultural norms and preferences. These barriers can keep children from receiving preventive services or timely treatment.[20]

When it comes to children's healthy development, the content of health services can matter a great deal. Children need dental care. They need regular screenings and developmental assessments to ensure that those who have disabilities or other special needs (or are at risk for disabilities) are identified early and get timely attention. California's School Readiness Master Plan, drafted in 2002, recommends universal access to screenings at birth, ages one and three, and at school entry. The twenty-year plan recommends access for all young children and expectant mothers to medical homes—primary care facilities where children can get a full range of medical and dental services, attention to developmental issues, referrals to specialists, and contact with a wide range of local agencies and service providers. The concept of a medical home for all children has been championed by the American Academy of Pediatrics.[21]

As a nation, we are years away from ensuring that every child has a medical home, but today, many pediatric practices are making efforts to help parents attend not only to their young children's physical well-being, but also to their full range of developmental needs. Given constraints on doctors' and nurses' time, this can be difficult. To address this problem, one national initiative has focused on infusing child development principles into pediatric practice. The Healthy Steps for Young Children Program is a national initiative that brings a "whole baby, whole family" perspective to prenatal and primary care for young children, and early returns suggest that the program is having a positive impact on children and their families. Healthy Steps adds to health care teams new members who have special training in child development and can fully address parents' concerns about their children's developmental and behavioral issues. The program also provides a range of supports for families, such as home visits, telephone help line, parenting groups, and referrals to community agencies. The Healthy Steps approach is being implemented and tested in pediatric and family practices across the country. The sites are coordinated by The Commonwealth Fund, and are funded by community-based foundations and local health care providers.

The Infant Health and Development Program (IHDP) also combines pediatric care with other services, including home visits, parent group meetings, and center-based early education programs. Designed for low birth weight and premature infants, the program follows children from birth through three years of age.

Some efforts to strengthen pediatric practice focus specifically on giving parents the tools they need to foster their children's reading readiness. In 1989, a group of pediatricians and early childhood educators gathered at Boston City Hospital to find a way to make early literacy development part of pediatric primary care. The result was Reach Out and Read—a program that makes reading and books a part of every visit to doctors' offices and clinics for children ages six months to six years.

The initiative has three key elements. First, volunteer readers are available to read to children in the waiting rooms of participating doctors' offices and clinics. The volunteers suggest and model easy ways to read and look at books with young children. Then, during the checkup, pediatricians counsel parents about the importance of reading with young children and suggest ways to make stories part of families' daily routines. As part of the checkup, older children are asked to read a developmentally appropriate book, and pediatricians have a chance to evaluate progress in speaking and reading. Finally, at the end of the visit, the doctor gives each child a new book to take home. By the end of the program, each child receives at least ten books. In this way, every family can add to (or begin) a library of children's books.

Children's Mental Health

A recent surgeon general's report on children's mental health begins with this vision statement: "Mental health is a critical component of children's learning and general health. Fostering social and emotional health in children as a part of healthy child development must therefore be a national priority. Both the promotion of mental health in children and the treatment of mental disorders should be major public goals."[22]

Beginning in infancy, young children have mental health needs that are often overlooked. There is strong evidence that even very young children can experience anguish and grief in response to trauma, loss, and personal rejection. Policy and practice in the early childhood field seldom take these findings into account. Few early care and education programs or pediatric health care facilities work closely with mental health professionals. And within the early childhood field, a severe shortage of professionals with training in children's mental health issues exacerbates the situation.

When prospective or new parents have access to mental health services, their children stand to benefit since babies' and toddlers' mental health is closely tied to that of the adults who care for them. An expectant mother who is very anxious or depressed may not eat well and may not be able to curb behaviors that can harm her baby, such as smoking, drinking, or drug use.

After birth, the consequences of maternal depression hinge on the child's stage of development. When mothers suffer from a brief postpartum depression, babies usually suffer no adverse consequences. But when depression persists beyond six months, it can be more problematic, interfering with a mother's ability to respond to her child. Researchers say that an infant whose depressed mother is withdrawn or unresponsive can show real distress, and an infant whose depressed mother is intrusive or hostile may avoid looking at or interacting with her. A toddler's playful interactions with a depressed mother tend to be briefer and are more likely to be interrupted (by the child or the mother) than with a nondepressed parent. Some depressed mothers are less able to provide structure or redirect the energies of excited toddlers, increasing the risk of behavioral or social problems.[23] The good news is that when mothers receive treatment for depression, their children generally fare very well.[24]

. . . .

Pediatrics Plus:
Colorado Parents Rely on Healthy Steps

By Joseph Alper

FOR EXPERIENCED PARENTS Peter and Elizabeth Nuncio, there is never enough help or advice to help them raise their children. Married for five years, the two Grand Junction, Colorado, residents each had children from previous marriages, so they knew what to expect when Elizabeth became pregnant.

Still, when Cathie Clark, R.N., approached the couple in 1997 to participate in the Healthy Steps program for children in the first three years of life, the Nuncios eagerly agreed.

Their now three-year-old daughter Irene has been the better for it, says Mom. "There's no doubt that Peter and I have been able to do an even better job with Irene than we did with our other children simply because Cathie has spent a lot of time with us over the past three years." Adds Peter, "How can you and your children not benefit from that kind of extra knowledge and help?"

On a sunny late summer day, the Nuncios have brought Irene in to the Western Colorado Pediatric Associates office for her three-year checkup with Clark, the practice's Healthy Steps specialist, and pediatrician Barbara Zind, M.D., who sees each of the practice's Healthy Steps families. It is Irene's last visit in the program, and the parents are a little emotional for they have grown to value Cathie as more than just their daughter's nurse. "Cathie is the best," says Peter. "She's always been available when we've had questions, and if nothing else the extra attention that Irene has gotten in the program has helped Elizabeth and me relax more about being parents. Everyone should participate in Healthy Steps."

That has been the program's goal from the start. Healthy Steps welcomes all comers regardless of income level, parental status, or number of children in a family. "The Healthy Steps philosophy is that all children, not just those from low-income families or those with single mothers, can use some extra attention during the first three years of life," says Clark. The only requirements are that parents must enroll their children at the ten-day visit to the pediatrician's office and promise to stay in the program for at least six months.

At Western Colorado Pediatrics, nine out of ten parents elect to join the program, and only a handful of parents have left over the past three years, all because they had moved out of the area. "And even then we still get calls from the parents when they have questions about their children," says Clark with a laugh. The program has recently expanded to include Grand Junction's largest family practice, and the goal is to have 750 families enrolled. "That would cover about half the newborns in Grand Junction and the surrounding towns," says Clark.

What parents get for enrolling their children is a steady diet of physical, emotional, and behavioral assessments for the kids and age-appropriate parenting tips beginning ten days after birth and continuing until the child reaches age three. While Zind performs the standard fifteen-minute in-office physical exams, Clark and colleague Rebecca Hobart, a licensed clinical social worker, spend more time observing the interactions between parent and child, as well as other family members, and going through a series of checklists with parents to ensure that no potential problems are overlooked. "Often, parents don't know what to ask, so the checklists work well at making sure that parents have as much information as they need to succeed at raising a healthy child," explains Hobart.

For example, when a child is nine months, either Clark or Hobart visits the family at home. At this age, many babies are getting ready to walk. Even if they are months away from taking their first steps, the attention they pay to mastering this skill often comes at the expense of eating or sleeping—a connection that parents may not make. "Many of our families become very concerned that their child has suddenly become a very fussy eater or that they've suddenly stopped sleeping through the night," says Clark. "What we do is provide them information on the transitions that children make at this age and how to start to organize the household, in terms of discipline and structure, to accommodate both the child's newly developing sense of freedom and the parents' need to establish routines and discipline."

The regular visits are also an opportunity to spot problems that parents may not know to look for in their children. Take speech lag, for example. "Particularly in families with older children, parents understand that each child develops differently," says Hobart. "But there's a difference between natural variation and a developmental problem, and we often pick this one up very early and get the child started in therapy right away to solve this before it actually becomes a problem."

What do Clark and Hobart, both experienced caregivers, get from Healthy Steps? "This is absolutely the best job I've ever had," says Clark, who was burning out as a psychiatric nurse before joining the Healthy Steps program almost four years ago. "I know that I'm having a positive impact on children and their families." Hobart agrees with her friend and colleague, adding, "This is the most important work that I've done in my professional life."

. . . .

Learning in the Context of Relationships

In the fifties and sixties, the scientists who studied child development tended to focus on the ways that individual children solve problems and stretch their mental abilities. They came up with ingenious ways to investigate how young children learn. These experiments tended to look at children's intellectual capacities—with relatively little attention to the social or emotional contexts in which those capacities evolve. In recent decades, researchers have taken more fully into account the fact that children learn in the context of close relationships.

Children's first bonds are usually with their mothers. From the first weeks of life, infants and mothers coordinate their behavior, reflecting close emotional communication. Their face-to-face interactions often approximate the give-and-take of conversation.

To study the attunement of infants and their mothers, a team of researchers set up an experiment using two real-time video cameras. Moms and babies interacted on-screen, watching the movements of each other's eyes and mouths and observing each other's gestures and other body language. When they were "in synch"—even over the video equipment—babies as young as six to twelve weeks were engaged and responsive. But when the equipment was adjusted so that the mothers' responses were out of synch, babies were more likely to avert their eyes and show signs of distress. Even when they looked at the image, they often seemed disengaged and confused.[25] This confusion—quite different from the state described by William James—reflects a pleasurable fusion between self and other.[26] Psychologists have used many words to describe it, including social syncretism, intersubjectivity, and attachment. Some refer to the "attachment system"—an inborn system that shapes and organizes infants' emotions and memories in relation to the adults who nurture them. It is this system that helps a young child establish a secure base in the world. On this base rests the capacity for emotional regulation, social relatedness, self-awareness, and meaningful communication.[27]

What happens when children do not form secure attachments in the first months of life? Once again, studies of children living in institutions provide insight. Children who leave orphanages to live with families can form a first attachment at any point during the early childhood years, and possibly later. The window of opportunity appears to be wider than some developmental psychologists have thought. However, the quality of these children's attachment relationships may be compromised. Some have trouble establishing secure attachments with adoptive or foster parents. As they move through childhood into adulthood, some find it difficult to form intimate relationships with peers. These findings add to a body of research showing that stable relationships during infancy play an important role in organizing the competencies that allow children to make strong emotional commitments later in life.[28]

Fortunately, nearly all infants form strong attachments during the first year of life. Most often, babies form "selective attachments"—limited to a few close people with whom they interact on a regular basis. While psychologists have long observed the importance of such attachments, only in recent decades have they begun to appreciate their impact on early development.[29]

To be sure, experiences throughout life affect the functioning of the mind, and strong emotional relationships remain important throughout the life span. For adults, attachment figures may be family members, romantic partners, close friends, or mentors. But early attachments play an especially important role, setting the stage for continued engagement in the world and continued learning. It is through day-to-day relationships with parents and other important caregivers that babies develop a sense of who they are and what they can expect of other people.[30]

LANGUAGE LEARNING

Long before children can say words or string them together, they are active language learners. Newborns who are only a few days old can differentiate between their own language and another.[31] In the early months, babies can distinguish all of the speech sounds that occur in natural language, but they soon begin to specialize. By their first birthdays, they can only distinguish the speech sounds of the language (or languages) which they hear consistently.[32]

By about seven to ten months, children begin repetitive babbling. At this age, deaf children also start to babble with their hands, producing sequences of sign-language syllables that parallel vocal babbling. Observations of deaf children have shed light on language learning, showing that the inborn human capacity for language acquisition goes well beyond learning to vocalize. Very early in life, babies begin to grasp abstract linguistic structure— whether by means of speech or other symbolic systems.[33]

Adults who struggle to acquire a new language have little doubt that young children are primed for language learning. By some estimates, children learn, on average, nine new words a day from age eighteen months to six years. By the age of six, many children have learned nine to fourteen thousand words.[34] But some children hear more words than others. Young children living in poverty hear, on average, 300 fewer words *per hour* than do children in professional families. This early "word gap" is linked with lower third-grade vocabulary and reading comprehension scores. It can also have an impact on children's conceptual understanding—what they know about the world around them. As they move through the elementary grades, this can affect their reading achievement and overall academic progress.[35]

Mastering thousands of words is an impressive accomplishment, but just as important is the system of rules that children master when they acquire a language. This system entails both rules and exceptions and becomes a template for many other rule systems that children will encounter in life.[36] Moreover, recent research has found that a successful use of language and communication helps to foster children's mental health. Impoverished verbal environments impede children's ability to perceive other people's mental states, which in turn affects their ability to make and sustain friendships.[37]

Communication skills do not develop in a vacuum. Babies learn language in the context of important relationships. For example, learning a new word depends on achieving "joint reference"—linking an unfamiliar word to the precise object, scene, or event to which a speaker refers. This is not easy, even if it is simply an object being labeled. After all, a baby's world is filled with objects, any one of which could be the "sweet potato" that Dad is naming.

Joint reference happens naturally if adult and infant happen to be focused on the same thing when the adult uses a new word. But if they are not, many parents will make an accommodation. Researchers who study mother-child interactions say that by the time infants are about nine months old, mothers frequently follow their line of vision and label the object that has seized their babies' interest. Studies suggest that most of mothers' utterances—as many as 70 percent—refer to an object already occupying the focus of a six- to ten-month-old's attention. As a baby reaches for a stuffed animal, Mom says: "Here's Sparky, here's your doggy. Say hi to your doggy." She may signal, with her intonation, which words name the object that has caught the baby's eye. This kind of responsiveness fosters infants' language acquisition. Researchers have found that mothers of infants who learn words at a normal rate are more likely to do this than those whose infants are slower language learners.[38]

Like the character in a Molière play who is surprised to learn that he has been speaking "prose" all his life, most parents practice "joint attention" without suspecting that the concept has a name or merits journal articles. For them, responsive care is intuitive, requiring no explanation or instruction. But for others, it is less obvious. When parents or other caregivers gain insight into language acquisition, they can make simple changes that may have far-reaching effects.

Expanding Parents' Opportunities to Nurture Infants

Childrearing practices and convictions about parenting evolve as nations and communities change. Our nation has seen dramatic change in public opinion and social policy on many issues. But one conviction remains constant: by margins of at least three to one, Americans prefer that a parent (usually the mother) stay home to care for infants and toddlers—unless the mother's employment keeps the family off welfare.[39]

In the realm of children and families, this is one of the rare topics that stirs little controversy: surveys show that nearly all parents (94 percent) think it is important for one parent to be at home during a child's first years. More than a third (35 percent) say that it is "absolutely essential." In focus groups, parents stress that "you can't take back this valuable time."[40] Convinced that pressures faced by working families are intensifying, 90 percent of Americans say that employers should do more, and 72 percent say that government should do more.[41]

In short, where infants are concerned, maternal care is considered preferable. But necessity, often called the mother of invention, has also required the invention of alternatives to mother (and father). Today, only a minority of parents have the option of attending to young children's needs on a full-time basis. In contrast to many of our peer nations, where parents have access to paid leave for substantial periods, in the United States few parents have access to paid leave. Paid leave would not only secure their jobs when they take time from work to raise children, but also replace enough of their foregone wages to make full-time parenthood possible during their babies' first weeks and months of life (or during adopted or foster children's first weeks and months with their new families).

Today, advocates and policymakers in the early childhood field are attending more closely to parents' views and preferences. They are taking measure of the gap between the ideal Americans profess and the reality they live with. And they are raising higher on the child care agenda two planks that have often been given low priority in the past: family leave and other forms of assistance for stay-at-home parents.

In 1993, the Family and Medical Leave Act (FMLA) was passed into law, giving eligible workers the right to take up to twelve weeks' unpaid leave to care for new children or sick family members or to recover from their own illness without risking their jobs. For working families, this initiative represented a major step forward. Each year, more than 4 million Americans take advantage of FMLA.

However, FMLA has two limitations. First, not everyone qualifies. FMLA applies to all public agencies, including state, local, and federal employees, local public and private education agencies, and to all businesses with fifty or more employees. According to some estimates, the FMLA does not cover 40 percent of private-sector employees.[42] Second, many parents who are eligible to take leave under FMLA cannot afford unpaid leave. According to a survey taken a year after FMLA was introduced, nearly two-thirds of employees who needed but did not take family or medical leave cited lost wages as the reason.[43] In *From Neurons to Neighborhoods,* the National Research Council recommended expanding coverage of FMLA to all working parents. It also urged policymakers to explore ways to financially support low-income parents who take family leave, since for them even a temporary loss of earnings can be a hardship. *From Neurons to Neighborhoods* further recommended that those states that require mothers on public assistance to work outside of the home soon after the birth of a newborn extend the period that infants can benefit from the care of their own mothers.[44] Today, many states are exploring options for providing paid family leave, but none has made a full commitment.

Working and stay-at-home parents have often been portrayed as distinct groups with very different interests and concerns. However, many parents—and especially mothers—move in and out of the labor force at different points in their children's lives. Many families who choose to have a parent stay home while their children are young forego a second income, and because of this, many face economic stress.

A number of policies already exist to help at-home parents. A per-child tax credit can be claimed by families with an at-home parent. In addition, the tax code offers a number of advantages to couples with only one earner. While two-earner families may incur a "marriage penalty" when they wed, single-earner couples have less tax liability after marriage than before.[45] However, for many families, these measures are not enough. Policies are needed that help both working parents and at-home parents survive economically while meeting their children's needs.

Infant and Toddler Care—Does Quality Matter?

In little more than a decade, we have changed from a society in which most infants and toddlers had at-home mothers, to one in which most spend long stretches away from their parents. Of course, in the real world of parenting and time clocks, child care issues are not new: millions of moderate- and low-income women have been juggling families and work for generations. Today, most families have to meet this challenge.

Here are the facts:

- *73 percent of infants and toddlers of employed mothers are cared for primarily by someone other than a parent* while their mothers are on the job, and they spend an average of twenty-five hours per week in nonparental care.

- *39 percent of infants and toddlers with employed mothers are in care full-time* (35 hours or more).[46]

These are averages. The proportion of infants and toddlers in full-time care is significantly higher for some groups of young children. For example, two-thirds of infants and toddlers in low-income working families (earning no more than twice the federal poverty line) are in full-time care. Two-thirds of those whose single parents work full-time are in full-time care. There are also sharp differences across racial and ethnic lines.

Moreover, the percentage of young children in full-time care varies markedly across states. For example, infants and toddlers in

Mississippi, Alabama, and Texas are much more likely than those in California or Massachusetts to be in full-time care. It is likely that numerous factors are at work, including differences in demography, culture, and policy. Given this variation, policymakers cannot rely on national data to guide their decision-making about the needs of young children and their families.[47]

Many infants and toddlers receive care that keeps them safe and healthy and meets the full spectrum of their developmental needs. Most do not. High-quality care for infants and toddlers is labor-intensive and very expensive, and most new parents have neither the earnings nor the savings to cover those costs. As a result, infants and toddlers receive early care and education that is, on average, worse than that available to older children.[48] Turning the situation around would therefore require significant public investment. But many Americans are wondering whether investments in early learning programs are best reserved for the year or two leading up to school entry.

Most people agree that, all things being equal, it would be wonderful for *all* young children in nonparental care to have highly trained teachers and a great deal of individual attention. But in the realm of policy, all things are rarely equal. Given fiscal realities, policymakers often must make tradeoffs between competing needs—among and within age groups. And so they may ask: does the quality of care matter less for infants and toddlers than for older preschoolers, who are closer to the thresholds of public schools? Given today's focus on school readiness, can we make do with untrained caregivers and custodial care in the early years and invest more heavily in pre-kindergarten, kindergarten, and the primary grades?

Researchers say that the answer to both questions is no. Pointing to new evidence of the opportunities and risks of the early years, they stress that the path to school readiness begins even before the preschool years. They also say that the well-documented achievement gap separating American students of different income groups opens up very early in life. Deborah Phillips, a leader of the National Research Council study of the science of early childhood development, testified to a Congressional committee in 2001 that "by the age of two years, striking differences in what children know and can do begin to distinguish low-income children from their better off peers."[49]

There is strong evidence that child care quality in the first year of life affects children's later development and school readiness, especially the social and emotional development that underlies other kinds of achievement. *The Handbook of Child Psychology* sums up the evidence this way: "Quality day care from infancy clearly has positive effects on children's intellectual, verbal, and cognitive development, especially when children would otherwise experience impoverished and relatively unstimulating home environments. Care of unknown quality may have deleterious effects."[50]

In its extensive study of center-based care for infants and toddlers, the National Institute of Child Health and Development looked at four factors: child-to-adult ratios; group size; caregivers' specialized training in child development or early education; and caregivers' formal education. In each case, NICHD considered whether the program met the guidelines recommended by the American Public Health Association and the American Academy of Pediatrics. They assumed that programs that met all four guidelines (we will call them four-star programs) would be of the highest quality, followed by three-, two-, and one-star programs.

The study found that settings for three-year-olds are of higher quality than those for younger children. More than one-third of classrooms for three-year-olds were four-star settings, compared to only one-tenth of classrooms for two-year-olds. The researchers wanted to know whether four-star classrooms actually produce better outcomes for children, and they found that they do. Even after controlling for family income and mothers' sensitivity to kids' needs, children who attended higher quality centers had fewer behavior problems at ages two and three and had higher school readiness and language comprehension scores at age three.

The researchers also looked at the effect of particular factors. They found that at age two, children whose centers met the recommended adult-to-child ratio displayed fewer behavior problems and more positive social behaviors. Some of the strongest findings concerned the benefits of having well-educated, well-prepared caregivers. At age three, children whose caregivers had more specialized training or formal education scored higher on measures of school readiness and language comprehension, and had fewer behavior problems.[51]

Other studies link caregivers' preparation to children's language development. Researchers have known for some time that when teachers or caregivers are better educated, the preschoolers in their care have stronger language skills.[52] Now they report that the same is true for younger children. When caregivers are better educated, infants develop stronger expressive language skills.[53] With better educated caregivers, both infants and toddlers are more likely to engage in language activities, complex play with objects, and creative activities in their classroom.[54]

Studies have documented not only the positive effects of good care, but also the adverse impact of low-quality care. After taking into account demographic and socioeconomic factors, researchers have found that children who have a history of poor-quality child care in the first three years were rated by their preschooler teachers as being more difficult and by their kindergarten teachers as being more hostile. They engaged in less social pretend play and were less likely to display positive feelings in their preschool settings.[55] All of this evidence suggests that improving the quality of early care and education for infants and toddlers can help to promote school readiness in all of its dimensions and prevent adjustment problems at school entry.

FOCUSING ON REGULATION

One key to raising quality is regulation. Those states with more effective regulatory policies offer their residents a larger supply of higher quality programs. Many states, however, need to strengthen regulation.

Most parents who enroll their small children in child care programs assume that they are regulated and inspected by the government. But this is not always the case. In some states, a large number of settings (both center-based and home-based) are exempt from regulation.

The National Association for the Education of Young Children (NAEYC), in its position statement on the licensing and public regulation of early childhood programs, states that any program providing care and education to children from two or more unrelated families should be regulated. It stresses that there should be no exemptions from this principle and explicitly opposes the exemption of part-day programs or programs sponsored by religious organizations because "such exemption does not provide an equal level of health and safety protection for all children."[56]

Even when programs are held to licensing standards, those standards may not be high enough. Some states set their basic floor of protection too low, creating rules that have little relationship to children's developmental needs. For example, adult-to-child ratios and group size are very important elements of quality in centers that care for infants and toddlers, who require more individual attention than older children. A number of professional organizations have made recommendations about ratios and group size. NAEYC recommends that all groups have at least two teachers. Infants should be in groups of no more than six to eight children, with at least one adult for every four children. For toddlers, groups should not exceed fourteen children and should have at least one adult for every seven children.[57] However, researchers say that few states have adopted standards that are consistent with the recommendations of professional organizations. Moreover, nationally representative surveys have found that average group sizes and ratios exceed recommended limits.[58]

Lack of enforcement is another barrier to improving infant and toddler care. Many states do not provide their licensing offices with enough resources or authority to enforce the rules.

The issue of regulation has come to the fore in part because so many taxpayer dollars, in the form of child care subsidies, are going to unregulated providers. The Foundation for Child Development has taken a strong stand on this issue, urging that public funding go only to providers or programs that are accountable for meeting quality standards.[59]

Raising and enforcing high standards might seem an obvious solution to the quality crisis in early care and education. But it has a down side as well. Some child advocates worry that raising the bar too high will intimidate many providers, especially those who offer informal care. The concern is that strict regulation could drive providers out of the field, narrowing options for parents in general, and low-income parents in particular. The questions of licenses and exemptions therefore warrant a closer look.

Who Is Licensed to Care for Children?

Arranging good quality child care can be tough for all families, but for those with infants and toddlers, it can be immensely difficult. First, parents must negotiate a maze of child care options—all of which have advantages and drawbacks.

- *Center-based care.* In this type of program, groups of children receive care in a facility that is not a home. The program may be operated as a for-profit business, or it may be run by a religious organization, not-for-profit agency, or parent cooperative. Some programs are part of public school programs. Others are run by employers for the children of their staff. Across the nation, there are about 99,000 licensed child care centers.[60] State laws generally require licensing, but centers may be exempt from licensing if they are housed in or run by a public school or religious institution or if parents are on the premises while their children are receiving care.

- *Family or group child care homes.* Not all center-based child care settings are licensed; by the same token, not all home-based settings are unlicensed. Across the nation, there are nearly 300,000 regulated or licensed family child care providers.

- *Kith and kin care.* This term refers to care provided by a friend or acquaintance (kith) or relative (kin) exclusively to children from one family, either in the provider's home or in the child's home. One-quarter of infants and toddlers with employed mothers are cared for by "kin." Usually this form of child care is not regulated. However, depending on the number of children being cared for in the home, some "kith" care must be licensed.

- *In-home care.* Care or "baby-sitting" may be provided by a nonrelative in the family home. This type of care is usually unlicensed, even though providers may be eligible to receive state subsidies.

- *Multiple arrangements.* In many cases, one child care arrangement does not provide the coverage that working parents need. They must often cobble together plans for their young children: one-third of their infants and toddlers are in two or more child care arrangements each week. All kinds of families have this need. Nationally, higher-income parents are just as likely as those who earn less to need multiple arrangements for their infants and toddlers. Many three- and four-year-olds also have multiple arrangements (such as preschool followed by several hours at a neighbor's house), but younger children are more likely to be in two or more *informal* arrangements.[61]

Widening the Policy Lens

When policymakers address early learning issues, they tend to focus on child care centers or preschools. Some are beginning to realize that the policy lens must be widened because the vast majority of infants and toddlers are not in those settings. Of young children with employed mothers, 15 percent are in center-based care during the first year of life, 23 percent in the second, and 27 percent in the third.[62] In part, these statistics reflect limited availability. Many child care centers do not accept children until they are out of diapers. Those that do tend to be expensive, hard to get to, and of lower quality than programs for older preschoolers.

When infants or toddlers have significant disabilities or other special needs, the obstacles can be even higher. Despite changes in public attitudes and the law, many parents are hard pressed to find appropriate settings for these young children.[63] Many early care and education programs have expanded to become inclusive settings, capable of serving children with diverse abilities, but the challenge of full inclusion for all children has not yet been realized.[64]

Low enrollment of very young children in child care centers also reflects parental preferences. Generally speaking, parents prefer home-based care for their infants and toddlers. As things stand, most home-based care is unregulated. Parents alone must monitor their children's safety, care, and learning, and this is difficult to sustain, given new parents' limited experience and busy lives. In the absence of regulation, providers are also on their own. They may, understandably, count themselves fortunate to be free of oversight; however, they also lose opportunities to get assistance, feedback, and advice from regulatory agencies or to connect with other people in the same line of work.

Despite its importance, home-based care has received little attention from policymakers or researchers.[65] This began to change in the late nineties, in the wake of welfare reform. As the need for child care grew, many states could not afford to overlook kith and kin care as a child care option, especially for parents working during nontraditional hours. Suddenly, public subsidies for care were going to providers who had drawn little notice and generally had been exempt from regulatory standards. This sparked greater interest in the quality of home-based care.

What is known about the quality of home-based care? When a team of researchers recently looked at the findings of twenty-seven studies of informal child care, the results were mixed.[66] A number of the studies they reviewed found that informal care is, generally speaking, of poorer quality than care provided by licensed providers. For example, the National Child Care Staffing Study conducted a decade ago found that regulated providers were more sensitive and responsive to children than unregulated caregivers (but found no significant differences between relatives and other unregulated providers).

But other researchers have found that home-based providers, whether regulated or unregulated, are more likely to talk to children than child-care center staff. A 1996 study of infant child care by the National Institute of Child Health and Human Development did not find poorer quality care by home-based kith and kin providers. This finding reflects, in part, NICHD's emphasis on small group sizes and low ratios as keys to quality. Moreover, the NICHD study found no significant differences between licensed and informal home-based care arrangements in terms of the quality of the physical setting. It did find, however, that the quality of kith and kin care (unlike center-based care) hinges on family income—with low-income children getting worse care.[67]

Researchers do agree that informal care settings are less likely than center-based care to have an educational focus. Children in these settings spend less time with books or educational materials and more time watching television and videos of all kinds. The stronger educational emphasis of center-based care has been associated with better cognitive and language outcomes for children and a higher degree of school readiness.

IMPROVING FAMILY CHILD CARE HOMES

Many home-based providers are warm, conscientious caregivers, but most work in isolation, without assistance or opportunities to upgrade their knowledge and skills. They work long hours (averaging 53 hours per week) and receive wages that often leave them living in poverty. As a result, the turnover rate is very high—exceeding 35 percent per year.

Standards for licensed family child care vary greatly. Exemptions are often available for small family child care providers—those who offer care in their own home for six or fewer children. Larger family child care homes—typically for seven to twelve children in the home of a provider who employs an assistant—are more likely to be subject to regulation. In some states, standards are high and home inspections are required; in other states, self-certification is sufficient, even if the provider receives state subsidies; and in still others, all that is required is a background check to determine whether the provider has a criminal record.

When family child care homes are subject to regulation, group size is an important issue. In family child care, mixed age groups are common, so more complex formulas are needed than for center-based programs. For example, Ohio mandates a one-to-six ratio, including the provider's own young children, and allows no more than three children under the age of two. North Carolina allows regulated family child care providers to care for six children (including their own), plus an additional two children before and after school. In most cases, they can care for no more than two children under the age of two years of age.

Family child care providers are more likely to seek licensing or to stay in business despite regulation if they feel that they benefit from their new status. One solution is to create networks that help family child care providers meet regulatory standards and offer other advantages as well. Some networks are sponsored by states or cities, but businesses can also create child care networks linking their employees' child care providers. Employers who want to create such a network can now turn to organizations (for-profit or not-for-profit) that specialize in this area.

Case in point: Bright Horizons Family Solutions manages three hundred family centers across the nation. This group can work with employers who want to sponsor a Family Child Care Network geared to the needs of its workers. All of the providers in the network must maintain safety and quality standards and take part in individualized quality and improvement programs. All programs must meet the criteria developed by the National Association for the Education of Young Children. Bright Horizons recruits and screens providers and employs a dedicated full-time network administrator for scheduled and unscheduled home visits. It makes available to providers professional advancement and training, vacation and emergency respite, low-cost liability insurance, and discounted equipment and materials.

Community-based child care resource and referral services

are natural centers for family child care providers. In addition to matching families with providers in their communities, resource and referral agencies provide a wide range of support services both to families and providers. They frequently offer training to child care providers. In California, for example, the state's Child Care Resource and Referral Network manages a public/private partnership that has provided training to more than thirty-five thousand providers (including more than seven thousand Spanish-speaking providers).

The National Association of Child Care Resource and Referral Agencies (naccrra) has also created large-scale training initiatives for family child care workers—including on-line training courses. Through a partnership between naccrra and a Washington-based organization called Learning Options, family child care and kith and kin providers (as well as center-based caregivers) can now earn a Child Development Associate (cda) credential by completing courses on the Internet.

Many other organizations offer training to family child care providers. In Alabama, the Federation of Child Care Centers of Alabama (focal) brings together about two hundred family child care providers, along with center-based caregivers, for training several Saturdays each year. The purpose is not only to provide professional development but also to help family child care providers network with other home-based caregivers in their communities. In Santa Clara County, California, Choices for Children hosts bimonthly provider networking sessions for family child care providers. In Oakland, California, a collaborative project organizes peer training for family child care providers.

STRENGTHENING KITH AND KIN CARE

As they have for generations, many families depend on relatives, friends or neighbors for inexpensive or free child care.[68]

Some arrangements involve barter or exchange of services. It is often the ability or willingness of a friend or relative to provide low-cost or free care that allows low-wage earners to hold down jobs and move toward economic self-sufficiency.[69]

At the same time, it is important to dispel the myth that child care is not a problem because working parents can always leave their young children with relatives or friends. Today, the majority of working families have no kith or kin available to care for their children. Moreover, about one-third of employed mothers who turn to relatives for child care pay for that care.[70] Changes in welfare law have diminished the pool of providers who are available to provide free or inexpensive child care for friends or relatives. Many of the grandparents, other relatives, or friends who have volunteered their services in the past are now subject to work requirements and must find employment or training opportunities outside of the home.[71] These families need better options.

Like many other aspects of early care and education, parents' use of kith and kin care varies across states and across demographic categories. For example, children in Mississippi are more than twice as likely as children in Minnesota to be cared for by relatives.[72] Within states, families vary widely in their reliance on care by relatives. Low-income working families are more likely than other working families to rely on relative care. Black and Hispanic families are also more likely than other families to make child care arrangements with relatives. For families whose home language is not English, familiarity with the caregiver is a major factor in making a selection.[73] Half of working mothers with less than a high school diploma rely on relatives to care for their infants and toddlers, compared with 30 percent of those with a high school diploma and 16 percent of those with a college degree.[74] Informal care is preferred by parents who have several children and those who work outside the conventional nine-to-five workday or have rotating shifts.[75] Most families with seriously disabled or chronically ill children use relative or in-home care arrangements until their children go to school.[76]

In short, kith and kin care plays a very big part in the lives of millions of children during a very important stage in their lives. It plays an especially important role in low-income communities and therefore has a strong impact on families whose children are at greatest risk for poor outcomes.

While kith and kin generally have less formal training than regulated providers, some researchers have found that they have a strong interest in expanding their knowledge and sharing experiences with their peers. Outreach services can be organized around an existing program (such as a family resource center, food program, or mobile van/lending library service) and can be facilitated by means of technology (including television programming, videos, and Internet connections). How services are presented can often make a difference. A study in Rhode Island found that kith and kin providers emphatically rejected "training" but were interested in participating in "get-togethers."[77] Organizations in Atlanta and elsewhere have found that efforts to recruit kith and kin to become licensed and regulated were unsuccessful until they shifted gears, offering support to caregivers without the explicit goal of licensing. A survey conducted in Los Angeles found that the great majority of license-exempt providers indicated an interest in becoming regulated family child care providers.[78] Efforts to improve the quality of kith and kin care are in their infancy, but several initiatives appear to be promising. The Child Care and Family Support Partnership, a collaboration of five New York–based organizations, has brought together the Bank Street College's Center for Family Support, Child Care, Inc., and three community-based, comprehensive family support programs. Through focus groups and other activities, the partnership is learning about the needs of kith and kin providers, documenting its findings, and developing activities and curricula aimed at supporting their efforts to improve quality.[79]

Other efforts are using technology to reach out to kith and kin caregivers. The Public Broadcasting Corporation's Ready to Learn initiative is designed in part to strengthen the capacity of parents and caregivers to help children enter school ready to learn. It supplements television programming with websites, specially developed materials, and other activities.[80]

A wide range of technologies can help caregivers reflect on children's needs, the care they provide, and ways to improve it. Some educational programs for young children, such as *Mister Rogers' Neighborhood* and *Between the Lions,* have both printed and on-line materials, offering parents and caregivers tips for extending the ideas presented on TV through at-home activities.

Through the I Am Your Child Foundation, parents can get videos and booklets that provide a great deal of information on such topics as child safety, healthy development, early literacy, and setting limits. These can be shared with home-based child care providers.

Another strategy for strengthening kith and kin care is to use a center-based program as the hub of efforts to reach out to isolated providers. In rural Kansas, the Clay County Child Care Center, a large child care and Head Start program, wanted to open all of its workshops and training seminars to local kith and kin providers. Identifying these providers proved to be a real challenge. The Clay County Child Care Center purchased a list of all registered providers from the Kansas Health Department, including all license-exempt providers who receive subsidies from the state. The center has had a strong response from kith and kin providers, who now account for one-third to one-half of participants at their workshops.

Increasing demand for infant and toddler care reflects, in part, the welfare legislation of 1996, which had far-reaching consequences for families and young children. Many more parents are working or receiving job training and must make arrangements for the care of their young children.

Whether or not they have ever received public assistance, all low-wage earners who have young children face a dilemma: child care costs take a huge bite out of their incomes—up to 30 percent by some estimates.[81] While child care costs vary by location, full-day programs were estimated in 1998 to run from four to six thousand dollars per year in many cities, and infant and toddler care can run even higher. Good quality programs generally cost more.[82] Because these costs are so high, most low-income families are bypassing early education programs and are using informal arrangements.[83]

To help these families, the 1996 welfare legislation authorized states to use the federal child care funds and savings they realize from closing welfare cases to provide subsidies to eligible families. Many states limit these subsidies to families who are moving from welfare to work, while others offer them to all low-income families with young children. Subsidies can make a major difference in parents' ability to afford child care.[84] At the same time, they can make a dent in poverty rates: it has been estimated that if child care costs were fully subsidized for all families that would otherwise be poor, the 1996 poverty rate for families with children would have fallen from nearly 17 percent to under 3 percent.[85]

In recent years, the share of eligible children receiving subsidized care has increased. However, as things stand, most children who qualify for child care assistance are not receiving it.[86] In every

state that has tracked the progress of former welfare recipients, utilization of child care subsidies has been reported at under 30 percent. Of course, since some eligible families do not want or need
child care assistance, utilization rates are not expected to be 100
percent. But these figures suggest that a significant number of
families who could benefit from child care assistance after leaving
welfare are not receiving it.[87] Many families are on waiting lists.
Others do not know that they qualify. In surveys of families who
have left the welfare rolls, 40 percent or more said they were un-
aware of the availability of child care subsidies. Confusion about
rules may play a role.[88]

Some parents who receive public assistance simply cannot find
safe care for their young children. According to federal regulations, states are not supposed to penalize parents who cannot meet
work requirements due to a lack of acceptable child care. But policymakers have not consistently gotten this message across to the
people who staff welfare offices. A recent survey of New York City
welfare recipients found that only 19 percent of parents were informed that they cannot be penalized if they cannot work due to
lack of child care, and 46 percent were told just the opposite.[89]

State subsidies affect parents' decisions about their children's
care. But those receiving subsidy assistance are more likely than
other low-income parents to use center-based care.[90] This is not
entirely surprising, since some states pay subsidies only for children cared for in regulated settings.[91] It has important implication
for children's well-being, since regulated settings generally offer
more safeguards and higher quality.

The good news is that, as they develop or revise subsidy policy,
states can influence parents' choices and upgrade the quality of
child care and early education. This represents an important policy
opportunity: the subsidy system, if well designed, can provide

strong incentives for providers and consumers to focus on quality. Many states are now experimenting with offering increased reimbursement to providers who meet specific quality standards.

Early Head Start

Responding to research on the importance of the early years and shortages of infant and toddler care, in 1994 Congress established Early Head Start, a new program serving low-income families with children under age three and pregnant women. Early Head Start provides resources to community programs to offer opportunities to infants and toddlers, with and without disabilities, to grow and develop together in nurturing and inclusive settings. In Fiscal Year 2001, Congress appropriated $564 million for Early Head Start.

The services provided by Early Head Start go well beyond center-based child care. Early Head Start sites provide services according to a plan jointly developed by the parents and staff. These services can include a mix of home visits, experiences at the Early Head Start center, and experiences in other settings such as family or center-based child care. Pregnant women can receive comprehensive services through Early Head Start.

Like the Head Start program for older preschoolers, Early Head Start holds all service providers to high performance standards, provides ongoing staff development, stresses linkages with other service providers at the local level, and ensures parent involvement in policy and decision making. An intensive evaluation of the initiative is now under way. Early findings show that in several dimensions of development, participants made greater gains than similar children in a comparison group.[92]

. . . .

Of Tots, Teachers, and Mashed Potatoes: Early Head Start through the Eyes of One of the Nation's First Head Start "Graduates"

By Rachel Jones

OVER THE LAST thirty-five years, Head Start has developed a solid tradition of delivering comprehensive and high-quality services designed to foster the healthy development and early learning of low-income children. Its array of services includes medical, dental, mental health, and nutrition programs. Parental involvement is encouraged in a way that is responsive and appropriate to each child and family's developmental, ethnic, and cultural background.

Head Start can make all the difference. I know. In 1965, I was one of the three-year-olds who, each morning, clambered down the stairs to the basement of Sumner High—a formerly segregated school in Cairo, Illinois—to take part in one of the nation's first Head Start programs.

My recollections of those days mostly are lost in the jumble of early childhood memories. But last fall I had a unique opportunity to rediscover firsthand what early childhood supports can mean to children and their families. I spent four days visiting Early Head Start programs in two very different communities: the predominantly white and Mormon town of Logan, Utah, and the diverse, economically struggling region in and around Russellville, Arkansas.

After spending many hours with program administrators and staff, bright-eyed babies, restless two-year-olds, and their parents, it was time to head home. But before leaving, I was offered the same lunch being served to the children at the Morrillton, Arkansas, Early Head Start site—a heaping plate of creamy, smooth, instant mashed potatoes, turkey, dressing, and cranberry sauce.

The meal made me smile. It summoned my only clear memory of

my Head Start years. I have always associated those piles of mashed potatoes—far better than the plain, lumpy spuds my mother served at home—with the sustenance and support Head Start provided me and my working poor family. I was one of the lucky ones. Along with two of my sisters, I received an educational and social leg up that our seven older brothers and sisters did not get.

My eldest sister, Julie Newell, has much more vivid recollections of my Head Start years, because while I was chattering, napping, or playing, she was an office aide for Cairo's first Head Start director.

"You couldn't wait to get ready in the mornings," Julie tells me. "The little ones loved coming to Head Start, because it made them feel special. They felt so grown up going to school like all the big kids. In a town like Cairo, I think what made the difference is that somebody cared. A program like this made people feel like their children, black and white alike, could have a chance, like everybody else."

After a thirty-two-year career in the Cairo Public School System, Julie is now a member of the Head Start Policy Council for the seven southernmost counties in Illinois. She is convinced that Head Start is all about giving young children a chance by offering services that many might miss out on without the program.

Early Head Start in Logan, Utah

A rural community tucked between two mountain ranges and isolated from the more populous areas of Utah and Idaho, Logan was selected as one of the nation's first Early Head Start demonstration sites. The Bear River program serves Cache and Box Elder Counties in northern Utah and Franklin County in southeastern Idaho. Most residents belong to the Church of Jesus Christ of Latter-day Saints (Mormons), and most households contain two-parent families, many of whom are young parents juggling the demands of work, family, and faith.

The community is primarily white. Hispanics account for about 13 percent of residents, and many have moved to Logan in recent years, drawn by seasonal migrant work and growing numbers of blue-collar manufacturing jobs, like those at Logan's Icon Exercise Equipment Company.

Head Start is no stranger to Logan, Utah. The Bear River Head Start Agency has served preschoolers in the northern Utah and southern Idaho region since 1966. And yet, many eligible families in this close-knit community remain reluctant to take part in Head Start's center- or home-based programs.

"This is an area with very, very conservative people, and family means a lot," says Sarah Thurgood, Bear River Head Start's executive director. "They tend to believe that if you need help, you go to your family first, and then you go to your church. There's a lot of sentiment that if they can't help you, then you have to figure things out on your own."

By late 1996, a vigorous outreach effort finally recruited enough families to launch the Early Head Start program, but federal programs of any sort are viewed with a wary eye in Logan. "People wonder what the neighbors will think, or they fear that a program designed to help children might ultimately mean that the parents' role is diminished," Thurgood says. "We had a hard time breaking through those beliefs."

Low-income families in the area face plenty of hurdles, including low wages, scarce affordable housing, and spousal and substance abuse and illegal alien status. Hispanic families and those living in outlying areas experience more social isolation, which can increase family tensions.

A Lifeline for Caregivers

Three-year-old Letecia and her four-month-old sister Jacqueline spend six days a week with their aunt, Maria Avalos, while their mother works twelve-hour (4 A.M. to 4 P.M.) shifts at Logan's Icon factory. Maria also cares for her own children, two-year-old Julio and five-month-old Sylvia.

Avalos says that the support and camaraderie provided by Bear River Early Head Start are truly a lifeline. "For one, I get to talk to adults, which I don't get to do all day," she laughs. "Two, the people here really want to know what's going on with me and the children."

Every week, Avalos and the children head over to the Logan Baby Buddy Group center, a converted church, with a kitchen and several staff offices. Toys and play space predominate, but comfortable couches and chairs and a large dining room table make it clear that the center is for the entire family.

These gatherings are designed to give parents and other caregivers chances to ask questions, to air problems, to try out more positive interactions with their children, and to see effective strategies modeled.

It is clear that the primary focus here is on children. Toys and child-sized furniture and play equipment are prominent. There is also a kid-sized grocery store, complete with shopping carts, where children like Leticia Avalos and two-year-old Stevie Ahlemann compete for fruits and vegetables to fill their wagons.

At a nearby table, Julio Avalos and Hayden Nielson play with clay, as their mothers watch. Often, Baby Buddy staffers encourage parents to join in with the play. The children play games, gather for Circle Time, and then line up to wash their hands and brush their teeth before the day's grand finale—sharing a meal at the big dining table with their parents.

Jane De Spain is the Logan Baby Buddy Group leader and a former Head Start parent. She says the program offers important perspectives. "Many of the people who come here say they've never thought of their children as having needs besides food and clothing and shelter," she says. "When they come here, and we help them learn about their children's learning needs and nurturing needs, it's like a light goes on in their minds."

"That's what made the Early Head Start piece so important," Thurgood explains. "So many of our staff here realized that by the time they were working with the three- and four-year-olds, there were so many problems that if we could just get to them earlier, it could be a totally different story."

Family educators like Seija Puikkonen partner with parents like Avalos to share child development knowledge. They talk about children's need for secure attachments to important adults in their lives and discuss the kinds of learning that can be fostered through play.

"I think about the families the first thing when I wake up, and at night before I fall asleep," Puikkonen says. "They are working so hard all the time, to keep their families healthy. When I see the way they want to give their children a good start in life, it makes me know that we are doing the right thing."

Home visits are another important component of the program. As parents play with their children, family educators encourage and model positive interaction. The family educator also serves as an advisor for parents who need information about child development or just a shoulder to lean on.

That shoulder can be especially welcome for parents like Carol Nielson, whose two-year-old son Hayden was born with a life-threatening hernia. An experienced mother with four older children, she nevertheless found all-consuming the strain of caring for a baby who needed ten operations before he turned two.

"They've taught me how to relax," Nielson says as Hayden scampers nearby. "They've taught me that he won't break, and that I don't have to keep him locked up away from other children. I really appreciated the fact that they listened to me and didn't think I was crazy."

The Bear River program shows that the kind of support, encouragement, and resources Early Head Start has to offer can make a difference, even in settings where they may not be initially embraced.

Early Head Start in Six Arkansas Communities

The communities near Russellville, Arkansas, have a very different demographic profile. There is an almost equal split between African Americans and Caucasians in the thirteen counties served by Child Development, Inc. (CDI). CDI has been a Head Start grantee since 1986 and is headquartered on the Russellville campus of Arkansas Technical University.

"We did it for the sole purpose of developing comprehensive child care centers available to anyone based in our rural communities," says Joanne Williams, CDI's executive director. "There was practically no child care available in any of our rural communities, and we wanted to develop one-stop child care centers for parents across the spectrum."

CDI operates an Early Head Start program serving children ages six weeks to three years at six of its sites: Clarksville, Dardanelle, Morillton, Paris, Ozark, and Russellville. The program also serves expectant mothers, who receive prenatal care, as well as information about children's growth and development, parenting, nutrition, and other topics. Infants and toddlers get well-baby checkups and home visits from site coordinators. The children attend full-day, center-based programs for nine months of the year.

In contrast to Logan, there was no problem recruiting parents for CDI's Early Head Start program. "It made an overwhelming impact in our community," says Jana Gifford, Early Head Start director. "It got to the point that a lot of times, it was very difficult for us to even decide who would get in and who wouldn't, because we had such a large waiting list of families who wanted the services."

Poultry processing is the major industry in and around Russellville, and many of the parents with children enrolled in Early Head Start work long hours in these plants. Increasingly, Hispanic families are moving into the area to take on these jobs, and they lack the extended family support to help with children. While most Early Head Start children in Logan come from two-parent families, two-thirds of Russellville area children come from single-parent homes. Many are teen mothers struggling to finish their high school education.

"This is a working community, and people here would much rather work to provide for their families," CDI director Williams says. "Among the single working mothers in our program, there's a real desire to provide a better life for their children, and when they heard about the Early Head Start program they were excited." Of the 103 families, only 9 received federal TANF funds. The average family income is $7,393 per year, and 81 percent of the children are on Medicaid.

Program administrators also got permission from many of the local factories and the public schools to allow Early Head Start teachers to meet with mothers at lunch time, during study hall period, or on work breaks to dispense information and advice. Many of the teen mothers leave school grounds during the day to check on their children, and other young pregnant mothers spend time at the centers because they have never had experience with babies and want to prepare themselves for parenthood.

"We believe in the 'continuity of care theory' in Early Head Start," Gifford explains. "When we assign a teacher to a pregnant mother, she will be that baby's teacher in the classroom, and she'll work with that mother and child throughout their stay in the program."

Each of Russellville area centers also has a Family Enrichment specialist, like Lois Kimbriel at the Clarksville center. They help provide transportation, direct families to social service agencies, and serve as an important touchstone for parents.

"In this community, where it's so hard to find quality affordable child care, it means so much for parents to have a place where they

feel comfortable leaving their children, and to know that they themselves are important, too," Kimbriel says. "We don't just take care of
the children, we take care of the family as a whole."

Compared with the Baby Buddy Group center in Logan, the
Clarksville center, and the ones in Morrilton, Russellville, and Ozark,
have more of a classroom feel. Numbers are larger here, too. Where
the average Baby Buddy Group consists of five children and their parents, some the Arkansas centers have ten or more children.

But the focus is clearly on children—like eighteen-month-old
Shy-Anne Carnicle, an impish toddler in a pink sleeper who is trying
to climb into her mother's lap at the Russellville site. A bold, outgoing
child like Shy-Anne has plenty of room to explore the center's two
large rooms, and aides like Kayla Traylor, whose two-month old baby
Maggie is also in the program, keep a careful watch.

"If it wasn't for this program, I wouldn't be able to work at all,"
Traylor explains. She received her degree as a home health aide from
Arkansas Tech but became pregnant shortly thereafter. She had met
Early Head Start director Gifford during a parenting class she had
taken in college and decided to pursue a job with the program so she
could keep her infant daughter close by.

"They really go out of their way to help families here," Traylor
says. "In this community people don't want a handout, but when they
feel that someone is supporting them while they're working hard trying to provide for their families, they really appreciate it."

Family enrichment specialist Kimbriel of the Clarksville Center
agrees. "I've had parents tell me there was no food in the house, or the
electricity has been cut off, and they don't know where to turn," Kimbriel says. "They work so hard, and they're so proud. They're doing
everything they can to raise their children, and we just want to give
them that extra support."

New Memories of Head Start

The images I will remember most from my visit to Utah and Arkansas are of parents pulling into driveways in the early morning, stifling yawns while dropping off babies and toddlers on their way to long shifts at local factories. Or a father walking through the door in the early evening, the fatigue dulling his eyes instantly erased by the sight of his grinning baby boy.

My parents worked long hard hours to provide for their family. I understand now it must have made a difference that they could leave me at the Head Start program. I wish I could remember more than the taste of mashed potatoes, but as I watched the crawling babies and scurrying toddlers at the Utah and Arkansas Early Head Start programs, I could not help feeling that I knew exactly what they were thinking—and where their lives might be headed.

. . . .

Protecting Young Children from Injury and Illness

The vulnerability and intensive needs of infants and toddlers makes their care especially challenging. Simply creating a safe and sanitary environment that is interesting to children and can be maintained efficiently can be extremely difficult. As they gain mobility, excitement and curiosity put them at risk of injury. Caregivers need to know pediatric first aid and rescue breathing. Moreover, because getting multiple infants and toddlers out of a building is not easy under the best of circumstances, emergency evacuation procedures must be established and practiced.[93] Many parents worry about their children's safety in early care and education settings. In too many cases, their concerns are warranted. In 1997, about thirty-one thousand children under the age of five were treated in U.S. hospital emergency rooms for injuries in early care and education settings. More than a quarter of these injuries resulted from falls on playgrounds.[94] While injured children represent only a small percentage of those in nonparental care, the number is much too high considering that most of these injuries are preventable.

A study by the U.S. Consumer Product Safety Commission (CPSC) looked at 220 licensed child care settings across the nation, including both child care centers and family child care homes, and found that two-thirds of them had at least one safety hazard (unsafe cribs or bedding, unsafe playground surfaces, windows without child safety gates, window blind cords, drawstrings in children's clothing, or recalled children's products). And these were all *licensed* programs. Parents can help to protect their children by asking providers to resolve any and all safety problems. The following is a safety checklist for parents and child care providers from the U.S. Consumer Product Safety Commission:

Cribs. Make sure cribs meet current national safety standards and are in good condition. Look for a certification safety seal. Older cribs may not meet current standards. Crib slats should be no more than two and three-eighths inches apart, and mattresses should fit snugly.

Soft bedding. Be sure that no pillows, soft bedding, or comforters are used when you put babies to sleep. Babies should be put to sleep on their backs in a crib with a firm, flat mattress.

Playground surfacing. Look for safe surfacing on outdoor playgrounds—at least twelve inches of wood chips, mulch, sand, or pea gravel or mats made of safety-tested rubber or rubberlike materials.

Playground maintenance. Check playground surfacing and equipment regularly to make sure they are maintained in good condition.

Safety gates. Be sure that safety gates are used to keep children away from potentially dangerous areas, especially stairs.

Window blind and curtain cords. Be sure miniblinds and venetian blinds do not have looped cords. Check that vertical blinds, continuous looped blinds, and drapery cords have tension or tie-down devices to hold the cords tight.

Clothing drawstrings. Be sure there are no drawstrings around the hood and neck of children's outerwear clothing. Other types of clothing fasteners, such as snaps, zippers, or hook-and-loop fasteners (such as Velcro) should be used.

Recalled products. Check that no recalled products are being used and that a current list of recalled children's products is readily visible.[95]

Policymakers also have a role to play. The CPSC reviewed state licensing requirements for child care and found that most of the hazards addressed in the study were not covered. For example, many states did not require day care centers to use cribs that meet federal regulations or voluntary safety standards. While virtually all programs use equipment like high chairs and strollers, none of the states reviewed had requirements for fixing or replacing recalled nursery equipment.

Linking Providers with Health Services

Those who care for infants and toddlers need to keep a constant focus on preventive health. Because their immune systems have not fully developed, very young children are more susceptible than older children to infectious disease. Providers need to be vigilant about sanitary measures in settings where many diapers are changed each day. They must consult with families about special health concerns and about immunization schedules.

Providers need to have a medical contact for every child in their care. Many health experts believe that in addition the providers themselves need to have an ongoing relationship with a pediatrician or clinic that can become a medical home for the program.[96] The American Academy of Pediatrics and the National Association of Pediatric Nurse Associates and Practitioners have urged their members to "adopt" an early care and education program.

Childcare health consultants can form vital partnerships with child care providers. The state of Iowa, for example, has five full-time and twenty-two part-time child care health consultants—registered nurses who respond to the needs of providers, whether center-based programs, public school–based programs, family child care providers, or kith and kin. By calling local child care resource and referral agencies or by phoning a toll-free number, providers can get help over the phone or arrange for an on-site visit at no cost to the provider. Funding comes from the Department of Public Health, the Title V Maternal and Child Health Program, and the quality portion of the Child Care Development Fund.

The consultants handle a wide range of concerns: food or playground safety, infection control, immunization, development issues, behavioral problems, and other health-related issues. They can work with providers and parents to address individual children's specific health issues, and they can help them plan and practice emergency procedures. Consultants can also help unregistered providers meet the requirements for registration.

A Compass for Early Childhood Policy

To a greater degree than ever before, policymakers now appreciate the importance of positive, strong early relationships, and how they scaffold language acquisition, early literacy, and many kinds of later learning. For those concerned about meeting kids' needs, the aim of warm, positive relationships has become a steady north star.

Decision makers in the public and private sectors are beginning to locate themselves in relation to that star. At the same time, our nation has only begun to create constellations of programs and services capable of strengthening young children's bonds with the adults who nurture and teach them.

Policymakers have found that it is much more difficult to create early learning "systems" for infants and toddlers than for older preschoolers. While states and communities have taken strides toward early learning systems for older preschoolers, progress toward large-scale programs or integrated services for younger children must be measured in baby steps. While the nation is moving toward consensus that the public has an interest in school readiness, that center-based care makes sense for preschoolers, and that the public schools ought to play a role, there is no such consensus about the care and education of younger children.

To be sure, there has been progress. Intensive public engagement efforts have increased awareness of young children's developmental needs. Maternal and child health are on the agendas of many more policymakers. And in the realm of early care and education, there is greater awareness of the number of infants and toddlers in out-of-home care and of the need to improve the quality of that care and give working families better options.

But the most daunting challenges have yet to be addressed. There is little consensus about the best way (or the best place) to care for the infants and toddlers of working parents or the best ways to support new families. Despite large infusions of public dollars into child care subsidies for low-income children, policymakers are hard pressed to solve the quality problem, in view of the fact that the great majority of young children spend their days in unregulated settings.

In short, the project of creating better options for parents with young children is very much a work in progress. However, in the years since *Starting Points* appeared, four realities that were once blurred have come into sharp focus:

First, parents want and need time with their young children. Research findings on the impact of child care on children's learning and behavior tend to be controversial. But this much is clear: *families,* not child care providers, have the most important and most long-lasting influence on children's life trajectories. In today's round-the-world, round-the-clock economy, ensuring that parents can both earn a living and spend time with their children is an urgent challenge that decision makers in the public and private sectors need to confront.

Second, policymakers, employers, and educators need to face facts: most infants and toddlers have no parent at home to care for them for much of the day. Millions are in full-time nonparental care. Today's policies and programs do not meet the crying need for expanded access to affordable, good quality care.

Third, a comprehensive approach to infant and child care will have to incorporate many types of care, accommodating those families who want to care for their own infants and toddlers, those who are only comfortable leaving young children with people they know and trust; those who prefer a home setting; and those who want the predictability and professionalism of center-based programs.

And fourth, improving the quality of nonparental care means coming to terms with the need for stronger accountability, especially when public dollars support care. More providers need to be held to standards designed to protect children's health and safety and to help them build a good foundation for later learning.

Wherever they occur, efforts to enhance the well-being of infants and toddlers must take into account the two dominant characteristics of our youngest children: first, that they can do so little, and second, that they can do so much.

Because they can do so little, infants and toddlers need almost constant attention and care. Keeping them nourished, warm, dry, and safe requires prodigious effort. Families have always needed help.[97] Today, that need is more intense than ever.

But because they can do so much, simply keeping them nourished, warm, dry, and safe is not sufficient. The kind of care young children receive, and the settings in which they spend their days, matter a great deal. Children have always needed to be nurtured, protected, and taught. They have always needed a secure relationship with at least one caring adult. Today's challenge is to base policies and programs on a clear understanding of what kids need.

CHAPTER 3

The Preschool Years

The last decade has witnessed such a proliferation of policies and programs for young children and their families that it is tempting, in describing them, to turn to zoology. It might be said, with apologies to larks and leopards, that recent years have witnessed an exaltation of research evidence and a leap of legislation. We have seen a pride of preschool programs—and an ostentation of reports documenting them.

In 2000, an international commission reported, across the nation and across the age span, "an abundance of collaborative initiatives and innovative practices, particularly at the local level, a remarkable array of energizing forces intent on improving the overall situation of young children and their families."[1]

In the early childhood field, no realm of policy or practice has witnessed more activity than the education of children as they get ready to enter school. During the nineties, the number of children participating in state-funded prekindergarten programs increased two and a half times—from about 290,000 to nearly 725,000.[2] Most states now fund some kind of prekindergarten program for some of their children.

In the process, our nation has taken steps toward improving school readiness for some children, at least in some places. But when it comes to creating an early learning system that can work for all children, we have a long way to go. As things stand, one state (Georgia) offers universal access to prekindergarten, and that program only serves four-year-olds. Major finance challenges remain. By creating Smart Start, North Carolina significantly advanced the early childhood education agenda, but the state continues to spend only $350 per child for Smart Start, compared with $5,000 per child for K-12 education.[3]

Building the political will needed to support state spending on early education remains a high priority, especially in view of the fact that some states have made virtually no investments in prekindergarten programs.

But there is movement in the right direction. Driving progress is growing concern, across the political spectrum, about today's three R's: Readiness, Reading, and Results. There is growing confidence that universal, voluntary prekindergarten is not only a worthy aim, but a realistic one. There are also signs of a shift in public sentiment on the public interest in early learning. History offers a valuable lesson. Our nation did not get serious about creating a higher education system that would work for all Americans until after World War II, when returning GIs were determined that societal support for education should not end when young people leave high school. Today, many Americans are reaching a similar conclusion about the other end of the educational spectrum: support for education should not wait until children enter elementary school.[4]

Moving on Two Tracks

From a preschooler's viewpoint, the stretch of years from three to five are part of the continuum of childhood. From the standpoint of policymakers, it is looking more and more like a distinct stage of life. In the mid- to late nineties, the early childhood field reached a junction: policies and programs related to infants and toddlers chugged along on one track; prekindergarten initiatives proceeded on another.

Movement on the infant and toddler track has been sluggish. Here, the most daunting challenges have yet to be addressed. There is little consensus about the best way (or the best place) to care for the infants and toddlers of working parents or the best ways to support new families. Despite large infusions of public dollars into child care subsidies for low-income children, policymakers are hard pressed to solve the quality problem, in view of the fact that the great majority of young children spend their days in unregulated settings.

There are fewer impediments on the prekindergarten track. To be sure, unresolved issues abound. There are conflicting views of what it takes to prepare children to succeed in kindergarten and beyond. The extent of taxpayers' responsibility for educating other people's preschoolers remains a subject of controversy. And there is ongoing debate about the relationship between Head Start—a federally funded initiative for low-income children with a historic commitment to parents and close links to community organizations, and state prekindergarten initiatives—programs funded largely by states that tend to have strong ties to public education systems.

But consensus is strong that the public has an interest in promoting school readiness, and most Americans believe that children benefit from group learning experiences in the year or two before entering kindergarten. In 1999, 70 percent of four-year-olds were enrolled in preprimary education, up from 62 percent in 1991. Enrollment rates for three-year-olds rose more gradually over the decade—from 43 to 46 percent.[5] While many children in this age range receive care in home-based settings, such as family child care homes, kith and kin care, or other informal arrangements, the great majority are in center-based programs, such as Head Start, public school prekindergartens, or nonpublic (profit and non-profit) preschools.

A rise in the number of mothers in the workforce, as well as welfare policies requiring mothers with preschoolers to attend work or training outside of the home, have helped to drive the pre-kindergarten movement. An equally powerful force is widespread concern about school readiness. The public is more aware than ever before of the risks and opportunities of the preschool years and is encouraged by evidence showing the impact of high-quality early learning programs on the prospects of low-income children. Americans are also concerned about disappointing achievement in K-12, especially in view of the heightened demands of an information-based society. For all of these reasons, there is now wider consensus that the public has an interest in supporting care and education for three- and four-year-olds. Crucial support has come from diverse sectors of society and all branches of government.

A network of state policy reformers has helped to advance the prekindergarten agenda, and governors have led the way in several states. In Georgia, for example, the leadership of former governor Zell Miller, who staked his candidacy on the potential of a state lottery to fund early education, was largely responsible for the realization of a universal prekindergarten program in his state. Georgia's universal prekindergarten is based on the premise that a universal program is more likely to generate broad and sustained political and public support than a program targeted only toward certain groups. While most states rely on an inconsistent and complex blending of federal, state, and local funding for early care and education, Georgia has substantial and consistent lottery-generated funding based on an amendment to the state constitution stipulating that lottery funds be spent on specific educational programs. Georgia's Lottery for Education opened in 1993. At first the program served low-income students. In 1995 the eligibility requirements were dropped and oversight of the program was moved from Georgia Department of Education to a newly created Office of School Readiness.[6]

One of the toughest challenges for a system of universal prekindergarten is integrating services of private nonprofit and for-profit providers into a state-based early education program. As program implementation proceeds in Georgia, many issues such as reimbursement rates, enrollment requirements, and curriculum standards need to be negotiated between program administrators and child care providers. A concerted effort has also been made to build a partnership with Head Start.

Other former governors, notably James Hunt in North Carolina, George Voinovich of Ohio, and Christie Todd Whitman of New Jersey, raised early education high on their agendas. In other states, such as Rhode Island and West Virginia, "children's cabinets" created within the executive branch with governors' support have taken the lead.

In some places, legislative bodies have also moved the preschool agenda. Numerous states have explicitly tied early childhood appropriations to school readiness goals. A case in point is Connecticut, where in 1997 the General Assembly passed an early childhood grant program tied to school readiness goals. According to child advocates, legislators were spurred to action by three facts: first, elementary school children with preschool experience were scoring better on standardized tests; second, fewer than half of all children in the state's three biggest cities were enrolled in prekindergarten programs; and third, state spending on prevention was very low. Prekindergarten is a key element in the state's early childhood initiative. The idea of a free program did not go over well in a state that is skewed economically, with large numbers of high-income and low-income families. There is a sliding scale intended to ensure universal access to the program.[7]

In the nineties, support for expanding high-quality early education has come from a less predictable but equally powerful source—the judiciary branch. In the landmark decision *Abbott v. Burke,* the New Jersey Supreme Court ordered public provision of high-quality preschool in several districts as a remedy to educational inequity. In North Carolina, the courts have likewise played a role in establishing children's right to high-quality early care and education. This trend has the potential to dramatically alter the policy landscape.

Finally, the electorate has been a decisive factor. During the nineties, polls consistently reflected voters' concern about early childhood services, and candidates once content to kiss babies found themselves delving into research on child development and school readiness. Voters have also cast ballots directly for early childhood initiatives. In November 1998, California voters passed Proposition 10, which dedicates approximately $650 million a year toward building a comprehensive early childhood development system. The initiative created the California Children and Families Commission, a statewide leadership agency that oversees its implementation. The initiative also created fifty-eight local commissions to provide the local guidance and decision-making on how the funding is directed in each county. A centerpiece of Proposition 10 is a School Readiness Initiative that is setting up local school readiness centers where families can access prenatal care, parent education, and a range of services aimed at fostering early learning.

Treating the span from three to five as a distinct developmental stage, with a well-defined set of policy challenges, has helped to accelerate progress. The two-track strategy has allowed states and localities to begin addressing the politically more palatable concept of school readiness, while the nation grapples with the thornier ideological and programmatic problems of infant and toddler care. The split has also given new prominence to public school districts as providers of early care and education and may over time lead to a redefinition of public education. By sharpening the focus on school readiness, the two-track strategy has drawn much-needed attention to the content of early education curricula, the professional development of teachers, and the child outcomes that new investments might promote.

The split has also had a significant downside. The two-track approach has raised equity issues by directing substantial resources to some children in need of early care and education and not to others; in some cases, it has fostered competition among groups who are vying for the same funding. It has removed many three- and four-year-olds from mixed-age programs, leaving providers to fill their places with younger children whose care is more labor-intensive and therefore more expensive. This may have an unintended, adverse effect on the quality of infant and toddler care.

At the same time, the focus on school readiness for three- and four-year-olds—interpreted more narrowly in some states than in others—had added to existing pressure to make preschool curricula more "academic," orienting activities and curricula more explicitly to the goal of reading readiness. Among education officials, there is now considerable conversation about bringing Head Start into the fold both pedagogically (making it a reading readiness program) and institutionally (positioning it within the U.S. Department of Education, rather than the U.S. Department of Health and Human Services).

A Head Start official interviewed for this book commented:

"I'm seeing a giant leap toward a more academic focus coming from all sides—from members of Congress, higher education, federal people who administer Head Start. . . . You hear it in every meeting, at every conference, that's the kind of discussion taking place."

In reality, the principles of child development that guide parents and teachers in the first three years of life hold true as children approach the age of school entry. Like babies and toddlers, preschoolers thrive when they have loving, responsive, well-informed parents; good health and protection; caring communities; and diverse opportunities to explore, learn, and develop their unique gifts, growing and maturing at their own pace.

The two-track strategy has also affected efforts to create an early childhood infrastructure—a coordinated set of behind-the-scene supports (such as professional development and facilities licensing) that can expand access to high-quality programs for all families with young children. Increasingly, early education for the two age spans is governed by different laws and regulations, supported by different funding streams and overseen by different agencies (including agencies responsible for special education). The challenge is to create a coherent, integrated early care and education system, meshing all of the services—public and private—that now serve young children and their families and holding them to high quality standards.

Federal Preschool Initiatives

Since the sixties, public support for preschool has reflected a deficit model—not a strategy for meeting every child's need for a good start in life but a way to compensate for early deprivation. Established by the Economic Opportunity Act of 1964, Head Start, the nation's largest preschool program, was intended for economically disadvantaged preschoolers. It remains the only significant federal program that directly funds preschool experiences for children who have no special health or developmental needs.

From its inception, Head Start has taken a comprehensive approach to school readiness, providing educational, health, nutritional, and social services, primarily in a classroom setting. Most Head Start programs operate on a part-day, school-year basis, although many local programs either provide or coordinate all-day care. Head Start has focused intensively on the social and emotional development and on the mental health of the children it serves. Although the primary focus of the program is the child, the program takes an ecological approach, recognizing the importance of parents and communities. Parent involvement is a hallmark of the program, and 30 percent of staff are parents of current or former Head Start children. Local community agencies are responsible for implementing the program. Program implementation varies from site to site.

Head Start has never been permanently authorized by Congress and requires annual appropriations in the budget. It has expanded significantly in recent years. In Fiscal Year 2001, the federal Head Start appropriation was approximately $6.2 billion. Other federal early learning initiatives (with considerably smaller budgets) include the Even Start family literacy program, Title I programs for children from economically disadvantaged families, and IDEA special education programs.

State Preschool Initiatives

For many years, when it came to public preschool, Head Start was just about the only game in town. But Head Start had sufficient resources to serve only a fraction of children who qualified; today, it serves less than half of all eligible children.[8] Across the nation, a handful of localities and a very few states invested in public preschool programs for low-income families, but most working families—including the vast majority of middle-class families—have had to make arrangements at their own expense. Until the eighties, the idea of states investing their own money in early education was practically unheard of.[9]

That is why the explosion of state prekindergarten initiatives may be the last decade's boldest educational headline, despite the fact that most serve only a fraction of the preschool population. As of December 2000, a total of forty-three states were funding prekindergarten programs, either by supplementing the federal Head Start program, providing their own prekindergarten programs, or both. Progress was especially rapid in the late nineties. Since 1998, three states have created their own prekindergarten programs and four states that already had programs for preschoolers added Head Start supplements.[10]

The definition of prekindergarten has remained extremely broad: state initiatives represent a wide array of goals, administrative structures, financing, eligibility criteria, quality standards, and scope of services and supports available to children and their families. They have in common a focus on school readiness during the year or two before kindergarten entry. Most serve only a fraction of the state's preschoolers—often those considered to be at-risk of low school achievement. Most only operate for a few hours a day, leaving working parents to make other arrangements for the rest of their preschoolers' day. Few aim to be comprehensive child and family services.

Over the last decade, state spending on prekindergarten initiatives rose by more than $1 billion.[11] In FY 2000, states spent $2.1

billion for preschoolers—a 24 percent increase from the FY 1998 figure. (This figure includes all child development and family support programs for children from age three to six—the vast majority of which are prekindergarten programs.)[12]

Public schools have played a key role in this expansion, as many school districts opened the doors of elementary schools to young children. Today, an estimated one million preschool children attend public schools. The number is growing. Responding to a General Accounting Office survey that defined preschool as programs that "generally operated as part of the public school system," thirty-two states reported funding preschool in 1998–99.[13] And most school districts offer some form of voluntary prekindergarten, including special education, general education, Head Start, and Even Start. Some are using Title I funds to serve prekindergarten children.[14]

Despite the dramatic expansion of preschool initiatives, today's school-based programs are not large enough to serve all families who qualify and want to enroll their children. Most programs are geared to preschoolers considered to be at risk for low achievement. Even programs that restrict eligibility usually have long waiting lists.[15]

State Prekindergarten Models

As states design prekindergarten programs, they have several options. They can:

- *Expand or supplement Head Start.* Four states have chosen to supplement Head Start programs, keeping in place a well-established model capable of coordinating a range of health and social services. This option also offers a built-in accountability system, since every Head Start program must meet federal performance standards. However, since each site can choose its own curriculum, there can be great variation in program content and quality.

- *Build a prekindergarten program separate from Head Start.* Twenty-one states have taken this route. Typically, these are classroom-based, educationally focused, half-day programs (although many have expanded to full-day programs), and while they may draw upon the Head Start model, they are not Head Start programs. They vary markedly in size, funding, eligibility, and components. The number of children served varies from a few hundred per state to more than forty thousand per state in California, Georgia, Illinois, New York, and Texas. Some provide prekindergarten funding exclusively to public schools; most fund a variety of providers who meet state standards, including community-based organizations, schools, or private preschools.

- *Combine a state prekindergarten initiative with Head Start (or with another community-based program).* A third group of states —eighteen in all—have designed state programs that coordinate all of the preschool resources in their state, including Head Start programs. In order to serve all eligible children whose parents want them to participate, Ohio has invested significant resources in funding Head Start expansion, establishing state prekindergarten programs and incorporating locally implemented preschool programs, with a very strong emphasis on coordination efforts. In Connecticut, state prekindergarten funding may go to schools, family resource centers, private preschools, or Head Start agencies. All must become accredited by the National Association for the Education of Young Children.

- *Give school systems flexibility to redirect K-12 funds to prekinder-garten programs.* Of the eight states that invest no state dollars in prekindergarten programs, only Pennsylvania gives school districts leeway to use aid provided for K-12 education to serve four-year-olds.[16]

The Case for Universal Preschool

For decades, the United States has lagged behind our peer nations in the provision of publicly supported early learning programs. Our preschoolers' educational opportunities continue to hinge on where kids live, not what they need. Moreover, low-income children are more likely to qualify for public preschool programs than children from middle-class families—a source of contention in many parts of the country. Parents are well aware of these inequities, and many are concerned about their children's prospects in a society that increasingly demands and rewards educational achievement.

As a result, the case for universal, voluntary prekindergarten has grown stronger with each passing year. In 1996, the Carnegie Task Force on Learning in the Primary Grades made headlines when it recommended universal, voluntary preschool programs for three- and four-year-olds.[17] Today, universal preschool is finding new, powerful champions from outside the ranks of child care educators and advocates. In 1999, the Council of Chief State School Officers, an organization of state superintendents of education, replaced a decade-old policy statement recommending free early childhood programs only for children at risk of poor educational achievement with a statement calling for universal access for all three- and four-year-olds. The states' highest ranking education officials concluded that "efforts to reform and strengthen K-12 education cannot succeed without a concerted effort to support the people and improve the programs entrusted with the care and education of our youngest children."[18]

The business community is also recognizing the logic of investing in universal early learning programs. In 2002, the influential Committee for Economic Development released a report entitled *Preschool for All*, calling for universal, voluntary access for children age three and up to center-based preschool programs that meet recognized standards for promoting education and school readiness. The report stressed social and physical development, as well as academic goals, and noted the importance of safe environments for children.[19]

Some in the private sector are investing now in potential employees who will not begin contributing to their bottom line for at least two decades. In 2000, the Lucent Technologies Foundation announced a $1 million grant to encourage universal preschool in thirteen cities or counties across the nation. According to the foundation, the aim of the Lucent Preschool Initiative is "to support the current move toward universal preschool education as a part of whole school reform."[20] Grants were made to thirteen partnerships that provide early childhood education and care to preschool children, based on the quality of collaboration with schools and community child care and the readiness of the community to support universal preschool and early care and education policies.

To date, Georgia is the only state that makes prekindergarten available to all four-year-olds in all communities, regardless of family income or other characteristics. To accomplish this, Georgia created a public-private partnership, incorporating private child care providers and preschool programs into a public system. Today about 70 percent of Georgia's families with four-year-olds enroll their children. The program operates six and one-half hours per day, five days per week, during the school year. Providers can be public schools, private preschools, or nonprofit preschools.

All providers are required to offer a "complete" educational program and use a curriculum approved by the Office of School Readiness (OSR).

Other states are moving in the direction of universal access. Voluntary preschool is on the table in Maryland, which already has a state program for low-income four-year-olds, and in California, where in 2002 a statewide working group on school readiness recommended to the state legislature a phased-in universal preschool program for the two years leading to school entry.[21] Washington, D.C., has long had free public prekindergarten operating on a first come, first served basis.[22]

New York has had an experimental prekindergarten program in place for thirty-five years. This program provided a foundation for Universal Prekindergarten (UPK), a half-day program that was launched in 1997 with a year of planning. Funding for the program goes to the public schools, which must then subcontract at least 10 percent of their funds to other agencies (such as Head Start or private providers). The program requires all lead teachers to be certified and offers a strong curriculum to local districts. Although envisioned as a universal program, UPK has a five-year phase-in, and there are concerns about funding and capacity. In 1999–2000, the program served only 13 percent of the state's four-year-olds. By law, New York's prekindergarten initiative must give each district enough funds to serve all children who wish to participate. However, the state allows districts to opt out of offering prekindergarten programs.

The gap between the goal of universal access and capacity appears to be wide in other states as well. Oklahoma recently opened its state prekindergarten to all four-year-olds, requiring a dramatic expansion of services. However, many districts are not yet able to serve all of the children who would like to enroll or are not offering programs at all.[23] A number of other states have no eligibility requirements for their state prekindergarten programs, but they either cap funds at a level that does not cover all of the preschoolers whose families want to enroll them or require that communities cover such a large percentage of program costs that many provide no prekindergarten services or offer them only to a limited number of children.[24]

In some cases, prekindergarten programs are hampered as well by political and ideological concerns. In South Carolina, a prekindergarten program was launched in 1984, funded with an additional one-cent sales tax. It called for half-day programs for four-year-olds considered to be at risk of academic problems, or those for whom English is a second language. According to a recent report, the program has been challenged by "conservative voices" who "often questioned whether such early childhood programs were undermining the family by encouraging women to work outside of the home."[25]

Today's Three R's

A decade ago, the National Education Goals Panel proposed as the nation's number one education goal that "all children in America will start school ready to learn." The fact that young children topped the nation's list of education goals dramatically changed the national debate on early childhood services, shifting the focus from child care geared to parents' work needs to early education geared to children's learning needs.

At the same time, scientists, policymakers, and child advocates were joining forces to spread the message that young children are even more "ready to learn" than most people realize. Pointing to scientific evidence that early experience lays the groundwork for later achievement, they argued that school readiness needs to figure prominently in the nation's education reform efforts.[26] Media attention to the early years—including an ABC television special and cover stories in *Newsweek, Time,* and *U.S. News & World Report*—helped to persuade many Americans that our nation cannot afford to forfeit the opportunities of the early years or postpone efforts to raise achievement until children reach the primary grades.[27]

Ongoing concern about underachievement further fueled interest in school readiness initiatives. There has been particular concern about reading achievement, given that only 31 percent of 4th graders, 33 percent of 8th graders, and 40 percent of high school seniors reached the "proficient" level on the 2000 National Assessment of Educational Progress (NAEP). Many parents and educators are alarmed by the wide gap in reading achievement between children attending America's lowest-performing schools and their peers in other schools.

Research supports the notion that efforts to build a foundation for literacy must begin early. And reading readiness looms large on the early education landscape because, as the National Research Council has concluded, "A devastatingly large number of people in America cannot read as well as they need to for success in life. Large numbers of school-age children, including children from all social classes, face significant difficulties in learning to read."[28]

Experts say that children who experience early difficulties in learning to read can certainly make progress later, but they often have difficulty catching up with their peers.[29] And reading problems can affect children's overall school experience. Most school-age children who are evaluated for special education services are referred because of unsatisfactory progress in reading.[30]

Given these facts and the attention they have received, today's three R's are readiness, reading, and results. There is a powerful impulse to institute policies that concentrate our nation's efforts in the realm of early education on a narrow set of skills that underlie children's ability to master the traditional three R's, especially reading. The question remains: will these efforts produce the results that families and teachers so fervently desire?

Readiness

Over the decade, school readiness moved from the realm of rhetoric to the sphere of policy. Many prekindergarten initiatives throughout the country, such as state programs in Texas and Florida and local efforts like Seattle's Family and Education Levy, have identified school readiness as their explicit aim.[31] And virtually all prekindergarten programs have school readiness as an implicit goal.

When "readiness" first arose as an educational issue, there was considerable debate about what was meant by this term. In *Ready to Learn: A Mandate for the Nation,* an influential book published in 1991, Ernest L. Boyer argued that efforts to improve children's readiness for school needed to be comprehensive, encompassing not only quality preschool but also empowered parents, a responsive workplace, health services, improvements in children's television, neighborhoods that contribute to learning, and connections across the generations.[32]

Today, few school readiness efforts embrace a vision as broad or bold as Boyer's. But there is wider consensus that what kids need to benefit from school goes well beyond "academic" skills. A view shared by many early educators, and endorsed by the National Education Goals Panel, is that school readiness has five key dimensions:

1. *Health and physical development.* Maternal health, prenatal health, child health, and nutrition have all been found to influence later performance in school. Early educators also stress optimal motor

development in children, from the large motor movements children use on the playground to small motor skills required for holding a crayon or assembling puzzles.

2. *Emotional well-being and social competence.* This dimension fosters the relationships that give children a sense of personal well-being and give meaning to school experience. Early educators stress the emotional support and secure relationships that help children function in groups and become self-confident learners.

3. *Approaches toward learning.* Children's success in school reflects not only their skills but also their attitudes toward learning and their ways of approaching new tasks. Because approaches to learning can vary within and between cultures, children with very different inclinations can all be ready for school. A key is curiosity—and a willingness to exert effort to satisfy that curiosity. Creativity, independence, cooperativeness, and persistence are some of the approaches emphasized by early educators.

4. *Communicative skills.* Children's transition to school is easier when they have experience with language in all of its forms (including being read to). These experiences give kids the tools to interact with other people and to represent their thoughts, feelings, and experiences.

5. *Cognition and general knowledge.* To get ready for school, children need chances to explore and learn from their surroundings. From these experiences children construct knowledge of patterns and relations, such as cause and effect. They also discover ways to solve problems in day-to-day life.[33]

Since all of these dimensions have been shown to influence school performance, initiatives aimed at strengthening children's readiness need to take all of them into consideration. Moreover, elementary schools that want to be ready for the children who enter their kindergartens need to focus on all of these dimensions.[34]

Most Americans take for granted that school readiness depends on communicative skills, cognition, and general knowledge. The following pages therefore take a closer look at other dimensions whose importance is often underestimated.

HEALTH AND PHYSICAL DEVELOPMENT

Health is an essential but often overlooked aspect of school readiness. Cognitive development and school performance can be affected by a child's overall health status, accidents and injuries, chronic illnesses such as asthma, dental problems, and by unrecognized or untreated mental health problems.

Compared with past generations, today's young children face many fewer health risks. During the twentieth century, breakthroughs in medicine and sanitation sharply reduced child mortality. The steepest drop came between 1960 and 1990, thanks largely to strides in preventing and treating infectious diseases. During this period, the death rate fell by 57 percent for children aged one to four and by 48 percent for children aged five to fourteen.[35] By the century's end, infection was no longer the most serious threat to children's well-being. Not all segments of the population have benefited equally, however. To a large extent, the racial and ethnic disparities in child mortality that prevailed a century ago have persisted, with African American children bearing more than twice the risk of white children. Research has not uncovered all the reasons for these disparities, but they appear to have more to do with the ecology of whole communities than with susceptibilities or behaviors of particular individuals.[36]

Public health and community-building initiatives therefore have a role to play in improving school readiness. Preventive health is especially important. As the chief state school officers have emphasized, when children enter kindergarten with preventable developmental impairments or delays, schools cannot be as effective as they should be in helping them reach their full potential.[37]

In addition to studying broad trends in public health that affect children's learning, medical researchers have begun to identify very specific health factors associated with developmental delays and poor school achievement. For example, researchers have found that children who have low levels of thyroxine (a hormone secreted by the thyroid gland) during the first week of life have a 30 percent increase in their risk of having neurological problems at age five and very low achievement at age nine.[38] Researchers are also learning about other biological markers that can help them identify, during the early years, children at risk for school failure. For example, there is some evidence that a slowed capacity to recognize and match a visual pattern (complex reaction time) and heart rate variability are associated with behavioral and attention problems that can interfere with school success. Though such risk factors cannot fully explain academic problems, they can help to identify groups of children who may need additional help in the early years.[39]

Dental health is also crucial. Early childhood caries (ECC), a distinctive pattern of severe tooth decay caused by bacterial infection, is one of the most common diseases of early childhood, affecting 5 percent of children under the age of six. Because there is no universally accepted definition of ECC, estimates vary. Some studies estimate that ECC is much more common, affecting one in four preschoolers. Children from low-income households have higher rates of ECC. The problem is especially severe among American Indian children.[40] While dental problems do not worry policymakers as much as low birth weight or asthma, they can make children miserable, causing constant pain and sapping energy.[41] Tooth decay and early tooth loss can interfere with good nutrition, speech development, the ability to pay attention, and self-esteem. Yet, many preschoolers have never seen a dentist. A California study showed that 44 percent of preschoolers had never had a dentist visit.[42]

Nutrition is another building block of school readiness. It has long been known that severe, prolonged malnutrition can have lasting effects on children's intellectual growth. But even moderate malnutrition—the kind most often seen in the United States—can jeopardize healthy development and school readiness. Poor nutrition triggers a natural rationing system in children's bodies. Scarce food energy goes first to maintaining critical organ function and then to physical growth. When survival is at stake, social activity and cognitive development are lower priorities. That is why undernourished children tend to have low energy levels and show little interest in the activities and people around them. They may seem apathetic and unresponsive. This in turn affects their social interactions, their curiosity, and their overall intellectual functioning. But improved nutrition and environmental conditions can modify the effects of early malnourishment, reducing or eliminating long-term consequences.[43]

EMOTIONAL WELL-BEING
AND SOCIAL COMPETENCE

The educators, pediatricians, social workers, and mental health professionals who shaped Head Start thirty-five years ago were convinced that an "academic" preschool program would not fully prepare children to succeed in elementary school. They designed a program that would address children's needs across the developmental spectrum, with an emphasis on social competence. They were guided as much by experience as research, but scores of studies conducted in the interim confirm that social competence and emotional growth are essential aspects of school readiness.[44]

Mental health problems can affect school readiness as well. For example, depression can, over time, mildly impair children's verbal performance, as well as their social adeptness.[45] Today, there is more appreciation of the need to connect early care and education programs with mental health services. In the late nineties, one such effort was developed by the San Francisco Starting Points program. The Starting Points Early Childhood Interagency Council (ECIC), composed of service providers, policymakers and community leaders, formed a partnership between the county mental health agency and the child care community. The goal was to train and deploy a team of mental health consultants who could provide services to early care and education programs, working with children, families, and staff. Helping child care providers handle stress or cope with emotional issues that could affect their work with children proved to be an important part of the effort. In developing this initiative, San Francisco Starting Points built on existing local resources, including a mental health initiative by the Miriam and Peter Haas Foundation that had previously supported mental health services in child care centers. Starting Points significantly expanded the effort, increasing the participation of the county mental health agency and expanding the network of mental health consultants.[46]

ATTENTION DEFICIT
HYPERACTIVITY DISORDER (ADHD)

ADHD is the most commonly diagnosed behavioral disorder of childhood and often shows up during the preschool years. Scientists using brain scan technology have found distinctive patterns of brain activity associated with ADHD in children as young as four years old—although these methods are almost always used for research, not for diagnosis.[47]

It is possible to diagnose ADHD during the early years, but it is not easy because the symptoms listed in diagnostic manuals sound very much like behaviors found in any preschool classroom, such as fidgeting and not paying attention. According to the National Institute of Mental Health (NIMH), when children are very young the diagnosis of ADHD should be made cautiously by experts well trained in child neurobehavioral disorders, because it can be hard to distinguish developmental problems, especially language delays and adjustment problems, from ADHD.[48] Very active, easily distracted children are not considered to have ADHD unless these behaviors seriously impair their functioning in more than one setting for at least six months.[49]

While the causes of ADHD are not completely understood, doctors have been prescribing stimulant drugs to treat hyperactivity since the 1930s. These stimulants affect brain chemistry, supplying the central nervous system with a more adequate level of dopamine, a neurotransmitter that increases motivation and alertness. Heredity also plays a role in ADHD, and researchers are focusing on genes that are dopamine receptors or transporters. Stimulants like Ritalin (methylphenidate) can work well during the preschool years, and they have been shown to reduce oppositional behavior and improve mother-child interactions. However, the chances of adverse side effects are higher in these years than in later childhood, especially for preschoolers who have developmental disabilities other than ADHD. Many of the stimulant drugs prescribed for children with ADHD, including Ritalin, have not been approved for use by preschool children.[50] According to the National Institute of Mental Health, stimulants should be reserved for severe cases or for preschoolers who are unresponsive to all other interventions.[51] NIMH recommends that preschoolers with ADHD be enrolled in structured preschool programs and that parents be offered training and support.

Despite these findings, Ritalin prescriptions for preschoolers have increased sharply—by 310 percent over a five-year period. Prescriptions for other medications used for ADHD, such as Clonidine, show even greater increases.[52] Given the steep rise in the number of children of all ages who are taking stimulants, concerns have been raised that children, especially active boys, are being overdiagnosed with ADHD and are receiving stimulants unnecessarily. A report on mental health by the Surgeon General concluded that the rise in stimulant use reflects better diagnosis and more effective treatment but added that some of the increase may result from inappropriate diagnosis and treatment. Many children treated for ADHD meet some, but not all, of the diagnostic criteria widely accepted by the medical profession.[53]

Some parents of preschoolers find themselves wondering which is the greater risk: accepting an inexact diagnosis or failing to deal with a disorder that carries a high risk of social, behavioral, and academic problems if left untreated. As things stand, many parents with hyperactive or impulsive preschoolers have few effective treatment alternatives. According to the NIMH, more research is imperative, and early preventive interventions for young children at risk for these problems are urgently needed.[54]

APPROACHES TO LEARNING

For decades education reformers have focused on dropout prevention, with good reason. Without strong preparation, our young people cannot participate fully in the twenty-first-century world and workplace. Economists report shrinking opportunity for those without diplomas.

But today, there is growing recognition that parents and educators need to focus as intensively on motivating children to "jump in"—to throw themselves wholeheartedly into learning activities—as they do on preventing them from dropping out. According to the National Dropout Prevention Center, the social and task-related behavioral problems that develop into school adjustment problems can have roots in the preschool years and cannot be addressed exclusively at the middle or high school levels.[55]

A group of experts who were convened by the National Education Goals Panel to work on Goal 1 urged attention to children's approaches to learning: "the inclinations, dispositions, or styles—rather than skills—that reflect the myriad ways that children become involved in learning and develop their inclinations to pursue it."[56] Their report observed that this dimension of child development is the "least understood, the least researched, and perhaps the most important. . . . Because approaches toward learning frame the child's entire being and are at the core of social/emotional and cognitive interactions, the dimension warrants more serious attention."[57]

A decade of research and practice has revealed a great deal about helping children master the skills needed to read well and succeed in school. It provided another powerful lesson as well: motivation is a key—if not *the* key—to achievement. As the National Research Council has concluded, if children are not willing or able to exert effort, no education reform initiative can succeed.[58]

As parents and teachers know, it is often easier to foster skills than instill motivation. Recently, the National Research Council proposed a strategic plan for improving education research, which urged greater attention to motivation. Their report said, "If ways can be found to increase the amount of effort that students, and particularly young students, expend on learning, the effects on educational achievement would be exponential."[59] Reading experts agree, saying that it is crucial for children to have not only the prerequisite language and early literacy skills but also the motivation to read.[60]

Scholars have devoted considerable attention to understanding what motivates older students to persevere. This topic tends to gain urgency once students approach the levels of schooling where delinquency, dropout rates and school-to-work transition become pressing issues. But there has been much less research on motivation in the early years.

There is a tendency to assume that young children are, throughout the first decade of life, eager to learn, and that problems occur in the second decade. However, there is considerable evidence that the problem of disengagement in fact begins much sooner.[61] When high schoolers drop out, it does not happen out of the blue. Rather, it is the culmination of a process of disengagement from classroom learning that can often be traced back to children's earliest encounters with school.[62] Researchers have pointed to the transition into full-time schooling as a critical period for children's academic development.[63] In the past, that transition generally occurred at age five or six; now it is likely to happen much earlier.

Kindergarten teachers say that motivation is already a challenge in their classrooms. A large-scale study of America's kindergarteners conducted by the U.S. Department of Education has found that, in teachers' estimation, many "do not have a particularly positive attitude toward classroom tasks: one-quarter are 'never' or 'sometimes' eager to learn, and one-third have difficulty paying attention in class."[64]

Motivation has always been a challenge, but today, parents and teachers are struggling to get a generation accustomed to lightning speed—children who may feel that a pixel is worth a thousand words—to find not only interest, but also pleasure, in reading, math, and other activities that take time and considerable exertion. All children are eager to learn. But as children get ready for school, curiosity must be accompanied by a willingness to slow down, to stay focused for a little longer, to tolerate some frustration, to work cooperatively with other children and engage with adults other than their parents, and to attend to objects and patterns that may not dazzle—at least at first. School readiness encompasses all of these challenges. Preschool teacher Rebecca New has written that after years of reflection on what really mattered to her in her work, she settled on two "rules": "When I was a classroom teacher, I struggled with my own need for social and academic reference points that were appropriate for the diverse population of children in my care. Ultimately, two rules were constructed that helped us—the children and me—negotiate countless decisions that we faced during our time together: 1) Make this room a nice place to be . . . for everyone. 2) Everyone has to do something hard every day."[65]

How Ready Are Today's Preschoolers?

One way to answer this question would be to test children as they enter kindergarten. The National Education Goals Panel definition suggests what should be measured to gauge school readiness, but the how remains problematic.[66] Standard paper-and-pencil tests are not appropriate for children entering school.[67] And assessing young children is notoriously difficult, because their growth is rapid, uneven, and strongly influenced by the kind of care they receive and the settings in which they learn.[68] Many states and communities are struggling to find ways to document children's readiness and gauge the success of their early childhood initiatives. For early educators, assessment remains one of today's most pressing challenges, and a great deal of work is underway in this area.

In the meantime, we are not completely in the dark. To find out about the state of school readiness across the land, many researchers have taken a common-sense route, consulting the real experts: kindergarten teachers. Surveys of kindergarten teachers have asked them to identify the skills needed to succeed in their classrooms and the percentage of children who are able to do so. Estimates have varied, depending on the scope and content of particular surveys.

Generally, teachers say that most children are well prepared but a significant minority will have a hard time coping with the challenges of elementary school. A decade ago, kindergarten teachers across the country estimated that about one-third of children were unprepared for the challenges of school entry.[69] In North Carolina in 1995, the estimate was about one-fifth.[70] A recent survey of thirty-six hundred kindergarten teachers nationwide, conducted by the National Center for Early Development and Learning (NCEDL), found that nearly half of all new kindergartners (48 percent) have moderate or serious problems as they enter school.[71]

When kindergarten teachers are asked to list the characteristics of children who are ready for school, cognitive ability and prereading skills do not top their list. In the NCEDL study, the most common answer was the ability to pay attention. When researchers put the same question to kindergarten teachers across the state of North Carolina, the three top answers related to children's emotional and social readiness: "listens and pays attention" (46 percent); "has good social skills such as sharing and taking turns" (44 percent); "follows directions and instructions" (37 percent). Having basic knowledge, like being able to name colors and provide their own address and phone number, was fourth on the list.[72]

Elementary school teachers want preschools to help children learn behaviors needed to succeed in school, like listening, taking turns, and getting along with other children.[73] Teachers stress the link between social and cognitive skills. Children who are rated by teachers as able to complete tasks and follow directions tend to also be rated higher in academic achievement in general and in reading and math in particular.[74] And research confirms that children who are able to work undisturbed, to persist at tasks, and to sustain their attention, go on to achieve better in reading and mathematics and have an easier adjustment to school.[75]

Like kindergarten teachers, parents tend to be more concerned about the social and emotional aspects of school readiness than about cognitive skills. They are also very adept at spotting behavior problems during the preschool years that can interfere with school readiness. One study followed three-year-olds through the primary grades and found that mothers' high ratings of hyperactivity and behavioral problems predicted later school adjustment problems.[76]

Ready Schools

Today's readiness agenda has two goals: ready children *and* ready schools. The aim is not only to get children ready for elementary school; it is also to ensure that elementary schools are prepared to meet the diverse developmental and educational needs of the kindergartners who pass through their doors. In 1999, the National Goals Panel identified key attributes of ready schools.[77] It stressed that ready schools are committed to the success of every child, understanding that children will arrive at their doorsteps in varying stages of readiness. They have high expectations of all children but build into their organization and curriculum sufficient flexibility to respond to significant variations within a class and to meet the changing needs of individual children over time. They meet children with curricula and teaching methods that are ready for children—that are open, flexible, and engaging.

One of the most important aspects of ready schools is their focus on the transitions that children (and their parents) make as they move from the familiar home setting to the pubic school classroom and from preschool or child care to kindergarten. The cultural divide between home and school can be treacherous for children who are not native speakers of English; it can also be problematic for low-income and minority families.

Practices that ease the transition to kindergarten have been shown to benefit children, parents, and teachers. Some districts and schools contact local families well before children reach age five. In written or personal communications, they suggest steps that parents can take in the first years of life to get their children off to a good start. Some schools plan home visits by teachers or principals before children enter school. As the school year begins, there are many ways that schools can extend a warm welcome to children and families. Despite research showing their importance, transition activities like these remain the exception rather than the rule.

Even the warmest welcome cannot ensure continuity as kids move from one level of schooling to another. Children benefit when preschools and elementary schools collaborate on a regular basis not only with families, but also with each other—holding joint workshops to discuss curricula and teaching strategies and to share insights about the kids in their classrooms. Kindergarten and primary grade teachers can profit from the knowledge of parents and educators who already know the child well. Some early childhood programs such as Head Start, and early intervention programs such as the Abecedarian Project and Project Giant Step, have made consistent efforts to establish links with the schools that their "graduates" attend.[78]

For children who have disabilities or other special needs, moving into kindergarten or an alternative elementary school placement may be especially challenging. Their families may experience more stress during these transitions. Transition plans are therefore an important element in children's individual learning plans.[79]

The National Center for Early Development and Learning has produced a manual entitled *Enhancing the Transition to Kindergarten: Linking Children, Families, and Schools.*[80] This manual stresses that helping children and families make a smooth transition to school requires a careful planning process that entails these key steps:

- *Form a collaborative team.* The team should consist of preschool teachers, kindergarten teachers, family workers, principals, parents, and other community representatives.

- *Identify a team coordinator.* The transition practices and plans for a given school or program should be coordinated by a school professional, who can act as a bridge with families from the preschool to the kindergarten year.

- *Create a timeline.* Decide when specific transition activities will occur, including coordination efforts, preparation of class lists, visits to school, summer programs, family literacy activities, open houses, parent-teacher meetings, and ongoing contacts between preschool teachers, parents, and kindergarten teachers. The timeline should stretch from September of the preschool year through the kindergarten year.

- *Implement transition practices.* As the process proceeds, the strategies can be fine-tuned for maximum effectiveness.

- *Evaluate and revise.* The collaborative team should assess results at both the district/community and school/neighborhood levels, making necessary adjustments.

Reading

Children's language development in the early years is an astonishing intellectual feat, and experts continue to explore the pathways by which children grow from wordless newborns to sophisticated storytellers in just a few short years. At the same time, researchers are studying the developmental pathways that lead, just a few years later, to competent reading. They are studying how, over time, young children come to understand the abstract notion that certain lines and circles on a surface have something to do with sounds, that a flow of such signs can convey words, and that those words can be linked together to record events, tell stories, or express thoughts. These are ideas we may take for granted, but they are by no means self-evident. Indeed, they eluded humans' grasp for most of the time that we have walked the earth.

What is the best way to get children ready to read? And when should formal reading instruction begin? These questions have sparked controversy as proponents of different strategies urged different emphases and methods. Some have stressed phonics—an approach that stresses teaching children how sounds and letters are related. Others de-emphasize phonics training and drill, considering phonics to be one of many ways that new words may be recognized. Preferring a "whole language" approach, they say that since the aim is to help children wrest meaning from text, early educators should concentrate on immersing children in a linguistically rich environment.[81]

The reading debates have gone on for some time—perhaps since a reading expert named Icklesamer published a book in Germany called *The Shortest Way to Reading*, which proposed introducing children to speech sounds associated with well-known words before teaching them letters as the basic unit of instruction. It was published in 1527![82]

The good news is that most children will learn to read no matter which approach is used. In fact, when they have a chance to experience the benefits of literacy—by watching older children and adults read for pleasure and information and by sharing books and stories with them—some children begin to grasp the relationship between oral and written language with no formal instruction at all.[83]

Today, most reading specialists recommend a balanced approach: children develop into readers gradually and at different stages of the process different skills come into play.[84] Becoming a good reader—gaining sufficient mastery that it can become an effective learning tool throughout life—requires two sets of skills.

SHAPE-AND-SOUND SKILLS

To learn to read, children need to be able to recognize the shapes that designate letters, and they need to understand the rules for translating those letters into sounds. These "shape-and-sound" skills include:

- *Phonological awareness.* This means being able to listen carefully and to think about how words sound, apart from what they mean. When children realize that the word "sunny" has two spoken parts, that it begins with the same sound as "soup" and "circus" or that it rhymes with "funny," they are making a crucial step toward grasping the alphabetic principle and ultimately toward learning to read.[85] Researchers have found that children's rate of acquiring reading skills is related to their phonological awareness. Children who are better at detecting syllables, rhymes, or phonemes are quicker to learn to sound out words—even when researchers control for other differences such as intelligence, memory skills, and social class.[86] These findings confirm that reading readiness skills can be taught. They are not just a matter of ability.

- *Print awareness.* For preschoolers, this means not only recognizing at least some letters of the alphabet but also knowing that writing goes from left to right and from top to bottom. Preschoolers who pretend to read are more likely to become successful readers later, because as they turn pages and recite familiar stories, they are becoming familiar with the format of books and practicing print awareness.

  Researchers know a lot about children's shape-and-sound skills at kindergarten entry: about two-thirds of new kindergartners can recognize their letters and nearly one-third recognize the beginning sounds of words. More girls than boys enter kindergarten with these skills, and children whose parents have higher incomes and more years of education enter kindergarten with more shape-and-sound skills.[87]

WORD-AND-WORLD SKILLS

To become good readers, children also need the language and conceptual skills that let them make sense of the words they have decoded and to relate them to objects, ideas, or experiences that are part of their world. Word-and-world skills include:

- *A store of words and concepts.* The store of words children recognize—including not only people, places, and things, but also concepts.

- *Semantic knowledge.* Understanding enough about the structure of language to make sense of a string of words.

- *Contextual knowledge.* Comprehension of all but the simplest writing requires knowledge that cannot be found in the word or sentence itself. The child must bring to bear knowledge of the world, semantic knowledge, and knowledge of the written context in which the particular sentence occurs. They have to connect information and events to real-life experiences.

Without word-and-world skills, texts can be readily decoded but not understood. Consider this passage from a well-known children's book, which was highlighted in *Starting Out Right,* a recent National Research Council publication on learning to read:

> Madeline soon ate and drank.
> On her bed there was a crank,
> and a crack on the ceiling had the habit
> of sometimes looking like a rabbit.[88]

Children may have all the shape-and-sound skills needed to sound out the words and still not read this passage successfully. They would need to understand words like "crank" and "habit." They would have to grasp that an inanimate object like a crack can be spoken of as if it were human and can be said to form a habit—although not the kind of "crack habit" that came into public consciousness long after our passage was written. They would have to understand not only that a crack on a ceiling may look like a rabbit, but also that the resemblance is not fixed, but is perceived only "sometimes." These are very complex ideas, and all the phonological awareness in the world will not illuminate them.

Given these considerations, how can early childhood educators best lay the groundwork for the reading instruction that will begin in the primary grades? As children are learning to read, shape-and-sound skills may appear to be more important. After all, the first words that children read tend to be easily recognized. The emphasis is on decoding. Understanding how a crack can have a habit, or why a bed might have a crank, would not be much help as a child tries to sound out the word "rabbit."

In fact, during the first year of formal reading instruction, substantial differences in children's word-and-world skills—that is, their knowledge of words and grammar, conceptual understanding, and contextual knowledge—have no apparent effect on reading scores. Word-and-world skills do not play an obvious role until children encounter the kind of material that really challenges their semantic and conceptual abilities. They may be well into the primary grades before this happens.

As parents and preschool teachers look ahead to kindergarten and first grade, the impulse to focus intensively on shape-and-sound skills may be powerful. They know that the children who are likely to learn to read quickly and well are those who know the alphabetic principle, know their letters and some of the sounds those letter make, can print letters, and know a lot about how print works. This is as true for children from low-income backgrounds as it is for children of affluence.[89]

That is why the kinds of activities that strengthen shape-and-sound skills can be very helpful in the preschool years. Songs, rhyming games, language play, and nursery rhymes spark children's awareness of language and sounds. Three- and four-year-olds can be encouraged to pay attention to separable and repeating sounds in language and to notice the beginning or rhyming sounds in familiar words.

Three- and four-year-olds can also begin identifying letters of the alphabet, especially those in their own names.[90] But drilling children in the ABCs is no guarantee of early reading, because preschoolers are still developing the visual motor skills needed to coordinate their eye and hand movements. These motor skills are among the best predictors of children's reading achievement in the primary grades.[91]

One of researchers' most important findings about shape-and-sound skills is that they can be taught. Individuals differ in phonemic awareness, but this ability is not highly correlated with general intelligence. All children can benefit from enjoyable activities geared to developing an awareness of the constituent sounds that make up words. And with sufficient instruction and practice, the vast majority—including many who may have initial difficulty—can in time become able readers. The percentage of children whose progress is impeded by more serious disabilities is quite small. Estimates vary, but the figure is certainly less than 10 percent.[92]

For all of these reasons, an intensive focus on shape-and-sound skills can have an immediate payoff as children move into kindergarten and first grade. But here is the catch: the skills that help children become able decoders are not the same ones that allow them to understand and integrate what they read. Shape-and-sound skills need to be developed as children approach the age of school entry, but an overemphasis on these skills may lead to a temporary improvement in academic performance at the cost of missed opportunities for long-term growth in reading performance and overall achievement.

Over time, children with strong conceptual understanding and contextual knowledge are more likely to become good readers and good students. These skills may not affect reading scores until well into the primary grades but need to be developed much sooner. This is a challenging goal, since word-and-world skills are harder to define and teach than shape-and-sound skills.

Some of the knowledge good readers have can come from books, and from discussions that spring from the stories. That is why the single most important activity for building the foundations of literacy may be reading aloud, especially when children are active participants. Adults can ask questions about what has happened in the story, and what may happen next. Children may talk about the pictures, retell the story, discuss their favorite parts, and hear favorite passages over and over again.

It is the talk that surrounds the storybook reading that gives it power, helping children to bridge what is in the story and their own lives. Adults can help children develop higher-level thinking by moving experiences in stories from what the children may see in front of them to what they can imagine. They can help children retell the story from the viewpoint of a particular character or object.

But books alone are not sufficient. Good readers have knowledge that comes from a wide experience of real life. Knowledge of the world and its complexities begins in the family—around the dinner table, at get-togethers with friends and neighbors, or during visits to interesting places near and far. But many families do not provide a rich variety of experiences. Some live in unsafe neighborhoods and nurture children by insulating them from the world rather than exposing them to it. Some are not sure how to explain abstract ideas to small children or how to talk about daily life in ways that will expand their knowledge of the world. Others have little relaxed time with their children.

That is why family support initiatives and prekindergarten programs play a strong role in reading readiness. As one first-grade teacher has said, "My biggest obstacle in teaching reading is the lack of experiences that some children are bringing to school—lack of language experiences involving reading, print, and concepts. Experiences like having your mother explain the types of fruit at the grocery store or playing with funnels in the bathtub. Experiences that come with having been talked to and read to."[93] Word-and-world skills may not show up in early reading assessments, but they are like money in the bank, accumulating and growing until they are needed.

There is no need to transform Head Start, or any other prekindergarten program, into a reading program. All high-quality preschool settings that have well qualified staff and a strong, diverse curriculum are, in fact, reading programs. A rhyming game is a reading readiness activity, but so is a visit to another neighborhood, a discussion of Ryan's unusual pet, an outing to the store where Samantha's dad works, or a story set in a far-off land. Singing the alphabet song is a reading readiness activity, but so is a puppet show, a guided tour through a family photo album, or a trip to the supermarket. Looking at picture books is a reading readiness activity, but so are chances to share the stories, songs, drawings, and experiences of people from other cultures.[94]

Family income affects achievement throughout children's schooling—including the preschool years. Children's socioeconomic status is one of the strongest predictors of performance differences in children at the beginning of first grade.[95] The achievement gap opens up early, as low-income children have more difficulty learning to read. How does this happen?

Part of the answer relates to less familiarity with shape-and-sound skills. A survey of today's kindergartners compared the reading readiness skills of children whose families had received public assistance, with those of children whose families had never been on welfare. They found that the children of welfare recipients were far less likely to recognize letters of the alphabet (41 percent vs. 69 percent) and to be able to identify the beginning sounds of words (11 percent vs. 31 percent).[96]

But this study did not consider word-and-world skills—the vocabulary, conceptual skills, and contextual knowledge that make so much difference as children move through elementary school. Another study followed 338 low-income children from Head Start preschool programs through the primary grades, and found that preschoolers who mastered shape-and-sound skills scored higher on reading tests in the second grade. But they found an even stronger correlation between preschoolers' word-and-world skills and their second-grade reading achievement. Moreover, their study of word-and-world skills found that "children who start school behind in these areas are likely to stay behind."[97]

As children move through elementary school and encounter more challenging material, those who can read with understanding will read more and, as a result, acquire more knowledge in various subject areas. But those with a limited store of words, concepts, or experiences will begin to have difficulty with comprehension, even if they are fluent decoders, and will resist reading. This is how the literacy-rich get richer while the literacy-poor get poorer.[98]

This research suggests that during the preschool period, children who are at high risk of reading difficulty need three kinds of literacy-building activities:

1. *They need many opportunities to develop and experiment with oral language.* A growing body of evidence suggests that children have a better likelihood of becoming good readers if they arrive in kindergarten with a greater ability to use oral language and to adapt their speech to a variety of listeners (such as family, friends, and teachers)

and a variety of purposes (such as telling a story, reporting an event, or giving directions).

2. *They need access to experiences that enrich their conceptual understanding and contextual knowledge.* These experiences should continue over the course of the child's development.

3. *As they approach school entry, they need activities that help them gain phonological and print awareness.* Children at risk for reading difficulties benefit from direct instruction in matching sounds and letters. Whenever possible, skill practice should be embedded in tasks like telling stories or narrating events—activities that are meaningful to children and help them communicate in real-life settings.[99]

READING READINESS
FOR ENGLISH-LANGUAGE LEARNERS

Young children with strong oral language skills are more likely to grow into able readers and students. But what about preschoolers whose first language is not English? Should these children attend bilingual or English-only preschools? Can the development of oral language skills in a native language get children ready to read in English? Will reading readiness activities conducted in the native language transfer to English reading? What should be the initial language of reading instruction?

These questions are crying out for research. Few have definitive answers, given the current state of knowledge. Like most questions concerning bilingual education, they are very controversial. They also have considerable urgency, given two key trends in early education. First, there has been a sharp rise in the number of young children who speak other languages and have limited proficiency in English. In 1997, 8 percent of kindergarten children spoke a native language other than English and were English-language learners.[100] And second, Hispanic children, who constitute the largest group of English learners, are at high risk for reading difficulties. Over the last two decades, Hispanic students have made progress in achievement, but they are still twice as likely as non-Hispanic whites to be reading below average for their age.[101]

Some researchers have looked at the impact of English-only and bilingual preschool settings on children's overall language and cognitive development. These studies suggest that children who use their first language in preschool are better able to understand and use opportunities in their classrooms and do as well as, if not better than, similar children who attend English-only preschools. For example, an evaluation of the Carpinteria Preschool program, which conducted classroom activities in Spanish, showed that as participants graduated into elementary school, they acquired English-language fluency faster, transitioned out of bilingual education sooner, and achieved better in English-language classrooms and on English-language standardized tests.[102]

Research on reading readiness is less clear. Preschoolers who can recognize and manipulate the bits of sound that make up words—who can rhyme words, name things that begin with a given sound, and identify similarities in sound—usually succeed in the early stages of reading. But what about language-minority children? Will phonemic awareness in their first language get them ready to read in English?

As things stand, early educators have little evidence on which to base their reading readiness strategies. According to a report from the National Research Council, there is some evidence that phonemic awareness transfers across languages under certain circumstances. But researchers have not determined whether mastering shape-and-sound skills in a first language is a sufficient basis for initial literacy in English, or whether those skills need to be developed in English first.[103]

Many teachers believe that children should first learn to read in a language they already speak, and there is evidence that immigrant children who have had two to three years of initial schooling in their native countries fare better academically than those who have not. Some studies in bilingual education show that learning to read in one's native language avoids the obstacles presented by limited English proficiency and can lead to high achievement.[104]

On the other hand, experience also shows that many children first learn to read in a second language without encountering serious problems. After looking at all the evidence, the National Research Council report on teaching language-minority children concluded: "We do not yet know whether there will be long-term advantages or disadvantages to initial literacy instruction in the primary language versus English, given a very high-quality program of known effectiveness in both cases."[105]

Other researchers gathered by the National Research Council offer more confident advice. In *Starting Out Right*, leading authorities on reading stress that spoken language comes before written language and that it is very hard to read a language that is incomprehensible to the ear. They say that whenever possible, children should be taught the basics of reading in their native language while acquiring oral proficiency in English; they can then be taught to extend their first-language literacy skills to English-language materials. When it is not possible to offer reading instruction in the native language, the priority should be to help children develop oral proficiency in English. Reading instruction should be postponed until an adequate level of oral proficiency in English has been achieved.[106]

Starting Out Right also addresses the needs of children who grow up speaking nonstandard dialects of English. Like bilingual children, they must develop the ability to switch codes—to summon different words and obey different rules depending on the setting. There is some evidence that the need to understand and use more than one language system increases children's symbolic processing capacity and strengthens their literacy skills.

However, children who speak other languages or dialects are often placed at risk of poor achievement as teachers develop low expectations for them. For example, an African American child who insists that "deaf" sounds the same as "death," who rhymes "ask" and "jacks," or is sure that "sold" ends with an "l" sound, may frustrate a teacher who is unfamiliar with dialect. Teachers who have a grasp of the rules that govern dialect can help children develop strong shape-and-sound skills and grow into able readers.[107]

Vartan Gregorian, president of Carnegie Corporation of New York, has said that literacy can move children "from where they are to a place elsewhere."[108] Whether the author is Dr. Seuss or Dr. Einstein, a text does not simply present a landmark to be noted by passersby. Rather, it offers possible worlds beyond the reader's ordinary reach. To experience a place elsewhere, you have to jump in— carrying all of the accumulated baggage of a lifetime, however long or short. Children need maps to find their way to those other places and to negotiate the new terrain once they arrive. Curriculum is the atlas that good teachers, including good early educators, create to contain and order those maps.[109]

Small children bring to emergent literacy knowledge of the world gleaned in the context of important relationships with their parents and extended families. Preschool curricula can supplement or extend these experiences, helping children to learn, think, and talk about new domains of knowledge. They can infuse into their curricula, in developmentally appropriate ways, all of the disciplines that appear as formal content areas in elementary school.[110]

Children can explore social studies by learning about their neighborhood, polling parents, or making sculptures. As beginning scientists, they can explore the physical properties of familiar things like water and sand; they can observe how a computer mouse moves on its mouse pad; they can discuss how time works and how it feels. They can study math through cooking projects, or by using blocks or toys. In all of these realms, teachers can challenge children to explore ideas and use language in new ways by asking open-ended questions: Why? How? What if?[111]

Preschool curricula can combine language activities with content area learning. The Head Start on Science and Communication (HSSC) Program was designed to promote success in science for children in preschool, kindergarten, and first grade. It emphasizes the development of children's language skills as they learn about scientific inquiry, apply this approach in school and at home, and acquire knowledge about life science, earth science, and physical science.

The baggage children bring to the texts they read (or pretend to read, or hear) is not limited to vocabulary or contextual information. In the case of the Madeline story, curriculum does not simply explain the difference between crack and crank or explain why certain old-fashioned beds have cranks. It unpacks some of the sensual, emotional experiences that children bring from home—feelings and fantasies associated with their own deepest, most important experiences. As Madeline eats and drinks, lies on her bed, and contemplates her cracked ceiling, children may bring to the scene contextual knowledge that includes the sensual experiences of eating and drinking and lying in bed and perhaps their own habit of changing something worrisome into something comforting. As Madeleine Grumet has observed, curriculum is what helps children find connections between the private self and the public text. By inviting children to talk about, extend, paint, act out, or dance stories, teachers can make room for the textures of children's own daily lives, honor their most important feelings and connections, and provide "a rich and varied sensory and interpersonal ground for learning."[112]

Results

Maternal employment and concern about school readiness are not the only forces driving the prekindergarten movement. There is a third factor—a growing body of evidence showing that preschool programs for children are a good investment.

Research shows that intensive, high-quality preschool programs can enhance the abilities of children from low-income families as they enter kindergarten and set into motion a cycle of increased success, producing permanent gains in achievement in school and in social behavior.[113]

Some have argued that children are being "hot-housed" in such programs, resulting in short-term gains that quickly fade when intensive services are removed. Steven Barnett, an economist at Rutgers University, reviewed all of the studies that follow preschoolers at least through third grade, measuring outcomes against those of a comparison group. He found that effects on IQ do fade and that evidence about the impact on achievement scores is mixed. But he argues that when you look at indicators that are easier to measure and less prone to analytic error, such as grade repetition, special education placement, and high school graduation, it becomes clear that high-quality preschool education does indeed have long-term positive effects. He believes that they may actually grow over time.[114]

A recent government report called *School Involvement in Early Education* offers another perspective on fade-out. Citing the work of Doris Entwisle, it emphasizes that even short-term IQ gains may lay a foundation for success by boosting children's performance during the critical transition into school. Higher ability during early schooling can raise teachers' expectations of children—a crucial factor in school success—while protecting primary grade pupils from being placed in lower-ability groups and retained in grade.[115]

These findings suggest that concern about fade-out should not discourage investment in high-quality preschool programs; rather, it should inspire greater collaboration between early childhood and primary grade educators, with the aim of ensuring high-quality standards on both sides of the kindergarten divide, developing curricula that stretch across that gap, and taking steps to smooth the transition to school.

The research also shows that to get large benefits, programs must be intensive and well funded. In his review, Steven Barnett also considered whether only model programs—the kind created by researchers, with small classes, highly qualified teachers, and close supervision—improve school success. He concluded that ordinary public school Head Start programs do produce the same kind of long-term effects, but they are distinctly smaller than the effects of model programs. Differences in the amount of resources devoted to children in the two types of programs appear to account for differences in the size of the impact.[116]

In 2001, a page-one story in the *New York Times* announced new evidence that a large-scale, public preschool program can indeed have lasting benefits. It described the findings of a landmark study published in the prestigious *Journal of the American Medical Association*. This study followed, over a fifteen-year period, nearly a thousand children from low-income families who took part in the Chicago Child-Parent Center study in the mid-eighties. It found that participants showed long-term gains, when compared with similar children who did not take part in the program. The researchers attributed the program's long-term effects in part to the fact that it provided services to children from age three (preschool) through age nine (second or third grade). The program focused not only on children's cognitive growth, but also on their physical, social, and emotional development. It was broad in scope, providing educational services, a multifaceted parent program, outreach activities (including home visitation), and health and nutrition services (including health screening, speech therapy, and nursing and meal services).[117]

As states invest significant public resources in preschool initiatives, they must come to grips with accountability. States that expand access to prekindergarten by extending their public school offerings can adapt existing accountability structures to accommodate preschool. States that expand Head Start can rely on that program's federal performance standards. But as states move toward universal prekindergarten, most find that they must utilize every possible resource, including public school prekindergartens, Head Start programs, and private preschool programs (operated by not-for-profit and for-profit providers). Given this mixed delivery system, how can states ensure or improve quality?

Virtually every state that has launched a prekindergarten initiative has set standards for them, not only to promote accountability but also to help consumers gauge the quality of a particular program. Several approaches are possible.

States can require providers to meet the standards set by a national accrediting body. For centers, the most widely used accreditation system was developed by the National Association for the Education of Young Children (NAEYC). In 1999, the National Association of Family Child Care (NAFCC) created an accreditation system for family child care homes. Various other organizations, including some faith-based groups, also accredit early childhood programs.[118] States have taken varied approaches to supporting the accreditation process, often by providing grants to help providers gain accreditation or by providing financial incentives to states that meet the standards.

Some states have adopted federal Head Start performance

standards for their state-run programs. And some have crafted their own prekindergarten standards, which differ from Head Start and national accreditation standards, but typically include some of the same key elements: health and safety, child-to-staff ratios, staff qualifications, curriculum and practices, and parental involvement.

As states begin to evaluate preschool initiatives launched in the 1990s, researchers will learn more about the long-term effects of early childhood education. Early returns are encouraging, show-ing positive effects on children's cognitive, social, emotional, and physical development. Early evaluations of Georgia's universal prekindergarten program found that participants had higher aca-demic and social ratings, better school attendance, and improved parent satisfaction. A survey of kindergarten teachers found, in 1997–98, that program participants were more ready for school, es-pecially in pre-reading, pre-math, fine and gross motor develop-ment, independence and initiative, and interactions with adults and other children.[119]

Studies in several states, including Connecticut, Maryland, Michigan, Texas, and Washington, compared participants in state prekindergarten programs with similar children who had not en-rolled and found that the programs had produced positive results. A study in Colorado evaluated the impact of its prekindergarten initiative on school readiness by screening children at the begin-ning and end of the prekindergarten year to assess language skills, identify developmental delays, and determine who needed refer-rals for special education. The post-test scores showed positive gains beyond those that would be expected due to maturation alone. A majority of these children began kindergarten on par with their classmates.[120]

A recent North Carolina study offers insight into the compo-nents of prekindergarten programs that affect school readiness. A six-county study of 508 children who began kindergarten in fall

1999 after participating in North Carolina's Smart Start program concluded that participating children's thinking and language skills were stronger than those of a comparison group. Children in the comparison group were nearly twice as likely to have low cognitive skills (17 percent vs. 9 percent) and were much more likely to have behavioral problems (18 percent vs. 10 percent).

There was an important qualification. The positive outcomes were not found for all Smart Start participants—only for those attending centers that had received assistance with quality enhancement, such as teacher training, mentoring, and curriculum materials. Smart Start children whose centers received other kinds of assistance (such as special library programs, first-aid training for teachers, or playground safety reviews) showed no advantages over the comparison group. While these forms of assistance in all likelihood benefited children, by themselves they did not improve cognitive or social outcomes.

In short, to improve school entry skills, it is necessary to tackle specific aspects of quality—those that relate directly to the quality of classroom experience. According to Donna Bryant of the Frank Porter Graham Center at the University of North Carolina at Chapel Hill, some of the centers benefited from grants that better outfitted classrooms and improved materials, especially when teachers were trained in the use of those materials. But intensive teacher preparation appeared to be the most powerful factor in improving school readiness. For example, several counties went beyond workshops, assigning mentors to spend time in classrooms and help teachers practice and incorporate new ways of working with young children.[121]

Investing in the Early Childhood Workforce

Improving results for young children will take significant investments in the development of current and new early childhood teachers. All teachers of young children need good, foundational knowledge of language acquisition, including second-language learning, the processes of reading and writing, early literacy development, and experiences and teaching practices contributing to children's optimal development.[122] Today, low standards and low rewards are the norm for early childhood teachers.[123] Efforts to upgrade the qualifications of the early education workforce, and improve its compensation and career options, are essential elements in any plan to improve early education.

Recently, the National Research Council's Committee on Early Childhood Pedagogy recommended that in early learning programs, every group of children should have a teacher with a bachelor's degree in some aspect of child development or special education. The committee further recommended that each state establish a single career ladder for early childhood teachers, specifying credentials and pay levels for teaching assistants, teachers, and supervisors.[124]

As things stand, our nation has no uniform preparation requirements or licensure standards for prekindergarten teachers, and state policies on teacher credentials vary widely. The states with the most rigorous standards require teachers in state-funded prekindergarten classrooms to have certification in early childhood education or elementary education with some coursework in early childhood education. Most states do not require certification but require teachers to acquire some kind of credential indicating a background in early childhood development. For example, many state prekindergarten programs (including all of the Head Start models) require at minimum a CDA credential. Four state initiatives have no statewide teacher requirements. Most states mandate some in-service training for their prekindergarten teachers, and some have very specific guidelines, but here too, requirements vary significantly.[125]

Salaries paid to preschool teachers tend to be too depressed to attract or hold better-qualified staff. Employment in preschool programs provides living wages and career opportunities for a small segment of the workforce, including some who staff Head Start, military child care, or public school prekindergarten programs.[126] But nationally, the average annual salary for child care workers is about $14,500. Few have health or retirement benefits. According to the U.S. Department of Labor, about one-third of those employed in the early education workforce leave their jobs after one year.[127] And many school districts that are experiencing shortages of elementary school teachers are hiring away the early childhood field's best trained and most qualified teachers.[128]

The trend lines are not encouraging. A recent study that tracked staffing patterns in the same California child care centers in 1994, 1996, and 2000 found that the centers, and the child care industry as a whole, are losing well-qualified teaching staff and administrators at an alarming rate and are hiring replacement teachers with less training and education. Despite recognition that higher wages contribute to greater staff stability, compensation for most teaching staff has not kept pace with the cost of living over the six-year period. Teaching staff and directors say that high turnover impeded their ability to do their jobs, and, for some, contributed to their decision to leave. Centers that employed highly trained teachers were more likely to sustain a high level of quality over time.[129]

A variety of programs now underway at the federal, state, and local levels hold the promise of incrementally improving child care workers' salaries and/or benefits.[130] For example, twelve states have implemented TEACH, a program that gives scholarships and bonuses to early childhood workers who complete college-level training, but such programs have affected only a small fraction of the workforce.[131] State compensation initiatives in North Carolina, Rhode Island, Washington, and Wisconsin; county initiatives in Alameda County, California, and Nassau County, New York; and local programs in San Francisco and Seattle are beginning to make headway in improving worker compensation in the early childhood field. But to date, such initiatives have affected only a fraction of the workforce, and little is known about their impact. This is an area where, despite recent progress, the most important challenges lie ahead.

The Challenge

Each year produces new evidence that high-quality early education and care can indeed promote later achievement. Recent research reports and policy statements have bolstered the case that early childhood learning—in all of its dimensions—affects school readiness and later achievement. More is known about how children's health, beginning with prenatal care, affects later learning and about the role of social and emotional readiness in school success.

The challenge is to factor all of this evidence into the crucial decisions about early learning programs that will be made in the months and years ahead. The case for universal, voluntary preschool is compelling, but public engagement efforts must not let up—especially since new decision-makers are entering state legislatures all the time with little background in early childhood policy. Moreover, efforts to pursue school readiness in all of its dimensions must be sustained. To be sure, today's emphasis on readiness, reading, and results has had some salutary effects. For example, it has spurred the early childhood field to consider more carefully the results it is pursuing, and to look more rigorously at program content and the transition to school. But the research shows that a narrow focus on cognitive skills cannot achieve the vision of school readiness embodied in the nation's number one education goal.

Parents, educators, and policymakers are all eager to strengthen children's reading skills and boost academic achievement, but we must not lose sight of the big picture. Given all we know about school readiness, prenatal care is in fact a reading readiness program. Programs that bolster social competence and emotional well-being are reading readiness programs. And of course early literacy initiatives are reading readiness programs. What is needed is a balanced approach with sensible outcome measures—one that combines the "healthy development" goals that have been set out in recent years with reading goals.

How can this approach be achieved? Collaboration is an important part of the answer. As we move forward, the entire education establishment needs to come together, addressing the challenges of the preschool years as an essential plank of the nation's larger education reform agenda. This is going to take some fresh thinking. As things stand, our nation has an immense, imperfect system of elementary and secondary education, and an immense, imperfect nonsystem of early childhood education and care. The challenge is to reform them both and to bring them together.

CHAPTER 4

Common Ground, Higher Ground

American families have often done their best thinking around the kitchen table, bringing all of their ingenuity to bear on solving problems and realizing a shared vision of how life could be. Today, concern about children is moving communities across the nation to "supersize" the kitchen table—creating children's councils, forums, or alliances, or engaging diverse groups in efforts to address the needs of young children and their families. In some places, ambitious systems change efforts are under way. In others, people are taking part in early childhood initiatives through the Internet, forming virtual communities that allow them to reach across geographic boundaries, and often across cultural, political, and ethnic and racial borders as well.

This chapter is about how our nation can build on the progress of the last decade, so that localities, counties, and states can improve prospects for their young children. No family, government body or agency, no community organization, no school, business, labor union, or congregation, can single-handedly create the comprehensive, integrated initiatives needed to help young children thrive. Collaboration has long been considered a cornerstone of any effort to improve results for children. Today it is more often viewed as the whole foundation.

The Accident of Geography

Our focus must widen from children and families to communities because to a greater degree than ever before, place matters. In the United States today, where you end up may well hinge on where you start out—quite literally. As new policies and programs proliferate in states and localities around the nation, so do concerns about fairness.

Of course, the accident of geography has always affected Americans' life prospects. Children born in Stillwater, Minnesota, have always had some different formative experiences than those raised in suburban Cobb County, Georgia, or in the urban landscape of Oakland, California. But today, where you call home is likely to have an even greater impact than in past decades. Large economic trends play lead roles in this story. The robust economy of the last decade benefited many American families and communities but had different effects in different settings. The same is true for globalization and technological advance. In particular, the nineties saw continued movement of manufacturing and higher income populations (mostly white) out of central cities. On the whole, these cities and older close-in suburbs have become less livable and more isolated. There has been diminished opportunity as well for rural residents.[1]

Children born in America's big cities face higher hurdles on the path to adulthood than those who grow up in the rest of America, especially those born in its more affluent suburbs.[2] But even within the universe of large cities, children born in different parts of the country have different life prospects. A baby born in Dallas, Texas, is four times more likely to have a mom who dropped out of school than is a newborn in Seattle, Washington. An expectant mother is three times more likely to go without timely prenatal care if she lives in Columbus, Ohio, than if she lives in Nashville, Tennessee.[3]

And these differences pale in comparison to discrepancies among neighborhoods within the same city. For instance, a Chicago child living in a high-poverty neighborhood (where at least half of the children are poor) is twelve times more likely to suffer abuse and forty-three times more likely to be placed in foster care than a child in the most affluent parts of the city.[4]

The nexus of race and class account for some of these differences, cutting deep channels around the worlds inhabited by many low-income children and their families. Kids who live in neighborhoods that are cut off from the economic and social mainstream begin life with the deck stacked against them. Researchers have found that as predictors of children's intellectual development, neighborhood characteristics count (though not as much as family characteristics such as income or mother's level of education).[5] They are beginning to understand where, when, and how neighborhoods influence family life and child development.[6]

Some of the factors are unsurprising, like the public services available to residents, the peer groups available to children, the presence of substance abuse, and the level of violence to which children are exposed. Other factors are less obvious but extremely important, like the sense of connectedness and responsibility people feel for each other and each other's children and the capacity of residents to join together to make good things happen for the community.[7] To improve children's lives, communities need not only economic and intellectual capital but also social capital, and today many community-mobilization efforts are working hard to accumulate more of it.

Bowling Alone

In recent years, bowling alone, the metaphor evoked by sociologist Robert Putnam to describe a paucity of social capital in American communities, struck a nerve. Putnam and like-minded scholars have pointed to a decline in civic engagement across the nation, assigning a good share of the blame to the appeal of electronic entertainment.

It is true that Americans spend a great deal of time watching television or videos, enjoying electronic toys, and surfing the Internet. But there is also an intense desire for connectedness. The very technologies that sometimes isolate Americans also reflect a desire for contact. Decades ago, when futurists predicted what the world would be like in the twenty-first century, they imagined fantastic contraptions—individual jet packs for supersonic commuters and education machines that would feed knowledge directly to the brains of passive children. They did not predict fax machines or the Internet. They did not foresee that the most ubiquitous technologies of our day would be those that connect people and ease communication.

While there are undoubtedly many individuals who bowl alone, millions of Americans are getting involved in their communities, especially when children are the beneficiaries. In some cases, they are taking new routes to community participation. Many parents continue to attend PTA meetings, but others keep in touch with the school and other parents through websites or e-mail. Many families learn about neighborhood resources for their children during church picnics, but others get this information on the job, at workshops, or at lunch-hour meetings. Within the early childhood field, groups involved in public engagement and community mobilization report a great deal of excitement and activity bubbling up at the local level.[8]

··

For West Virginia Families,
"Starting Points" Is Just around the Bend

By Meredith Sue Willis

THE TREES are just turning bronze and orange along the curving West Virginia roads up the mountain to Kingwood, site of the Preston County Starting Points Center. A beautiful, sweeping ridge has been cleared and developed with new colonial style homes, but, in typical West Virginia style, around the bend is a rundown frame house, porches stacked with discarded tires. A mile further, in the center of Kingwood, are the landmark granite courthouse and bank building.

Such side-by-side contrast is typical of the Appalachian region. When West Virginians improve their income, they do not pull up stakes and flee to a distant suburb. Rather, they improve the house they have or build one next door. Affluence and poverty here are not strangers, but neighbors and relatives. This intimacy of social and economic status has made the Preston County Starting Points Center a perfect match for its community.

Located on the bottom floor of an office building around the corner from the courthouse, it has become a central community institution. Part of a consortium of organizations that includes Head Start, the Board of Education, the County Health Department, the Valley Health Care System, the Family Resource Network, and three private day care centers, the Starting Points Center has become the first stop for many families to have their needs met speedily, specifically, and flexibly. It is one of the several family resource centers established in West Virginia as part of Carnegie Corporation's Starting Points Initiative and managed by the Governor's Cabinet on Children and Families.

At the center, there are no inquiries about financial need and no forms to fill out. When the Catholic Community Services had thirty extra school book bags, the staff at Starting Points picked up the phone and distributed the bounty. Coordinator Kay Dewitt can give a family the name of an actual human being to talk to at a county agency, and she will call ahead with her referral so the family is expected. In response to requests from agencies and families, she has set up training sessions on home safety, nutrition, and attention deficit disorder. While parents are in the training sessions, her staff provides child care and snacks.

Kelsie Dixon, mother of a four-year-old in a Starting Points playgroup, says, "If you're in a pinch, this is the place." Kelsie also makes the point that in Preston County, it is often middle-income families who feel the pinch. Kelsie and her husband both work, but they needed help with a mortgage for a new home. They did not meet the income requirements for an FHA loan or for Habitat for Humanity, but Kay Dewitt directed Kelsie to the West Virginia Housing Plan, a mortgage support program for middle-income families. This kind of help is extremely important in northeastern West Virginia where middle income can mean a married couple together bringing in less than twelve dollars an hour with no health insurance. The average income in Preston County is under twenty thousand dollars and unemployment and children qualifying for free lunch are extremely common. Working families can easily come up short of funds at the end of a month.

Here again Starting Points offers help. People can drop by any time the center is open, like the young woman whose knock came during playgroup. She had run out of diapers, she said, and did not have money until her check came. The only question Kay Dewitt asked was whether she needed anything else from the Baby Pantry, a walled-off corner of the room with baby formula, jarred baby food, donated clothes, strollers, potty chairs, a baby bed, and toys, as well as new shelves built by volunteer labor. The staff at the center also has the key to a church-run food pantry across the alley, which is only open a few hours a week. If a family needs food as well as supplies for children, Kay takes them over for groceries.

The Starting Points Center offers material goods, expert advice, personal referrals to public and private agencies and institutions, and an enriching educational program for small children. It also offers the full-time devotion of Kay Dewitt herself. Small, dark-eyed, and intensely cheerful, Kay is an early childhood educator with nineteen years of experience as a Head Start teacher and a deep knowledge of her county and her community. She efficiently ticks off the areas covered in the playgroups: large motor coordination, small motor coordination, music, stories and books, nutritious snacks, creative movement, crawl-through tunnels and parachute games, and this coming week, a trip to a local game farm. With the help of Debbie Braham from Americorps and center aide Tammy Sphar, she runs a vital, five-day-a-week program.

Barb Thorn, head of the Family Resource Network (and coincidentally the grandmother of a playgroup regular), shares space and planning with Starting Points. She agrees with Kay about how to reach people in Preston County. This is the county in West Virginia with the most miles of unpaved road and where many families do not have a telephone. To make people aware of the Starting Points services, Kay and her staff use home visits, trips to the courthouse and welfare offices, lots of word of mouth, and the *Penny Saver*, a free publication with a circulation of thirteen thousand that is stuffed in virtually everyone's mailbox.

It is also important to know, say both Kay and Barb, about people's pride. People in Preston County do not like to ask for help. The playgroups offer a way for them to ease their way into finding support they might not have admitted or even known they needed. The playgroups were the activity that everyone agreed would be the first priority of the Starting Points Center. For families who do not meet the income restrictions of Head Start, yet cannot afford private day care, the playgroups can be the first place children socialize with their own age group.

So far, there are three playgroups a week, with forty-three children. One is a satellite group that meets a half hour up a mountain in the tiny community of Terra Alta. Tammy Howe, who lives there, discovered Starting Points at the county WIC office when Kay Dewitt came marching in and asked whether Tammy's little girl might like to be part of a playgroup. Tammy was not sure, but later that day, she dropped by the center and liked what she saw and heard: the blue plastic tunnel, the big green sandbox, the posters, the music, and the books. Her daughter did not want to leave! Indeed, many children cry when it is time to leave, and they press close to Kay as if she were a heating stove on a cold morning.

Tammy herself spends her days caring for the children of family and friends but says she wanted something more educational for her child. She is participating in the Terra Alta playgroup partly to learn new techniques for working with young children. She enthusiastically describes the shaving cream and paint and how the children had a rousing good time and also learned that colors, when mixed, make predictable new colors. Tammy will be the Terra Alta playgroup back-up teacher when the winter roads become impassable for Kay.

Kay says that many children in Preston County live in extremely isolated places. For some, the very interaction with other small children and adults who are not family members is a new experience. Among them are children who have never used glue or scissors. This is not the case for Kaelee, the daughter of obstetrics nurse Patty Degler, who lives a few doors down from the center and started dropping in purely for her daughter's socialization. The Starting Points Center, of course, welcomed Patty and Kaelee, just as it welcomes low-income families. But after a few weeks—and this is a typical Starting Points tale—Patty discovered that she was getting something directly for herself: respite from the rigors of single parenting. "Kay is a model," says Patty, "for how not to lose your cool." Kay has been a friend and support to Patty through her divorce, as well, and the center turned out to be the ideal place for little Kaelee's visits with her father.

Now, in one of the beautiful full circles that the Preston County Starting Points Center can create, Patty Degler refers new mothers from the hospital, telling them not to worry about being home alone with the baby, they can always drop in at Starting Points for companionship or to leave the baby in a safe place while they run to the Laundromat or the courthouse or just down the street for a cup of coffee.

In the best West Virginia style, then, the same people who use the services are enriching and expanding the services. People in Preston County, West Virginia, may be slow to ask for help, but once they are part of the Starting Points family, they never hesitate to give back and to share empowerment with their neighbors.

· ·

In communities across the nation, people from many walks of life are working together, pursuing broad-based strategies to improve the lives and prospects of children. Some efforts are beginning to show results, but in most places, many families have yet to be reached and many problems have yet to be solved. In some cases, initiatives are promising but have not been implemented on a scale that can begin to match the dimensions of the problems they are designed to address. In other cases, efforts have flagged due to shaky resources, inadequate planning, or a poor fit between problems and solutions, making reformers more sober about the complexity of the challenges they face.

Based on a decade of work, a great deal has been learned about what it takes to harness the energies of communities on behalf of children. Experience has pointed to ten key lessons:

   1. Focus on systems, not just programs. How can communities come together in common purpose? Why do some neighborhoods that want to do right by their young children succeed, while others do not? Why do some local programs or demonstration models achieve great results, only to falter as soon as they are expanded or scaled up?

These are among the questions researchers and practitioners have addressed in recent years. When Lisbeth B. Schorr, author of *Common Purpose: Strengthening Families and Neighborhoods to Rebuild America,* talked to people across the nation about the forces that get in their way as they try to strengthen families and communities, she found many fingers pointed toward the same culprit: the "system." She set out to understand what the system is and how it gets in the way. In the process, she found impressive examples of people who had managed to translate small successes into big ones by taking on the challenge of changing systems.[9]

Other researchers agree that community mobilization efforts need to aim at changing systems, not just programs.[10] That is very hard to achieve, and system changers find plenty of skeptics at every turn. But most approach their endeavor with the mix of common sense and resolve exemplified by educator Deborah Meier, who has said, "I don't know where this idea has come from that we can't collectively use our intelligence to create strong and effective public institutions."[11]

2. Build a constituency around a vision, *not just an institution; around* values, *not just issues; around a* theory of change, *not just an agenda for change.* A hallmark of system change is an explicit effort to build a constituency for change around a vision rather than an institution. Creating this vision is a collaborative process that allows community members to imagine how their children's lives and prospects might be changed; how their needs can be met; how existing resources can be utilized; and what each player's role might be.

Many organizations and initiatives devote time to brainstorming big-picture scenarios and drafting mission statements. Sometimes the thinking is broad enough, but not deep enough. According to veteran community organizer Ernesto Cortes Jr., Southwest regional director of Industrial Areas Foundation (IAF), "We organize people not just around issues, but around their values. The issues fade, and people lose interest in them. But what they really care about remains: family, dignity, justice, and hope. We need power to protect what we value."[12]

Systems change requires a vision deeply rooted in the aspirations of the people in the community. The vision needs to reflect the hopes and beliefs of people in every part of the community, including those who have seldom been consulted on policy or programs, and those who have not fully recognized their stake in improving results for children.

At the same time, the vision must take into account the priorities and cultural preferences of community residents. Given current demographic trends, one-size-fits-all solutions will not work. By the year 2020, "minority" children will constitute the majority of schoolchildren in the United States (and by the year 2050, "minorities" will account for the majority of the population). Since 1990, the number of children in immigrant families has risen seven times faster than the number of children in other families. Efforts to help communities help their children need to take fully into account the fact that different communities will do this in different ways and need the latitude to define and achieve results based on local strengths, needs, and preferences.

There is another question system reformers need to ask themselves: how and why will this approach make a difference? The Aspen Institute has been a leader in helping community-based initiatives foster systems change. Its Roundtable on Comprehensive Community Initiatives for Children and Families has promoted a "theory of change" framework for helping community collaboratives improve results for children and families. This approach proceeds from the notion that sometimes there is nothing quite so practical as a good theory. Community initiatives have a better chance of succeeding—and can better gauge their impact—if they state clearly, at the outset how they think their efforts will make a difference for individuals, families, and neighborhoods.[13]

Once a vision has been articulated, plans for realizing it can be elaborated and implemented. The organizers provide the time, place, resources, and processes needed to move the agenda. The children provide a powerful reason.

3. Cultivate leadership. The most visionary initiatives have been undertaken in states where political leaders, including the governor, grasped and communicated the importance of the early years. At the county and community level, efforts to improve results for children and families have been most effective where leaders from many fields—including some unexpected messengers—brought their influence to bear on early childhood policy. Grassroots efforts have been most successful in places where parent and citizen leadership training has been an intensive focus.

Changing systems takes strong leadership from within the community, but it may require more experience and expertise than community members possess. By definition, initiatives that engage many organizations and address multiple risks are complicated enterprises. People who may be accustomed to simpler community projects—say, organizing a blood drive or passing a school budget—may be daunted by more comprehensive efforts. Suddenly they find themselves dealing with large delivery systems and operating on many fronts at the same time.

Success may therefore hinge on an organization with able, committed staff who can help community members articulate a vision, secure funding, and develop an overall strategy that allows system changers to build on victories and learn from missteps. Making good things happen in communities takes know-how, but experience is often in short supply. Many community groups rely on a few energetic leaders and staff, and when these individuals move on or burn out, there may not be a plan for developing or recruiting their replacements.[14]

Building leadership requires a change in mindset, according to Jeff Kirsch of Families USA, an organization dedicated to better health care for all Americans. "Too often, organizations don't take community empowerment seriously, or just pay lip service to it," says Kirsch. "They see it as a fuzzy, non-accountable kind of activity. They don't define the outcomes they're after or the specific strategies needed to achieve them, as they would for other complex efforts."[15]

As a result, leadership development in general, and staffing issues in particular, often sink to the bottom of the agenda. The "outreach" or "community" dimension of a systems change project may be assigned to volunteers or part-timers without adequate training, supervision, or resources. Then effort flounders, reinforcing the notion that investments in community empowerment efforts do not pay off.

Leadership development is therefore a strong focus of community organizers. The Industrial Areas Foundation, the nation's largest and oldest institution for community organizing, has spent six decades building coalitions of Catholic, Protestant, and Jewish congregations (along with public schools and other community stakeholders), with an emphasis on identifying and supporting local leaders. Regional organizations like IAF or the Pacific Institute for Community Organization often work through existing local groups such as congregations or housing projects, helping their "movers and shakers" expand their role or agenda.[16]

There are also, across the nation, notable efforts to strengthen the qualifications and effectiveness of the people who staff community empowerment projects. Organizations like Chicago's Midwest Academy provide training and technical assistance to statewide and neighborhood organizations.

4. Empower families, do not just serve them. In many parts of the country, parents have taken the lead. Of course, national organizations have long been active in identifying and publicizing parents' concerns. Examples include the National Parenting Association and the National Parent Teacher Association (PTA), which has early childhood (or preschool) PTA's for parents with young children.

Other national parents' groups have gained influence by focusing on a specific concern. The National Head Start Association, National Center for Home Education, and National Parent Network on Disabilities exemplify this approach. Often out of necessity, parents whose children have disabilities and other special needs have become especially knowledgeable advocates for their kids—and ultimately for system changes that have the potential to improve prospects for all children. Some organizations have focused on the concerns of grandparents. The Center for Florida's Children, located in a state that is home to many older Americans, is particularly active in this sphere.

When system change is the goal, organizations generally seek to empower families, not simply to serve them. Parent leadership training has emerged as an especially effective model for engaging parents in local communities. The idea is to involve and train a core group of parent leaders, helping them learn how to influence legislative and other political processes, engage other parents, and reach the media. Such projects operate at the national, state, and local level.

Within its huge network, Family Support America encompasses thousands of family support programs, practitioners, and the families they serve, with the aim of helping participants gain the skills and tools needed to be effective agents of change. Free to Grow, a national substance abuse prevention initiative, works in partnership with Head Start programs across the nation, empowering parents and other community residents to identify and address local problems that exacerbate alcohol and drug problems.

A state program, Connecticut's Parent Leadership Training Institute, offers courses that help parents hone leadership and political skills, as well as a practicum in which participants apply new skills to attack problems in their communities. Minnesota's Parenting Association has a similar mission.

Local leadership training programs are taking root as well. In Boston, Parents United for Child Care focuses on parent empowerment. Another Boston effort, the Right Question Project (RQP), grew out of a dropout prevention program. Its organizers realized that parents wanted to be better advocates for their kids, but did not know what to ask. RQP teaches people the skill of formulating their own questions and helps them focus effectively on key decisions made by public institutions that affect them.

5. Create linkages across different delivery systems, levels of government, and programs serving different generations. A crucial task for system changers is to create linkages across delivery systems and bureaucracies. Case in point: the broad spectrum of agencies and activities known as the "human services." This category includes most nonparental efforts to nurture, educate, and protect young children.

American taxpayers spend hundreds of billions of dollars each year on services for children and families. Virtually every locality and county across the nation provides a range of publicly funded human services—not only child care and education but also health services and a wide range of social services. Low-income and high-risk children and families also have access to a variety of income supports, including social security, food stamps, Medicaid, SCHIP, and Temporary Assistance to Needy Families (TANF).

Private-sector organizations, philanthropic institutions, and faith communities provide or underwrite some of these services. However, most of the dollars spent to better the lives of children and families, especially in low-income neighborhoods, come from federal, state, and local tax revenues and bring with them many eligibility rules and regulations.[17] Moreover, agencies with different areas of specialization generally have a different knowledge base, organizational structure, and procedures.[18] As a result, existing systems of services are often fragmented and difficult to access. A single family may need to navigate several service systems. Members of the same family may qualify for a different array of services, depending on their age, educational status, work history, or other characteristics. It can be so difficult to negotiate this maze that only families that already function well succeed in accessing them. Imagine the obstacles faced by a working family, hard pressed for time, whose three children qualify for different health benefits, different child care services, and different nutrition programs.

In many places, system reform means linking all of the

health, education, and social services available in a given geographical area. It means bridging the gaps separating professions and bureaucracies in order to better serve children and families, especially those facing multiple risk factors. System changers approach family needs more holistically, stressing prevention and measuring success in terms of results, not services provided.

Because families need informal supports as well as professional services, the challenge goes well beyond linking professionals across bureaucracies. Increasingly, systems change efforts recognize the need to link the federal or state with the local; the private with the public; and the paid, professional service with the voluntary.[19]

Linking different levels of government is especially important. When it comes to helping children and their families, local efforts are often most effective. It takes a firm grasp of local realities to ensure a good fit between service systems and the people who rely on them. Community collaborations focusing on young children's issues (such as prenatal and infant health, school readiness, early care and education, mental health, and child safety) have proliferated around the country.

Counties have also taken the lead, sometimes in partnership with cities. Since 1991, with grants from Carnegie's Starting Points Initiative and the Heinz Endowments, Pennsylvania's Allegheny County and its largest city, Pittsburgh, have worked together to strengthen their strategic planning capacity, build public-private partnerships, increase public support for preventive approaches, and expand services for children and families facing multiple risk factors.

Most people who take part in local reform efforts come to the realization, sooner or later, that many decisions that affect their communities take place at a higher level—administratively and politically. And while the problems facing children are often plain to see at the neighborhood level, many of them are not rooted there. Even when change strategies are successful within a community, or even a county, they may be hampered by a lack of change in the larger systems in which local education, health, or family support services are embedded. For example, community-based efforts have been hard pressed to achieve the finance reforms that would free up money by giving them more flexibility and control in spending federal or state funds.[20]

Efforts to reduce risk for children and families therefore require close collaboration among different levels of government. In recent years, numerous states have launched initiatives to improve results for children and their families. Some, like California, North Carolina, Ohio, and Oregon, have set up local county or community councils charged with strengthening and integrating services for children and families. Typically, statewide officials set goals and benchmarks but give local councils flexibility in using resources to meet them. Children's councils may be new organizations, or they may come into being when an existing organization or agency, such as a mayor's office, a family support organization, a resource and referral agency, or a community development agency, expands its mission. To be effective, these councils must build good working relationships both within localities and with county and state officials. In most cases, councils rely upon resources and technical assistance from public and private sources to ensure that they are able to plan, implement, manage, finance, and monitor large-scale programs.

Developing more coherent community-based services generally requires changes in how existing public systems are managed and financed. The aim is to move these systems from restrictive regulations and funding requirements, which emphasize families' problems and needs, to approaches that foster collaboration and build on families' strengths. At the federal level, a number of large-scale programs under the aegis of the U.S. Department of Health and Human Services and the U.S. Department of Justice have made efforts to develop more comprehensive and less categorical approaches and have provided technical assistance to community collaborations.

A third challenge of systems change is linking programs that are geared to different generations. Head Start has played a leading role in developing two-generation programs to integrate employment and training services with child and family-oriented supports. Since its inception, Head Start has embraced economic self-sufficiency for the families of the children it serves. To advance this goal, Head Start initiated a two-generation self-sufficiency initiative in partnership with Project Match, an innovative, Chicago-based welfare-to-work program. Through this initiative, local Head Start sites can gain support as they develop services for parents and children. For example, since 1995, New York City's Mid-Bronx Head Start program has included a vocational counselor on its staff and has provided counseling, workshops, and job development to help parents improve their job prospects.[21]

6. *Form strategic partnerships with key institutions in the community.* Systems change efforts generally require both public investment and the participation of public agencies. Most must also tap the resources and knowledge of the private sector, both profit and not-for-profit. Public-private partnerships played a particularly important role in the early childhood initiatives launched in the nineties, such as Smart Start in North Carolina.

EARLY CARE AND EDUCATION PROGRAMS

Because most young children today are in nonparental care for at least part of the day, new parents look to early care and education programs for services. Some local child care centers have joined forces with other service providers, sharing facilities and working collaboratively. For example, in Scottsburg, Indiana, New Hope Kids Place houses under one roof an early childhood education program, county health services, and the Women, Infants and Children (WIC) nutrition program. These providers work together with parents and with other child and family programs across the county to improve new parents' access to the full range of services they need.

SCHOOLS

Many Americans think of their local school as the heart of the community and a gathering place for people of all ages, including young children and their families. Moreover, the idea of the neighborhood school as a focal point for social services has been around for many decades. Early in this century, an urban school superintendent argued that the school should "serve as a clearinghouse for children's activities so that all child welfare agencies may be working simultaneously and efficiently."[22]

How can schools serve the full range of children's needs, removing nonacademic impediments to school success? And can they do so without getting derailed from their core academic mission? These questions have sparked controversy over the last decade. The Committee for Economic Development, an independent organization of hundreds of business leaders, has argued that schools have neither the resources nor the time to tackle social problems: "Clear away the extraneous and the secondary. No institution can be everything to everyone, and no institution can succeed if it has too many competing goals."[23] Other concerns have been raised by the National Black Child Development Institute (NBCDI), which has acknowledged the potential benefits of using public schools as hubs for nonacademic services but notes that public schools have not served all children well or equitably and are not always perceived by parents as friendly or safe places. NBCDI argues that safeguards are needed to ensure that minority families are served appropriately, including assurances that a significant number of teachers will come from the children's communities and will be representative of the children's racial and ethnic backgrounds.[24]

Despite these concerns, many localities have experimented with innovative ways to link schools and communities, especially in distressed neighborhoods. Some are experimenting with community schools or full-service schools: they are making neighborhood schools (usually elementary or middle schools) hubs for a wide range of services, so that children and their families can access health and social services in settings that are familiar and nonthreatening. The trend within the field is toward making activities available to anyone in the community, rather than limiting them to enrolled students and their families. The projects may be managed by the school district or by another agency or organization. The Community Schools Coalition movement has enlisted a broad range of sponsors for the broader vision of schools as community resources and institutions.

A particularly powerful community school model comes from the Schools of the Twenty-first Century program, which since 1987 has expanded from two to more than six hundred elementary school sites. Participating schools offer all-day, year-round care and education for children ages three, four, and five.

The program supports schools' own efforts to extend their own mission to encompass young children or helps them partner with other community organizations to meet this goal. It takes different forms in different communities, based on local needs and resources. All share a commitment to children's optimal development.[25]

BUSINESS

Business leaders can play a crucial role in advancing an early childhood agenda—both as employers and as advocates. As employers, they can take the lead in instituting policies aimed at helping all employees meet their responsibilities at work and at home. These policies can be especially meaningful for the 25 million parents with preschool-aged children who are now in the workforce.[26]

In the tight labor market of the late nineties, family-friendly employment policies came to be seen as an aspect of good economic strategy. Even more intensive efforts to promote family-friendly policies will be needed in the more difficult economic environment of the new decade. Such policies can boost not only morale but also the bottom line. A study of three major corporations (Corning, Tandem Computers, and Xerox) funded by the Ford Foundation found that helping employees meet the dual pressures of work and family life by changing how employees work can also enhance efficiency and creativity.[27]

Three qualifications must be added. First, not all companies are equally supportive of or able to accommodate employees' family roles. White collar and knowledge-based employers often can provide flexibility in work hours and options, as employee work can be conducted in many settings and is deadline based. Alternatively, manufacturing and service industries have more set hours that require attendance at a particular time for the industry to survive. At the same time, it is families who are employed in those lower-paying service industries who often face the greatest challenges as they strive to mesh work and family responsibilities. According to the Families and Work Institute, companies in the finance, insurance, and real estate services industry tend to be the most generous, while the wholesale and retail trades tend to be the least. Large companies are more likely than small businesses to provide flexible work options and longer parental leaves, as well as wage replacement during maternity leave.[28]

Second, companies need to recognize that all of their employees—including low-wage workers—need time to be with their families and peace of mind when they are away from home. In a recent survey of low-income parents, one-third said that they have had to quit a job because they could not find child care that meshed with their work schedules or they had too little flexibility at work.[29]

And third, piecemeal programs and Band-Aid solutions do not work. To effect change, organizations need to realize that work-life issues are reflected in corporate cultures and require systematic, corporation-wide solutions. And that requires strong leadership—a willingness to rethink the way work gets done, with a view toward creating better quality jobs and a more responsive work environment that takes employees' needs into account and yields a more significant bottom line.[30]

Business leaders can be not only enlightened employers but also powerful, credible advocates for children. When they speak out on issues like the importance of prenatal care or the need for improved early education programs, decision-makers listen. There is an element of surprise, because people expect captains of industry to speak out on "pinstripe issues" such as employment trends or market shifts, not on "Pampers issues" such as child care or reading readiness. Business leaders are especially effective messengers when they present facts, problems, and solutions succinctly and can make credible arguments for investing in early childhood programs.[31] Such corporate leaders as the late Brad Butler, who was CEO of Proctor and Gamble, and Jim Renier, former CEO of Honeywell, spearheaded activities across many communities. Renier's Success by Six approach in Minneapolis has been adapted by hundreds of United Ways across the country.

Several Starting Points sites involved business leaders in efforts to build political will for investment in early childhood programs. Through "One Hour a Week for Kids," created by the Florida Starting Points site, experienced business lobbyists donated an hour per week during the state's legislative session to lobby on behalf of children. These efforts helped to convince the Florida legislature to significantly increase child care subsidies and pay higher rates to providers who meet high-quality standards.[32]

In some cases, corporations have banded together to support early care efforts. The American Business Collaboration for Quality Dependent Care (ABC) is a national initiative sponsored by many major corporations that support dependent care programs in communities where their employees live and work. This collaboration not only addresses work/family issues in the workplace but has also contributed to the behind-the-scenes supports that help to improve quality in programs.

LABOR UNIONS

Labor unions are an important force in the lives of America's working families. With nearly 14 million members, they represent more working families than any other organization in the

United States. Traditionally, unions have kept a steady focus on workplace conditions; however, meeting members' needs for child care rose higher on unions' agendas in the nineties. A number of unions took steps to expand the quality, affordability, and availability of early childhood services, and to increase parents' ability to care directly for their children. More union leaders are recognizing that child care and a flexible workweek are "bread and butter issues."

Labor unions have also formed coalitions with other groups, including advocacy and community groups, faith-based organizations, researchers, and legislators, to press for increased child care funding and support family leave legislation. Union leaders are finding that to appeal to a wide constituency, child care must be defined broadly—as part of a package of family supports that includes not just care for preschoolers but also after-school or sick care programs. In the San Francisco Bay Area, a union-led coalition has won many supporters by promoting a five-point agenda that calls for paid family and medical leave, flexible work schedules, quality child and elder care, living wages, and adequate health coverage for all working families.

Unions have also sought to increase the compensation and dignity of the child care workforce. Today, fewer than 5 percent of child care workers belong to a labor union, but unionization is on the rise. One notable success is the unionization of one thousand child care workers in Massachusetts by the Child Care Employees Union (United Auto Workers). Large-scale organizing drives are also under way in Seattle and Philadelphia. The dispersion of child care workers among many small employers and workplaces has been a major obstacle to unionization. To scale this hurdle, some organizers are trying to create an association of center directors and owners to recognize the unions and negotiate a master contract.[33]

FAITH-BASED ORGANIZATIONS

Across the broad spectrum of America's faith organizations, social services are provided not only by local congregations but also by national religious organizations, denominations, and their social service arms (such as Catholic Charities, Lutheran Social Services, or Jewish Family Services) and by a wide range of other groups that have a religious basis, such as local interfaith coalitions or ministries that address specific problems such as homelessness or substance abuse.

Faith-based organizations run food and clothing drives, provide shelter to the homeless, offer early care and education programs, and help families deal with emergencies. They also offer family support services, such as parenting education and counseling. Because record keeping is a luxury many of these organizations cannot afford and because the research base on faith-based service providers is thin, it is difficult to gauge the extent or efficacy of these efforts. Researchers estimate that nationwide, faith-based organizations serve tens of millions of people each year, devoting about 20 percent of their income from private contributions to social services—anywhere from $15 to $20 billion per year. Most of the beneficiaries of these services are not congregants or members of these organizations but are community residents. And most are neighborhood children.[34]

Today, more and more faith communities are realizing that when it comes to meeting the needs of high-risk children and their families, it makes no sense to go it alone. To a greater extent than ever before, they are partnering with public and private organizations, as well as with other faith communities. Three key factors are driving this trend.

First, most congregations cannot begin to provide the intensive, sustained services that many inner-city families need. They generally have limited budgets, administrative capacity, and paid staff and can only supplement resources or services that come from other sources. Moreover, faith-based organizations rely heavily on volunteer effort, often donated by older women. But in the wake of welfare reform, in some neighborhoods these women are increasingly pressed into service to care for the children of their daughters, sons, or other relatives.

Second, many faith-based organizations are recognizing the wisdom of integrated services for children and families faced by multiple risk factors. They are therefore coordinating efforts with other organizations or agencies that serve the same population.

And third, recent public policy shifts are channeling more social services through faith-based organizations. The Supreme Court has ruled that the government can contract with religiously affiliated institutions to provide social services so long as taxpayers' money is not used to teach religious doctrine. The charitable choice provision of the 1996 welfare law allows faith-based service providers to receive federal dollars without divesting themselves of their religious character or symbols.

Some partnerships with faith communities begin when a program launched by a church, synagogue, or mosque expands and reaches out to partners from other faiths or other sectors. The National Ten-Point Leadership Foundation (NTLF), based in Boston, grew out of the efforts of one charismatic Pentecostal minister. NTLF helps African American Christian churches gain the strategic vision, programmatic structure, and economic resources needed to serve high-risk inner-city youth. It addresses not only child abuse and neglect, street violence, drug abuse, and school failure but also the hopelessness that often accompanies these problems. NTLF works in partnership with other religious groups and congregations and runs programs in cooperation with social service and law enforcement agencies. It also maintains ties with numerous research institutions. By the year 2006, NTLF seeks to mobilize one thousand churches to form youth-outreach ministries.

In other cases, coalitions are formed when secular agencies or community development initiatives recognize the appeal and influence of faith-based organizations and their ability to reach across racial and class boundaries. By working with local congregations, the Industrial Areas Foundation has become the nation's most successful community organizing network.

7. Build a collaboration infrastructure. Just as states, cities, and towns need bridges, tunnels, and roads for transportation, they need an infrastructure for collaboration. Some statewide early childhood initiatives have focused on building capacity in counties and communities. For example, California planners are aided by funds provided by Proposition 10, a ballot initiative that created a state tobacco tax to fund community-based comprehensive child care, health care, and social services not provided by existing programs. Most of the money goes directly to counties, where local commissions allocate funds based on need, and the balance goes for statewide programs, including anti-smoking media campaigns and parent education programs. Proposition 10 funds also support a statewide School Readiness Initiative, designed to provide the "glue" that can pull these services together into a coherent system. Beginning in neighborhoods where schools need the most improvement, the Initiative is creating a network of School Readiness Centers. Their mission is to restructure and coordinate delivery of services that have been shown to promote school readiness, including: high-quality early care and education; health and social services; parental education and support; and efforts to get schools ready for young children.

Outside catalysts can link community organizations with other initiatives that are addressing similar challenges. For example, the National Community Building Network connects community-based economic development organizations. Outside catalysts can also provide access to research, training, evaluation and research services, and other forms of technical assistance. State or local initiatives can look for guidance to national organizations such as the National Governors Association, National Black Child Development Institute, National Latino Children's Institute, Center for the Study of Social Policy, or the Institute for Educational Leadership. Technical support may be available from such organizations as the Finance Project, the Aspen Institute Roundtable on Comprehensive Community Initiatives, the National Center for Service Integration Technical Assistance Clearinghouse, or the Harvard Center for Effective Services for Children. Many organizations with broader missions, such as Family Support America, the Child Welfare League of America, the American Public Human Services Association, and the Council of Chief State School Officers, have branches that focus on early childhood issues as well.

Assistance with capacity-building often comes from foundations and the initiatives they fund. Carnegie Corporation's Starting Points Initiative was designed, in part, to help states and communities across the nation forge collaborative efforts aimed at promoting children's healthy development. The initiative sought to help cities and states act on the recommendations of the *Starting Points* report, especially those that relate to vulnerable children and families. Each of the Starting Points sites has pursued a unique strategy for engaging key state and community leaders, strengthening policy and programs, and developing systematic strategies for tracking progress. For example, the San Francisco Starting Points Initiative, located in the Mayor's Office of Children, Youth and Their Families, has established the Early Childhood Interagency Council. This council is working collaboratively to develop and implement a citywide strategic plan for improving services for young children and their families. While the initiative has many goals, none is more important than facilitating this collaborative process.

Many other foundations, both national and regional, have funded significant efforts to expand capacity in the early childhood field. Traditionally, foundations have functioned independently, without much teamwork. In the nineties, however, program officers from many national and regional foundations that fund early childhood projects came together to form the Early Childhood Funders Collaborative. The collaborative works together toward shared goals, such as advancing the quality agenda in early care and education.

8. Focus on public engagement. Over the last decade, a number of early childhood initiatives have invested heavily in public engagement campaigns, based on the conviction that only broad support can generate the levels of investment needed to make real, lasting, widespread improvements in child well-being.

On the national scene, the Children's Defense Fund (CDF) has been a steady and forceful presence, making research on children's needs available to the public and influencing policy and programs at every level. Most recently, CDF launched the Leave No Child Behind campaign, enlisting more than one thousand organizations in an effort to support policies and enact legislation providing early learning opportunities, health insurance, and other key resources to all families with young children.

Another national organization, the Children's Partnership, seeks to inform leaders and the public about the needs of America's children and to engage them in ways that benefit children. The partnership forges new alliances among parents, policymakers, and the private sector to achieve tangible gains for children. At the same time, it conducts research and policy analysis and publishes reports and multimedia materials related to the needs of children.

States have also invested in public education campaigns. In partnership with the I Am Your Child Foundation, several states, including California, Pennsylvania, and Kentucky, have undertaken campaigns aimed at raising awareness of the importance of the early years and providing families with the information and resources they need to do a good job. These states are distributing to thousands of new parents family resource guides as well as videos covering many aspects of parenthood and child development.

Some promising public engagement efforts have been undertaken by cities. Greater Kansas City's Partnership for Children launched the # 1 Question campaign, urging institutions and individuals to ask themselves a single question before making any key decision: "Is it good for the children?" Through the use of grassroots engagement and advertising, the Partnership for Children has been able to build general awareness of the # 1 Question throughout our community. Many organizations have committed themselves to factoring the # 1 Question into their decision-making.[35]

Not every state, county, or locality has committed to a major early childhood campaign, but most have child advocacy organizations that are tackling early childhood issues and concerns. Many of these are members of the National Association of Child Advocates (NACA), which offers its members assistance in developing agendas and drawing on national resources as they plan and promote early childhood services.

9. Focus on results. A visioning process may begin with expressions of hope or determination; over time, these expressions can be translated into specific results that community members want to achieve. Communities can then develop benchmarking and accountability systems to ensure the effective use of resources. Whatever system is designed, it works best when communities frame and own their own vision, rather than having a framework imposed upon them from the outside.

In recent years, policymakers have sought new strategies for moving resources and authority closer to where the problems are—at the county or community level. In many places, negotiations between states and communities have resulted in greater responsibility and fund flexibility at the local level, but also greater accountability for results. Key questions have been: based on new understandings of human and child development, which outcomes matter for families and children? And who is responsible for achieving them?

Several states have focused intensively on strengthening accountability in recent years, creating outcome and indicator frameworks. Oregon's "benchmarks," Minnesota's "milestones," and Georgia's "results" have served as models for other states, counties, and communities. Missouri created the Family Investment Trust, a public-private partnership designed to mesh efforts by state agencies and local communities to create a new, more responsive system of services for the state's children and families. The state agencies and communities that are collaborating in this initiative focus on six core results and have reached consensus on a common set of eighteen benchmarks for which baselines are being established on a state, community, and neighborhood level.

Since 1992, Vermont has been a leader in developing community partnerships, with an emphasis on improving results for children and youth. These partnerships take many forms: some are collaboratives of service providers; others organize around a particular goal, such as reducing child abuse. What they have in common is a commitment to improving outcomes. The state defined an "outcome" as a measurable result that is sought by people across many disciplines and many organizations. It stressed three aspects of outcomes: local people help create them; they make sense to most people; and they impel people to act. In addition, outcomes can be measured, using specific indicators.

Beginning in 1993, the state published its first "well-being report"—*The Social Well-Being of Vermonters*. Residents could judge how their state was faring over time, and compare state outcomes with those for the nation as a whole. Moving accountability to the community level was the next step. In 1995, the state published *Community Profiles*, comparing well-being data for the state's sixty school districts. *Community Profiles* have been used to plan and improve human services at the state and community level.

State efforts to strengthen accountability have been bolstered by the Annie E. Casey Foundation's Kids Count initiative. Each year, Kids Count publishes a data book with national and state results for infant mortality, child poverty, health insurance coverage, parental employment, and other indicators of child and family well-being. It ranks the states on each measure, highlighting good and poor performance.[36]

10. Think big. A decade of research and practice has produced many lessons about how to improve children's lives and brighten their future. Perhaps the key lesson is this: there are no simple solutions. Large-scale change requires ambitious, multifaceted efforts. At the same time, it requires coherent responses.

Many researchers and policy analysts have called for a broad approach to the challenge of improving prospects for children and families. Some have recommended the creation of a comprehensive learning system for America's children, beginning in the early years. That was the key recommendation of the Carnegie Task Force on Learning in the Primary Grades in *Years of Promise*, a report on the status of children ages three to ten.[37]

Quality 2000, a project that took shape at about the same time, mapped out a step-by-step action plan for creating an early care and education system for the nation. Led by Sharon Lynn Kagan and her colleagues at Yale University, Quality 2000 represented the best thinking of many experts in the early childhood field about the kinds of supports (such as governance, finance, professional development, and accountability) needed to undergird early care and education programs in the United States.[38] In the interim, a number of states, notably Delaware and California, have undertaken strategic planning processes that build on the work of Quality 2000.

Many community-building efforts have also embraced broad, ambitious agendas. They have based their efforts on research showing that children and youth who face multiple risk factors need interventions that are intensive, integrated, coordinated, and comprehensive.[39] But experts do not always agree on the definition (or wisdom) of comprehensive approaches. If a project offers many services, geared to families' multiple needs, should every family and every child receive the full range of services? Or should services be targeted to those most likely to benefit? This issue has stirred debate among researchers and practitioners who focus on children and families.

Some point to disappointing results from specific large-scale programs (such as the Comprehensive Services Program) to argue against offering a full spectrum of services to each family. Others urge policymakers to "get bold about what 'comprehensive' means." Focusing on distressed communities in one Pennsylvania county, Charles Bruner and his colleagues at the Child and Family Policy Center analyzed the potential return on investment of programs sufficiently broad and powerful to cut rates of child welfare, juvenile delinquency, poverty, and violent crime. They concluded that investments in the tens, if not hundreds, of millions of dollars could be justified in these neighborhoods. They believe that to make a difference, policymakers need to take bold steps—investing enough resources "to create a critical mass of activities and opportunities so that residents begin to see new possibilities both in their own lives and in the lives of those around them."[40]

One very ambitious initiative has taken up the challenge. *Making Connections* is the centerpiece of the Annie E. Casey Foundation's multifaceted effort to improve the life chances of vulnerable children by helping to strengthen their families and neighborhoods. Bold in scale, the initiative began by making grants to neighborhoods in twenty-two cities. Applying a "place-based" strategy, *Making Connections* has not set a specific agenda for these sites. Rather, its grants were designed to engage a broad range of residents, civic groups, political leaders, grassroots groups, public and private sector leadership, and faith-based organizations in an effort to create and carry out their own vision for transforming tough neighborhoods into family-supportive environments.

Across the nation, many organizations are working to build public support for efforts to improve children's well-being, to increase public investment in high-quality services for children, and to create a "children's movement" aimed at keeping children's issues high on the national agenda. A *Time* magazine article observed that there is no "children's agenda" but rather a splintering of issues and organizations. That was in 1998. Today, efforts to supersize the kitchen table have a long way to go. There have been many disappointments and missed opportunities, especially where child poverty is concerned. At the same time, consensus appears to be building around key challenges, including child health, infant and toddler care, universal preschool, and reading readiness. There is more agreement about the kinds of system reform that are likely to lead to school success. In short, there is, in many parts of the nation, a growing commitment to understanding what kids need and to acting on that understanding.

CHAPTER 5

The Agenda for Change

The experts consulted during the preparation of this book had two main pieces of advice: don't make it too gloomy, and don't make it too sunny. Their counsel reflects the wish both to celebrate progress and to sustain momentum on behalf of children. It speaks to the difficulty of painting accurately a policy landscape that has always been rocky and has now been made all the more complex by changes in the nation's priorities, leadership, and economic outlook.

To be sure, there has been progress. Some large-scale, publicly supported programs have been expanded, like Head Start, or introduced, like Early Head Start and the Children's Health Insurance Program. The Family and Medical Leave Act of 1993 broke new ground in employment policy. The No Child Left Behind Act of 2002 included the Reading First initiative, increasing the federal investment in the language development and reading readiness of young children, especially those from low-income families.

In the field of health, the nation has succeeded in reducing overall the infant mortality and teen pregnancy rates—though in some states and communities they remain extremely high. In the realm of early learning, many states have made significant investments in school readiness initiatives, and some are moving toward universal, voluntary preschool. Initiatives like North Carolina's Smart Start have shown what can be done when leaders take political risks and policymakers think outside of the box. Additionally, there have been significant infusions of public dollars into early childhood initiatives, including not only funding for Head Start and Early Head Start but also billions of dollars in child care subsidies.

Voters have made themselves heard on the need to expand and strengthen services for young children. Public engagement campaigns have led to successful ballot initiatives. In Georgia, for example, voters approved the use of a state lottery to support free, universal access to preschool for all children whose parents want to enroll them. In California, voters supported Proposition 10, which expanded services for the state's young children.

Court decisions have made a difference as well. In past decades, the courts have played a strong role in addressing disparities in educational opportunity for public school students; in the nineties, precedents were set for judicial action to address disparities in opportunity for younger children. *Abbot v. Burke* in the state of New Jersey was an important case in point, mandating early learning programs for young children in low-income districts as a matter of equity.

Other important initiatives have come from the voluntary or philanthropic sectors. Organizations representing the private sector, such as the Committee for Economic Development, have taken a stand on the wisdom of significant investment in early childhood education.

If we were to judge the nation's commitment to children on the basis of rhetoric alone, we could rest on our laurels. If we were to judge it on the basis of parents' concern for their own children or their readiness to take part in community efforts to improve children's prospects, we could paint a sunny picture. If we were to judge it on the basis of policies and programs developed in some states and some communities, we could imagine that the vision presented in *Starting Points* and *Years of Promise* had been largely fulfilled.

But that progress has been uneven, and any effort to depict the terrain of early childhood must capture highlights and shadows. Across the nation, there is greater interest in school readiness in general and reading readiness in particular. The public appears to support readily strategies aimed at preparing young children to succeed in school and in the workplace. But this concern falls well short of a full social commitment to the well-being of young children and their families. Compared with children growing up in our peer nations, America's young children are much more likely to face economic deprivation and educational mediocrity. On average, their parents have less time to spend with them, and the adults who care for them while their parents work are less qualified to do so.

While many states are moving in the right direction, no state has yet achieved a coherent system of early childhood services. None has put in place the finance, governance, or professional development reforms needed to ensure that programs for young children and their families are of high quality or reach all who need them. Millions of infants and toddlers continue to receive care of inadequate quality while their parents work, and billions of public dollars are going to providers and programs that are accountable to no one. Improving this situation is very difficult, given the dearth of "licensable" facilities in many neighborhoods.

Lessons from a Decade of Progress

THE EARLY YEARS MATTER

The stretch of years that begins before birth and extends through school entry is very important. *From Neurons to Neighborhoods*, an exhaustive review of the science of early childhood development published by the National Academy of Sciences in 2000, took note of long-standing debates about the importance of the early years in the larger scheme of human development and reached this unequivocal conclusion: "What happens during the first months and years of life matters a lot. It does not matter because all early damage is irreversible, because missed opportunities can never be made up later, or because the early years provide an indelible blueprint for adult outcomes: early damage may be reversible, some missed opportunities can be made up later, and adult outcomes do not proceed inexorably from early experiences. Rather, the early years of life matter because early damage—whether caused by prenatal injuries or personal rejection—can seriously compromise children's life prospects." The report found that compensating for missed opportunities later in life can require "extensive intervention, if not heroic efforts."[1] America's children need policies and investments that take this finding fully into account.

A POLICY VISION MATTERS

Public policy and public investment affect both the daily lives and the long-term prospects of young children. Across the nation, most children are thriving—including some who are facing tough odds. But millions are not. There are clear, comprehensible reasons for this variation. When some groups of children fall short of their potential, it is not simply bad luck. It is often a matter of failed policy.

International comparisons are often marshaled to make this point, but comparisons among groups of children within our own country can be equally compelling. Children's outcomes vary widely across the United States. A 1999 study by Columbia University researchers has shown that states that provide low levels of support to children and families, considered as a group, have the highest child poverty rates.[2] Given today's understanding of how economic deprivation can jeopardize early development and learning, this finding highlights how high the stakes can be when legislators and other policymakers make funding decisions.

While many such decisions are made at the state level, national policymakers also shape children's futures. In coming months and years, members of Congress will be asked to consider new investments in young children's learning and well-being and to reauthorize welfare and Head Start legislation. As they do so, they will have historic opportunities to alter the daily experiences and life chances of millions of children.

PLACE MATTERS

As we move into the new decade, equity is a major concern. As previous chapters have shown, children in some states have access to more resources and greater educational opportunity than in others.

States make a difference, but so do communities (and even streets). A growing body of scientific evidence is confirming a fact that will surprise few Americans: healthy, vibrant communities are associated with good outcomes for children, while communities that are disorganized and have few resources tend to produce poor outcomes.[3] But what are the pathways that lead from detrimental conditions to poor outcomes? Recently, researchers from the National Institutes of Health undertook an ambitious effort to study how forces like economic hardship, racial discrimination, and segregation affect the likelihood that various groups of adults and children will suffer ill health, have accidents, or die. Using new research tools, they are now able to identify environmental "hot spots" for disease and mortality by linking child health outcomes to local-level and in some cases address-level factors, such as unemployment statistics, building code violations, or even the number of liquor stores in the area. With these new research tools, researchers will be better able to identify factors that undermine or promote children's health and safety.[4] As they do, policymakers need to respond.

PARENTS MATTER—A GREAT DEAL— AND SO DO THE RESOURCES THEY BRING TO THE CHALLENGES OF RAISING A FAMILY

Many people, including teachers, relatives, and friends, help to shape children's attitudes and behavior. But it is an early relationship between a child and at least one adult who is "crazy" about him or her that lays the groundwork on which social competence is built.

Starting Points and *Years of Promise* emphasized that when women and men are prepared for the opportunities of parenthood, they are more likely to provide the care and create the conditions that promote healthy development. This new agenda continues to stress preparation for responsible parenthood but focuses more sharply on the resources families and parents bring to the task, including not only material resources, knowledge, and access to service but also time with their children.

POLITICAL WILL MATTERS

Creating a flexible, choice-based system of health care, parenting supports, and early education will require large-scale, sustained public investment, and that is not possible without significant efforts to identify effective approaches and build public demand for them. The aim is not only to educate the public but also to inform legislators. Many policymakers have become familiar with early childhood issues in recent years. But given the prevalence of term limits, new legislators are constantly entering this arena. They need access to the information and scientific evidence that can lead to good decisions on behalf of the families they represent.

Increasingly, child development experts, media strategists, and advocacy groups are working together to develop powerful messages about the benefits of investing in the early years. Public engagement initiatives have made wide use of the media to inform the public about scientific research on the importance of the early years. More can be done. Efforts to improve results for children are hampered by continued underinvestment—and that can only be turned around if millions more Americans come to understand what is at stake and how public investment can make a difference.

But it is not just a matter of the American public understanding what professionals in the early childhood field believe and want. The field needs to have a much clearer sense of what Americans believe and want. Today, public opinion research is generating more information about where the public stands on these issues. More can be done both to inform public opinion and to align strategies and investments with widely held preferences and convictions.

FINALLY, QUALITY MATTERS

Each year produces new evidence that high-quality prenatal, preventive health, and preschool programs can indeed promote later achievement. A great deal of work has been devoted to improving single, small-scale programs. But too little has been done to develop an infrastructure for early care and education so that as a nation we can move beyond a scattershot approach and build an early education system. The excellent child care system established by the Department of Defense for the children of military personnel shows what can be done when commitment is high and a systemic approach is applied.[5]

Improving the well-being of infants and toddlers is an urgent need. It is therefore important to focus more intensively on improving the quality of family child care and other informal arrangements that most low- and moderate-income families with very young children find comfortable and affordable.

When it comes to older preschoolers, our country has made some strides. Across the nation, there is a new willingness to focus on three- and four-year-olds—especially if efforts to meet their needs are cast in terms of school readiness in general and reading readiness in particular. Most states are now funding some kind of program for preschoolers, and some are moving toward voluntary, universal preschool. A key challenge in coming years will be to ensure that preschool programs address all of the dimensions of school readiness. To be sure, making progress in reading is vitally important. But we know, and the research supports, that an overly narrow focus on reading will not likely bring about a nation of curious, eager, and engaged learners. We need to advance a balanced approach with sensible outcome measures—one that combines the "healthy development" goals articulated in *Starting Points* and *Years of Promise* with essential literacy and numeracy goals.

Today's Best Ideas

In *Starting Points* and *Years of Promise,* task forces of distinguished policymakers, scholars, and practitioners convened by Carnegie Corporation of New York called upon Americans in all walks of life to reconsider and address the needs of young children. Other influential reports published over the decade by other foundations and organizations have issued their own calls to action.

In the interim, individuals and institutions in virtually every sector have responded. Both Democratic and Republican administrations have convened White House conferences on early childhood development and learning. Universities and other research institutions have focused their powerful research capacities on early childhood issues. The nation's pre-eminent research institution, the National Academy of Sciences, has dedicated no fewer than five major studies to topics related to early childhood learning, development, and pedagogy, as well as important studies of immigrant children and English language learners. In the realm of health, professional associations such as the American Academy of Pediatrics have issued groundbreaking policy statements on children's health care. The surgeon general has reported to the nation on children's mental health. The Council of Chief State School Officers, the National Governors Association, and the National Conference of State Legislatures have all weighed in on early childhood issues. Associations of educators, such as the National Association for the Education of Young Children and the International Reading Association, have issued position statements on various aspects of early childhood development and learning. Many other groups, including associations of parents, law enforcement officers, and business leaders, have taken positions on various aspects of early childhood development and learning.

The agenda presented below brings the best, most recent thinking of these eminent bodies to bear on the recommendations offered in *Starting Points* and *Years of Promise*.

What Kids Need

I. A FAIR SHOT AT SUCCESS

If you work hard, you can succeed: this notion is basic to the American dream. But today, many dreams dissolve before effort can even become an issue. The prospects of millions of children are limited by a wide achievement gap—persistent disparities in academic performance by children of different backgrounds. We now know that this gap opens up very early in life. While kids are still in diapers, striking differences in what children know and can do start to set low-income children apart from their better-off peers.[6] Studies by the U.S. Department of Education have shown significant disparities in performance among kindergartners of different backgrounds.[7] Of course, it is always possible for children to make up for early delays, but a good start in life increases the odds of greater adult competence. As our nation shapes a school readiness agenda, equity must therefore be an overriding concern.

- *Judge policies and programs on the basis of their success in addressing outcome gaps.* In *From Neurons to Neighborhoods,* the National Research Council recommended that school readiness initiatives be judged not only on the basis of their success in bolstering the performance of the children they reach but also on their effectiveness in narrowing skill gaps among children of differing backgrounds that can be observed at school entry.[8] Providers of many kinds of early childhood services should be asked to report on their efforts to strengthen equity as well as improve results for children and families.

- *Fund research on the root causes of disparities in outcomes for young children.* Expanding access to high-quality early education programs is imperative but does not fully address disparities in child well-being. An outcome gap is apparent from the very start, as infant mortality data suggest. As of 1998, the infant mortality rate in the United States reached an all-time low.[9] But there are widespread geographic, racial, and ethnic discrepancies in the incidence of infant mortality. More than three hundred communities in the United States have rates at least one and one-half times the national average, with some as high as three times the overall rate. In particular, there is a persistent black-white differential. At any age, income, education, or socioeconomic level, an African American mother is twice as likely to lose her infant as is a white mother.[10] Research is needed to provide a more subtle understanding of pathways to infant mortality. In particular, studies are needed that take multiple factors into account, linking community characteristics with individual histories. Research on the causes of low birth weight are especially important.[11]

- *Strengthen public health efforts and public information campaigns aimed at narrowing outcome gaps.* Sustained support for both research and public information campaigns is needed. Again, infant mortality data offer an illustration. A recent study published in *Pediatrics* showed that in the United States, African American women are only 40 percent as likely to breastfeed as other new mothers. The study reports that a lower rate of breastfeeding accounts for a higher rate of infant mortality among African Americans, at least as much as low birth weight does.[12] A sustained campaign to promote breastfeeding is therefore a key strategy for narrowing the infant mortality gap, but the success of such an effort hinges on a better understanding of all of the factors that may encourage mothers to choose bottle feeding—including not only cultural preferences and family structures but also employment patterns and welfare requirements.

- *More equitable child care subsidy policies.* Today, most children who qualify for child care assistance are not receiving it. Moreover, low-income working families often have less access to subsidized care than those who are on (or in the process of leaving) the welfare rolls. In the absence of subsidies, many of these families must rely on unlicensed, informal arrangements. Their young children are less likely to experience high-quality care and education. As they reshape subsidy and reimbursement policy, policymakers can address barriers to participation. At the same time, they can strengthen incentives for providers to improve quality and for consumers to focus on quality. They can base reimbursement rates not on market rates (which reflect parents' ability to pay, not children's needs) but on the real costs of quality.

2. BASIC FAMILY RESOURCES

Children's development and learning in the early years are affected by the knowledge and skills of their parents or guardians and on the resources available to them.

- *Offer to all families with young children effective family support and parent education programs.* The Carnegie Task Force on Learning in the Primary Grades recommended that states and communities make effective parent education and family support programs, capable of promoting learning and child development, available to every interested family with preschool children. This recommendation stands. In the interim, research and evaluations have shed more light on the principles of effective family support and the specific types of initiatives that can benefit children. For example, more is known about the types of home visiting programs that are likely to improve outcomes for children.[13] At the same time, more has been learned about how various funding streams (federal and state, public and private) can be blended to support and expand effective programs.[14] As they make appropriations for family support and parent education programs, legislators should set aside funds for program evaluation and improvement.

Preparation for parenthood needs to begin long before a child is conceived. In a 1999 policy statement, the Council of Chief State School Officers asserted that the public schools have a major potential in helping prepare students for successful future roles in early childhood and family education. It emphasized that "each generation of secondary students is also a generation of future parents" and stated that "the quality of their overall education and the introduction they are given to their opportunities and responsibilities for their own children's learning are of great significance."[15]

- *Make a commitment to adequate economic resources for all families, with an emphasis on the working poor.* A family's capacity to do a good job raising children can depend on economic forces that are usually seen as outside the sphere of early childhood policy. *From Neurons to Neighborhoods* stressed the link between economic policy and children's outcomes. It recommended that the President's Council of Economic Advisers and Congress should assess the nation's tax, wage, and income support policies (including the earned income tax credit, minimum wage laws, Temporary Assistance to Needy Families, in-kind supports, and child support policies) to assess their adequacy in enabling families to provide for their children. The aim is a set of policies that can move the nation toward two basic goals: first, ensuring that no child who is supported by the equivalent of a full-time working adult lives in poverty, and second, ensuring that no family suffers from deep and persistent poverty, regardless of employment status.[16]

  Families' economic resources have also been emphasized in recent years by many research and policy organizations, including the National Center for Children in Poverty, Child Trends, the Urban Institute, and the Economic Policy Institute. They have called for policy and procedural changes aimed at expanding and strengthening the safety net for young children and improving the utilization of existing safety-net programs by eligible families.

- *Provide incentives for employment policies that allow parents time to nurture children.* Surveys suggest that across geographic and demographic boundaries, the great majority of parents share a desire for more flexibility in deciding how much time to spend with their young children.[17] In *From Neurons to Neighborhoods,* the National Academy of Sciences stressed a pressing need to "strike a better balance between options that support parents to care for their infants at home and those that provide affordable, quality childcare that enables them to work or go to school." In particular, it called for expanding coverage of the Family and Medical Leave Act to all working parents, pursuing the complex issue of income protection, and extending the exemption period before states require parents with infants to work as part of welfare reform.[18] Moving toward paid parental leave was also recommended by the distinguished advisory group that guided a comprehensive policy agenda set in 2000 by the Foundation for Child Development.[19] Parents also need employment policies that reflect today's realities and help them meet their family responsibilities, such as flextime and opportunities to telecommute. These work/life supports have also been shown to increase job satisfaction and reduce turnover. They may be especially important for the low-wage workers who are least likely to receive them. Tax credits and other government incentives for companies that create child care and work/life solutions should therefore target employers of low-wage workers.[20]

3. GOOD HEALTH AND PROTECTION

Medical and technological advances have improved health and safety for millions of American children. But these improvements have not equally benefited all segments of our population.

- *Move toward universal medical and dental coverage for children.* Today, most uninsured children are eligible for publicly supported health insurance coverage. The gap between eligibility and enrollment has been attributed to several factors: lack of knowledge about eligibility (both by families and those who can assist them), complex eligibility rules, difficult and confusing enrollment procedures, and lack of materials in a native language. To ensure that children have a good start in life, policymakers should move toward universal access to health care for children, including preventive and well-child services. *The American Academy of Pediatrics (AAP) has strongly endorsed this approach, noting that universal coverage that includes preventive care is affordable and cost-effective.*[21] A study sponsored by AAP showed that Medicaid can insure four children for less than what it costs to cover one adult.[22]

- *Ensure that children's health and development are closely monitored, and that problems or delays are identified and addressed in a timely way.* Guidelines for health and developmental screenings have been established by the Early and Periodic Screening, Diagnosis, and Treatment (EPSTD) program and the American Academy of Pediatrics. These screenings should be performed on a regularly scheduled basis, with greater frequency for very young children and those with disabilities or other special needs. All Medicaid-eligible children qualify for EPSTD screening; however, many eligible children do not receive screenings. Moreover, all children—not only those who qualify for Medicaid—stand to benefit from regular screenings that can detect not only physical health problems but also developmental, mental, emotional, behavioral, and substance abuse disorders. Children also benefit when states establish effective surveillance and tracking systems for specific aspects of health and development, such as early hearing loss.

- *Over time, ensure that every child and expectant mother has a medical home.* Timely intervention can be crucial when children have health problems or developmental delays. Healthy People 2010, the national strategic plan for improving Americans' health developed by the U.S. Department of Health and Human Services, recommends a medical home for every child with special health needs, capable of addressing the full range of each child's health and developmental needs.[23] Over time, this concept should be expanded to encompass all children. A medical home can take many forms, depending on the characteristics and preferences of particular communities or neighborhoods. It may be housed in a pediatric practice, community clinic, hospital, housing project, or community-based organization. In rural areas, it may take the form of a mobile unit. The key is that health and family support services are linked and delivered in a way that assures access to all families; address all dimensions of child and family health and development; reflect the cultural and linguistic diversity of the community; and facilitate continuity of care. The concept of the medical home for all children and expectant mothers has been championed by the American Academy of Pediatrics.[24]

• *Ensure a medical home for all early learning programs, including family child care homes.* All center- and home-based early education and care programs should have ongoing contact with a consulting health care provider. The American Academy of Pediatrics endorses this view and has encouraged its members to reach out to local programs.

• *Infuse today's understandings of children's developmental needs into health care.* Policymakers' concern about public health insurance and other safety-net programs has tended to focus on outreach and enrollment, because so many eligible children are not participating. But participation alone does not assure adequate health care. Policymakers need to ensure that participating children receive appropriate services and high-quality care.

Enhancing developmental services in pediatric primary care is a major challenge. Traditional modes of health supervision do not adequately address infants' and toddlers' social, emotional, and intellectual development. A number of new models of primary health care delivery for young children are designed to integrate developmental perspectives into well-baby care. Initiatives that are working to implement this approach include Zero to Three's Developmental Specialist in Pediatric Practice Project; the Healthy Steps for Young Children Program; the Touchpoints program, based on the work of pediatrician T. Berry Brazelton; and the U.S. Maternal and Child Health Bureau's Building Bright Futures project.[25]

- *Make the prevention and timely treatment of mental health problems a high priority.* A recent report on mental health by the surgeon general devoted a chapter to young Americans, highlighting self-regulation as a major challenge of the early childhood years. The surgeon general urged greater recognition of children's vulnerability to mental health problems and the importance of considering these problems in the context of children's social environments. The report paid special attention to the widespread use of pharmacological treatment for preschoolers with behavioral problems. It is important to expand families' access to health care providers who can identify and treat mental health and developmental risk in young children, beginning in the first years of life. Researchers note that entry points for mental health services can vary but need to build on existing community networks of early childhood services. Mental health professionals need greater insight into the cultural dimensions of regulatory development, which can decisively affect young children's understanding, regulation, and expression of emotion.[26]

- *Ensure adequate nutrition for all children and expectant mothers.*
  In the United States, no child should have to go hungry, rely on
  food from unacceptable sources, or suffer the ill effects of malnutrition. Three main programs aim to meet children's nutritional needs: the food stamp program; the Special Supplemental Nutrition Program for Women, Infants and Children
  (wic), which serves children up to age five as well as expectant
  and new mothers who are low-income and considered to be at
  risk of inadequate nutrition; and school-based child-feeding
  programs, such as school breakfast or lunch programs. Barriers
  to participation in all three types of programs need to be exam-
  ined and addressed. In particular, it is imperative to address
  the barriers that deprive immigrant children of adequate nutrition.[27]

4. RICH EARLY LEARNING EXPERIENCES

Virtually every state across the nation now has some kind of
early childhood initiative. The focus is especially sharp on improving school readiness and building the foundations of early literacy.
However, much more must be done.

- *Maintain an intensive focus on improving the quality of infant
  and toddler care.* According to the National Association of
  Child Care Resource and Referral Agencies, most families
  with young children have three key concerns about child care:
  Can I find it? Can I afford it? And can I trust it? Few families
  can answer yes to all three questions. Affordable, good quality
  infant and toddler care is especially difficult to find. Monitoring and improving the quality of infant and toddler programs
  must be given high priority, given evidence that these programs
  tend to be of very poor quality. Provider networks, run by well
  qualified staff, are a key to improving the quality of family child

care homes. Policymakers need to set health and safety standards for all providers or settings that receive public subsidies. Health and safety are of the utmost importance, but it is also important to focus on factors that influence caregivers' capacity to give responsive, individualized care to infants and toddlers, and to expose them to varied, engaging activities and rich language experiences. A long-term study by the National Institute of Child Health and Human Development is providing new evidence that caregivers' interactions with very young children can influence their cognitive development in general and language development in particular.[28]

- *Offer universal access to preschool programs during the two years leading to school entry.* Between 1979 and 1999, the number of states providing prekindergarten programs for three- and four-year-olds more than quadrupled. Some states are now taking steps toward universal preschool programs. The challenge is to expand both access to early childhood services and the quality of those services. The case for universal, voluntary prekindergarten has been powerfully made by many policymakers, researchers, employers, parent groups, and education leaders, including not only the Carnegie Task Force on Learning in the Primary Grades but also, more recently, the Council of Chief State School Officers and the Committee for Economic Development. However, only one state (Georgia) presently has a free, universal program and it is limited to four-year-olds. Other states are moving in this direction, but much more needs to be done. Building the political will needed to increase public investment is a crucial next step.[29]

- *Ensure attention to the full spectrum of developmental tasks.* Concern about building early literacy and reading skills is motivating many early education programs to focus heavily on cognitive development. While these skills are certainly important, reading experts stress that motivation and curiosity are very important aspects of reading readiness and school success. Many organizations, including Zero to Three, the National Academy of Sciences, the National Education Goals Panel, and the Child Mental Health Foundations and Agencies Network, have called for an approach to school readiness that addresses all aspects of children's development, including social and emotional development. Attention to the full spectrum of developmental outcomes is crucial for children with and without special needs.[30]

- *Support a broad, balanced approach to reading readiness.* According to numerous organizations, including the National Association for the Education of Young Children and the National Research Council, children benefit from early learning curricula that provide not only phonological and phonemic awareness but also the sturdy conceptual and informational foundation that children need in order to comprehend and build on what they read. This is especially important for those children who bring to early learning settings a knowledge base that is limited or not aligned with the content encountered in school.

By the year 2030, the majority of America's children will be from groups now thought of as "minorities." Many children will enter early education programs or kindergartens without previous exposure to the kind of language they encounter in the classroom. Intensive efforts are needed to identify and implement effective approaches to helping these children adjust to new settings and develop a solid foundation for literacy and school success while maintaining strong bonds with their families and positive identification with their cultures.

Some states and communities have taken specific measures

to improve early care and education for children who come from non-English-speaking homes; others are struggling with how best to serve these children. A joint position statement by the International Reading Association and the NAEYC states that for children whose primary language is not English, a strong foundation in the first language promotes school achievement in English. English learners are more likely to become readers and writers of English when they are already familiar with the vocabulary and concepts in their first language. Oral and written language experiences should be regarded as an additive process, ensuring that children are able to maintain their home language while also learning to speak and read English. Including non-English materials and resources can help to support children's first language while they acquire oral proficiency in English.[31] These positions are consistent with findings of a National Academy of Sciences study on literacy skills for language-minority children.[32]

- *Ensure a better qualified, better compensated early childhood workforce.* Many factors affect the quality of early education and care programs, including facilities, adult-to-child ratios, and group size, but no factor is more important than the preparedness, competence, and commitment of program staff. The relationship between caregiver characteristics and program quality is well documented.[33] Compared with elementary and secondary teachers, providers of early care and education have fewer opportunities to prepare for their roles, acquire ongoing training and support, or advance along a career path. They have fewer incentives, economic or professional, for staying in the field. Wages in the early childhood field continue to be very low, especially for those working outside of public school systems. High turnover rates, which threaten program quality, cannot be improved without addressing compensation. Tackling these issues is a vital step toward improving results for young children and improving their readiness for elementary school. In *From Neurons to Neighborhoods,* the National Academy of Sciences recommended that a portion of all child care funds be earmarked for efforts to support and strengthen the early childhood workforce.[34]

- *Strengthen the curricula of institutions that prepare early educators.* A great deal can be done to make the activities and content of early education programs more interesting, diverse, and challenging for all children, including those with disabilities and other special needs. Cognitive scientists have shown that even very young children are eager and able to explore not only objects, environments, and people but also concepts—if they are presented in a way that engages their interest. Teacher education programs can create or strengthen evidence-based curricula, preparing early educators to provide engaging, stimulating activities with an emphasis on rich language experiences. Early educators also need stronger preparation to work effectively in "inclusive" settings—where children with disabilities and other special needs play and learn alongside their typically developing peers.

- *Ensure the continuity of learning experiences as children move through early childhood programs and into elementary school.* A significant body of research, including a recent study of the Chicago Child-Parent Center program that tracked nearly one thousand children over a fifteen-year period, shows that high-quality preschool programs are most likely to have lasting effects if services are sustained as children move into the primary grades.[35]

  Attention to continuity was a key recommendation of the

Council of Chief State School Officers' policy statement on early childhood and family education, which stressed that children who receive consistent services as they move across institutional structures perform better on academic and social development measures well into the elementary, middle, and secondary grades.[36] The National Education Goals Panel has stressed that children need schools that are ready for them—that is, ready to meet individual boys and girls wherever they happen to be on the developmental spectrum; to provide continuity with early learning experiences; to involve families; and to ensure that children do not slip into the gap that often opens up between the culture of the home and the culture of the school. Policymakers need to ensure that core principles of early development are infused into elementary school curricula, teacher education programs, and professional development strategies.[37]

- *Create and fund an infrastructure capable of supporting a large-scale early care and education system.* An early childhood infrastructure includes many elements, as the Quality 2000 Initiative and other efforts have demonstrated.[38] They include: public engagement, parent engagement, professional development, finance, governance, and accountability systems. States can use discretionary funds available through TANF block grants and tobacco settlement funds to plan and build an early childhood infrastructure. Several states are engaged in efforts to move beyond a program-by-program approach and build systems of care for young children and their families. The challenges are immense, and federal participation is crucial to ensure quality and equity.

- *Strengthen accountability.* There is a trend toward stronger regulation in early care and education, especially for infants and toddlers. Many states are working toward this goal. Most have developed policies that support accreditation in various ways, primarily through increased funding, quality enhancement grants, and other incentives. But voluntary accreditation has not succeeded in improving low-quality programs serving low-income children. Many bodies, including the Council of Chief State School Officers, have recommended strengthening early childhood program standards and accountability.[39] The National Association for Education of Young Children has taken the position that any child care provider who receives public subsidies, whether home-based or center-based, should be held to standards that are aligned with research on young children's developmental needs. There should be no exceptions to this principle because "such exemption does not provide an equal level of health and safety protection for all children."[40]

5. CARING COMMUNITIES

• *Support effective community efforts to plan and implement comprehensive programs for young children and families.* In many states, there is a deepening commitment to creating comprehensive programs for young children. Some focus on infants and toddlers, and many report programs for older preschoolers. More than half of the states have introduced specific systems change and/or community mobilization strategies to strengthen communities, and many include explicit attention to the needs of children and families. Researchers also report growth in state funding of "enabling grants" to communities (or school districts) to develop early childhood programs and adapt them to local realities. These are positive developments. However, many states have yet to develop programs for young children, and overall levels of funding for such programs remain relatively low.

- *Foster ties among services and programs.* Communities can address barriers to service integration, fund efforts to improve collaboration, tie authorizations to increased funding to collaborative efforts, and require grant applicants to show how they will advance efforts to integrate early childhood services. States can also integrate their approach to welfare reform with early childhood programming and system development. They can provide tools and technical supports needed to facilitate collaboration.

6. A CHANCE TO BE CHILDREN

Given today's heavy emphasis on children's readiness for success in school and in the workplace, it is easy to overlook an essential need of all kids: a chance to be children. In addition to all of the resources, services, and learning opportunities described in this book, children need time to play, to fidget, to daydream, and to fuss. They need to spill their juice and have awkward accidents in the supermarket. They need to be protected from much of the stress and worry that the adults around them may experience. Babies need to be babied, and sometimes older children need to be babied as well. Finally, all young children need countless expressions of affection and frequent assurance of unconditional love.

Looking Ahead

The last decade has brought new attention to America's young children, heightening interest in such issues as early brain development, language learning, family support, and school readiness. But many public opinion researchers and political observers are quick to qualify the trend. They say that the American public is chiefly interested in early childhood development and learning not as an end in itself, but as an aspect of other issues—notably, education, crime prevention, and welfare reform. Moreover, the public's most passionate concern appears to be the quality of parenting and the capacity of today's mothers and fathers to imbue their children with sound values.[41] According to Public Agenda, only two out of five adults say that today's kids will make the world a better place.[42]

It would seem that many Americans who in the last decades of the twentieth century were asking themselves what kind of world we would be handing down to our children, who were focused on reducing conflict, shrinking the deficit, and protecting the planet, are now asking another question: to what kind of children are we entrusting our world? Will they have not only the intellect and skills, but also the moral compass needed to chart a course into the new millennium? As they cross into new frontiers, will they have the personal qualities—the mix of daring and discipline, ingenuity and industry—that have held previous generations of Americans in good stead?

Such questions are not new. Each generation has wondered about the capacity of the next to protect their legacy and perpetuate their values. But today, concern about young people appears to be especially urgent. This shift in focus may reflect, in part, an introspective mood that seems to have taken hold since the events of 11 September 2001. In part, it is fueled by concern about juvenile crime that grew in the nineties as headlines about children having children were overshadowed by reports of children killing children. And in part, it reflects worry about the demands of the twenty-first-century workplace and our nation's continuing prosperity.

These concerns have a very positive dimension. They have focused public attention on the full spectrum of developmental tasks that children must meet on the path toward adulthood—with an emphasis on social and emotional development. They have bolstered interest not only in reading and numeracy, but also in civic literacy—children's growing capacity to join in common purpose with those who share their household, school, or neighborhood. For some time now, children's advocates have been rethinking the brain; today, they are also rethinking the heart.

If We Were Starting Now

It was Albert Einstein who said, "We can't solve problems by using the same kind of thinking we used when we created them." That is as true in the world of public policy as it is in the realm of physics. The key institutions that affect America's children were designed long ago. They reflect many assumptions about children's needs and the best ways to meet them that are deeply entrenched in our society. So it is important to ask: if we knew then what we know now about children's development and learning, would we have arrived at today's arrangements?

If we knew then what we know now about the opportunities and risks of the early years and about how quickly children are set in academic trajectories, would we wait until age five or six to begin significant public investment in children's learning? If we knew then what we know now about the early foundations of literacy and numeracy, would we have today's disjunction between early childhood programs and K-12 education?

If we were starting now to create systems of care and learning that are in the best interests of the children and the nation they will inherit, would we arrive at systems of care that prepare and protect some but not all of our children?

Our nation cannot rely on yesterday's thinking to solve today's problems or to shape tomorrow's solutions. Starting now, we must make every possible effort to communicate, act on, and expand our understanding of what kids need.

NOTES

Introduction

1. M. K. Meyers et al., *Public Policies that Support Families with Small Children: Variation across the U.S. States*, paper prepared for the Luxembourg Income Study (LIS) conference on "Child Well-being in Rich and Transition Countries," Luxembourg, 30 September–1 October 1999 (New York: Columbia University School of Social Work, National Center for Children and Poverty, 1999).

2. D. Kutt Nahas, "Havens for Babies, Choices for Mothers," *New York Times*, 15 October 2000. More information about safe havens is available from the International Association of Voluntary Adoption Agencies and NGO's. See: www.iavaan.org.

3. N. K. Cauthen, J. Knitzer, and C. H. Ripple, *Map and Track: State Initiatives for Young Children and Families*, 2000 Edition (New York: National Center for Children in Poverty, 2000), 5.

4. N. Sazer O'Donnell and E. Galinsky, *The Seven Lessons of Early Childhood Public Engagement* (New York: Carnegie Corporation of New York; Families and Work Institute, 2000).

5. Cauthen, Knitzer, and Ripple, *Map and Track*, 7.

6. J. Knitzer and S. Page, *Map and Track: State Initiatives for Young Children and Families* (New York: National Center for Children in Poverty, 1998).

7. K. A. Johnson and S. Rosenbaum, *Making Medicaid and SCHIP Work for Working Families* (New York: Carnegie Corporation of New York, 2000).

8. National Governors Association, "First Three Years: State Early Childhood Initiatives," NGA *Issue Brief,* http://www.nga.org/center/divisions/1,1188,C__ISSUE__BRIEF^D__161,00.html, posted 6 June 2000, accessed 23 May 2001; National Conference of State Legislatures, *Children, Youth and Family Issue: 2000 State Legislative Summary* (Denver, Colo.: Author, 2001).

9. Cauthen, Knitzer, and Ripple, *Map and Track,* 5.

10. R. Takanishi, *Renegotiating a Social Compact Based on Children and Families' Requirements for a Decent Life,* paper presented at the Joint Center for Poverty Research, 1999 Commissioned Research Conference, Washington, D.C., 1999. See also G. T. Kingsley and J. O. Gibson, *Civil Society, the Public Sector, and Poor Communities* (Washington, D.C.: Urban Institute, 2000).

11. Knitzer and Page, *Map and Track.*

12. R. Schumacher, M. Greenberg, and J. Lombardi, *State Initiatives to Promote Early Learning: Next Steps in Coordinating Subsidized Child Care, Head Start, and State Prekindergarten* (Washington, D.C.: Center for Law and Social Policy, 2001).

13. Cauthen, Knitzer, and Ripple, *Map and Track.*

14. Cauthen, Knitzer, and Ripple, *Map and Track,* 10.

15. A. W. Mitchell and R. Shore, *Next Steps: Advancing the Early Care and Education Agenda* (Packard Foundation, 1999).

16. National Association for the Education of Young Children, "Governors' 2001 State of the State Addresses," www.naeyc.org/childrens__champions/state updates/2001/state-of-the-state-addresses.htm, accessed 27 July 2001.

17. The Child Care Partnership Project, 1998, http://nccic.org/ccpartnerships/home.htm, accessed 27 July 2001.

18. R. Shore, *Ahead of the Curve: Why American Businesses Are Meeting the Needs of New and Expectant Parents* (New York: Families and Work Institute, 1998).

19. A. Mitchell, "The Children's Hour: Hugging and Kissing Your Way into the White House," *New York Times,* 14 May 2000, Week In Review section.

1. What Families Need

1. L. Belkin, "Your Kids Are Their Problem," *New York Times Magazine,* 23 July 2000.

2. A. Dufett, J. Johnson, and S. Farkas, *Kids These Days: What Americans Really Think About the Next Generation* (New York: Public Agenda, 1999).

3. E. Galinsky, *Ask the Children: What America's Children Really Think About Working Parents* (New York: William Morrow, 1999).

4. P. Klass, "One Child, Many Influences" *New York Times*, 9 September 1998, Op-ed.

5. R. Weissbourd, *The Vulnerable Child: What Really Hurts America's Children and What We Can Do About It* (Reading, Mass.: Addison-Wesley, 1996), 27.

6. D. J. Macunovich, "The Fortunes of One's Birth: Relative Cohort Size and the Youth Labor Market in the United States," *Journal of Population Economics* 12 (1999):215–72.

7. Author's interview with Jack Shonkoff, 27 April 2001.

8. U.S. Department of Health and Human Services, *Mental Health: A Report of the Surgeon General* (Rockville, Md.: U.S. Department of Health and Human Services, Substance Abuse and Mental Health Services Administration, Center for Mental Health Services, National Institutes of Health, National Institute of Mental Health, 1999), 127.

9. S. Crockenberg and E. Leerkes, "Infant Social and Emotional Development in Family Context," in *Handbook of Infant Mental Health*, 2nd ed., edited by C. H. Zeanah Jr. (New York: Guilford Press, 2000), 63.

10. Ibid.

11. W. W. Hartup, "Having Friends, Making Friends, and Keeping Friends: Relationships as Educational Contexts," ERIC Digest (Urbana, Ill.: ERIC Clearinghouse on Elementary and Early Childhood Education, 1992).

12. D. N. Lloyd, "Prediction of School Failure from Third-Grade Data," *Educational and Psychological Measurement* 38 (1978).

13. S. G. Moore, *The Role of Parents in the Development of Peer Group Competence* (Urbana, Ill.: ERIC Digest, 1992).

14. R. Pianta, B. Egeland, and A. Hyatt, "Maternal Relationship History as an Indicator of Developmental Risk," *American Journal of Orthopsychiatry* 56, no. 2 (July 1986): 385–98.

15. E. L. Cowen, "The Enhancement of Psychological Wellness: Challenges and Opportunities," *American Journal of Community Psychology* 22 (1994):149–80.

16. L. C. Huffman, S. L. Mehlinger, and A. S. Kerivan, "Risk Factors for the Academic and Behavioral Problems at the Beginning of School," in *Off to a Good Start* (Chapel Hill, N.C.: University of North Carolina, University of North Carolina FPG Child Development Center, 2000).

17. Moore, *The Role of Parents*.

18. U.S. Department of Health and Human Services, *Mental Health: A Re-*

port of the Surgeon General (Rockville, M.D.: U.S. Department of Health and Human Services, Substance Abuse and Mental Health Services Administration, Center for Mental Health Services, National Institutes of Health, National Institute of Mental Health, 1999).

19. J. Knitzer, "Early Childhood Mental Health: A Policy and Systems Development Perspective," in *Handbook of Early Childhood Intervention*, 2nd ed., edited by J. P. Shonkoff and S. J. Meisels (New York: Cambridge University Press, 2000).

20. J. Rogowski, "Cost-Effectiveness of Care for Very Low Birth Weight Infants," *Pediatrics* 102 (1998): 35–43.

21. V. R. Chomitz, L. W. Y. Cheung, and E. Lieberman, "The Role of Lifestyle in Preventing Low Birth Weight," *The Future of Children* 5 (spring 1995).

22. Annie E. Casey Foundation, *The Right Start: Conditions of Babies and their Families in America's Largest Cities* (Baltimore: Author, 1999), 16.

23. J. Kleinman, B. Mitchell, J. H. Madan et al., "The Effects of Maternal Smoking on Fetal and Infant Mortality," *American Journal of Epidemiology* 127, no. 2 (1988): 274–82.

24. U.S. Department of Health and Human Services, *The Surgeon General's 1990 Report on the Health Benefits of Smoking Cessation* (Washington, D.C.: Author, 1990).

25. Institute of Medicine, *Nutrition During Pregnancy: Part I: Weight Gain, Part II: Nutrient Supplements* (Committee on Nutritional Status During Pregnancy and Lactation, Author, 1990).

26. U.S. General Accounting Office, *Early Intervention: Federal Investments Like WIC Can Produce Savings* (Washington, D.C.: Author, 1992).

27. K. Porter and W. Primus, *Changes Since 1995 in the Safety Net's Impact on Child Poverty* (Washington, D.C.: Center on Budget and Policy Priorities, December 1999).

28. V. R. Chomitz, L. W. Cheung, and E. Lieberman, "The Role of Lifestyle in Preventing Low Birth Weight," *The Future of Children* 5, no. 1 (1995): 121–38.

29. Institute of Medicine, *Prenatal Care: Reaching Mothers, Reaching Infants* (Committee to Study Outreach for Prenatal Care, Division of Health Promotion and Disease Prevention, 1988); U.S. Department of Health and Human Services, *Savings in Medicaid Costs for Newborns and Their Mothers from Prenatal Participation in the WIC Program* (Washington, D.C.: Author, 1989).

30. C. J. Hobel, M. G. Ross, R. L. Bemis et al., "The West Los Angeles Preterm Birth Prevention Project. I. Program Impact on High-Risk Women," *American Journal of Obstetrics and Gynecology* 170 (January 1994): 54–62.

31. Johnson and Rosenbaum, *Making Medicaid and SCHIP Work.*

32. The Infant Health and Development Program, "Enhancing the Outcomes of Low-birth-weight, Premature Infants," *JAMA* 263 (1990): 3035–42; D. Olds and H. Kitzman, "Review of Research on Home Visiting for Pregnant Women and Parents of Young Children," *The Future of Children* 3, no. 3 (1993): 53–92.

33. D. Hughes and D. Simpson, "The Role of Social Change in Preventing Low Birth Weight," *The Future of Children* 5, no. 1 (1995).

34. D. Hamburg, foreword to R. Shore, *Family Support and Parent Education: Opportunities for Scaling Up* (New York: Carnegie Corporation of New York, 1996).

35. S. K. Henshaw, "Unintended Pregnancy in the United States," *Family Planning Perspectives* 30 (January/February 1998): 24–29.

36. Annie E. Casey Foundation, *Kids Count 2001 Data Book* (Baltimore: Author, 2001).

37. K. Edin, "Few Good Men: Why Poor Women Don't Remarry," *The American Prospect* 11, no. 4 (3 January 2000): 26–31.

38. S. McLanahan, I. Garfinkel, and R. B. Mincy, *Fragile Families, Welfare Reform, and Marriage*, Welfare Reform Brief no. 10, The Brookings Institution, December 2001, 4.

39. R. J. Lerman, "The Impact of the Changing U.S. Family Structure on Child Poverty and Income Inequality," *Economica* (May 1996).

40. Allen Guttenmacher Institute, *Why Is Teenage Pregnancy Declining? The Roles of Abstinence, Sexual Activity and Contraceptive Use* (Washington, D.C.: Author, December 1999).

41. Forum on Adolescence, *Adolescent Decision Making: Implications for Prevention Programs* (Washington, D.C.: Institute of Medicine/National Research Council, 1999).

42. D. Olds et al., "Theoretical Foundations of a Program of Home Visitation for Pregnant Women and Parents of Young Children," *Journal of Community Psychology* 25 (1997): 9–25.

43. Wei-Yin Hu, *Welfare, Marriage, and Cohabitation: Experimental Evidence from California*, working paper, University of California, Los Angeles, 1998.

44. Efforts to eliminate the "marriage penalty" in the federal tax code fall into this category. Every state now allows two-parent families who meet eligibility requirements to receive public assistance. An important step would be raising the income level at which the Earned Income Tax Credit begins to phase down for married couples. See I. J. Lav and J. Sly, *Large Cost of the Archer "Marriage Penalty*

Relief" Provisions Reflects Poor Targeting (Washington, D.C.: Center on Budget and Policy Priorities, February 2000), available on the internet at www.cbpp.org/ 2–2-00tax.htm.

45. F. J. Furstenberg Jr., *The Effects of Welfare Reform on the Family: The Good, the Bad and the Ugly* (Chicago: Joint Center for Poverty Research, 1998), 12.

46. S. N. Bernard and J. Knitzer, *Map and Track: State Initiatives to Encourage Responsible Fatherhood* (New York: National Center for Children in Poverty, 1999), 11–12, 45–46.

47. I. Garfinkel et al., *Fathers Under Fire: The Revolution in Child Support Enforcement* (New York: Russell Sage Foundation, 1998).

48. Bernard and Knitzer, *Map and Track,* 55.

49. J. Bruner, "Tot Thought," *New York Review of Books,* 9 March 2000, 27–30.

50. Bruner, "Tot Thought"; A. Gopnik, A. N. Meltzoff, and P. K. Kuhl, *The Scientist in the Crib: Minds, Brains, and How Children Learn* (New York: William Morrow, 1999).

51. H. Schaeffer, ed., *Studies in Infant-Mother Interaction* (London: Academic Press, 1977), cited in *How People Learn: Brain, Mind, Experience, and School,* edited by J. D. Bransford, A. L. Brown, and R. R. Cocking (Washington, D.C.: National Academy Press, 1999), 90–91.

52. C. E. Snow, M. S. Burns, and P. Griffin, eds., *Preventing Reading Difficulties in Young Children* (Washington, D.C.: National Academy Press, National Research Council, 1998).

53. Public Agenda, *Kids These Days: What Americans Really Think About the Next Generation* (New York: Author, 1999).

54. Walker Percy, cited in R. Coles, *The Moral Life of Children* (Boston: Houghton Mifflin, 1986), 29–30.

55. E. E. Maccoby, *Social Development: Psychological Growth and the Parent-Child Relationship* (New York: Harcourt Brace, 1991), 607.

56. Maccoby, *Social Development,* 606.

57. J. Dunn, *The Beginnings of Social Understanding* (Cambridge: Harvard University Press, 1988).

58. Ibid.

59. Interview with Urie Bronfenbrenner conducted by the Families and Work Institute, 1996.

60. D. Baumrind, "Current Patterns of Parental Authority," *Developmental Psychology Monographs* 4 (1971): 1–103.

61. E. E. Maccoby, "The Role of Parents in the Socialization of Children: An Historical Overview," in *A Century of Developmental Psychology*, edited by R. D. Parke et al. (Washington, D.C.: American Psychological Association, 1994), 605.

62. U.S. Department of Education Office for Civil Rights, *1998 Elementary and Secondary School Civil Rights Compliance Report* (Washington, D.C.: Author, 2000).

63. Committee on School Health, American Academy of Pediatrics, "Corporal Punishment in Schools," *Pediatrics* 106, no. 2 (August 2000): 343.

64. Committee on Psychosocial Aspects of Child and Family Health, American Academy of Pediatrics, "Guidance for Effective Discipline," *Pediatrics* 101, no. 4 (April 1998): 723–28.

65. Centers for Disease Control, 1998.

66. U.S. Department of Health and Human Services, *SIDS Deaths Reach New Record Low in 1997, but Disparities Persist for Minority Communities* (Hyattsville, Md.: Centers for Disease Control and Prevention, National Center for Health Statistics, 1999).

67. Centers for Disease Control and Prevention, "Assessment of Infant Sleeping Position—Selected States, 1996," *Morbidity and Mortality Weekly Report* 47, no. 41 (1998): 873–77. According to this study, the percentage of African American mothers who put their babies to sleep on their stomach was 11 percent to 54 percent higher than for white mothers. The percentage of American Indian and Alaska Native mothers who reported usually placing their babies on their stomach ranged from 16.0 percent to 33.9 percent in the states studied, suggesting variations in sleep positioning practices among tribes. These results mirror the increased incidence of SIDS deaths found in these communities, with African American and American Indian/Alaska Native infants 2.4 and 2.8 times more likely to die of SIDS, respectively.

68. National Safe Kids Campaign, 1998. See: www.safekids.org/tier3__cd.-cfm?folder__=440&content__item__id+2290.

69. National Safe Kids Campaign, Injury Facts: Childhood Injury. See: www.safekids.org/tier3__cd.cfm?folder__id=540&content__item__id=1030.

70. National Highway Traffic Safety Administration, 1999.

71. National Safe Kids Campaign, 1998. See: www.safekids.org/tier3__cd.cfm?folder__id=171&content__item__id=215.

72. National Center for Injury Prevention and Control, 1999.

73. P. Cummings et al., "State Gun Safe Storage Laws and Child Mortality Due to Firearms," *JAMA* 278 (1 October 1997).

74. National Center for Injury Prevention and Control, 1998. See: www.cdc.gov/ncipc/factsheets/drown.htm.

75. J. D. Bransford, A. L. Brown, and R. R. Cocking, eds., *How People Learn* (Washington, D.C.: National Academy Press, 1999), 92.

76. Author's interview with Isabel Sawhill, 3 April 2000.

77. R. F. Wertheimer, *Working Poor Families with Children* (Washington, D.C.: Child Trends, 1999).

78. W. Primus, L. Rawlings, K. Larin, and K. Porter, *The Initial Impacts of Welfare Reform on the Incomes of Single-Mother Families* (Washington, D.C.: Center on Budget and Policy Priorities, 1999).

79. M. Lino, *Expenditures on Children by Families, 2000 Annual Report* (Washington, D.C.: U.S. Department of Agriculture, Center for Nutrition Policy and Promotion, 2001), table 9.

80. K. Taaffe Young, K. Davis, and C. Schoen, *The Commonwealth Survey of Parents with Young Children* (New York: The Commonwealth Fund, 1996).

81. J. Brooks-Gunn, G. Duncan, and N. Maritato, "Poor Families, Poor Outcomes: The Well-being of Children and Youth," in *Consequences of Growing Up Poor* (New York: Russell Sage Foundation, 1997).

82. Food Security Institute, *Summary of Existing Food Security Survey Studies* (Medford, Mass.: Center on Hunger & Poverty, School of Nutrition Science & Policy, Tufts University, 1999).

83. E. M. Lewit and N. Kerrebrock, "Child Indicators: Childhood Hunger," *The Future of Children: Welfare to Work* 7, no. 1 (1997): 128–37.

84. J. L. Brown and E. Pollitt, "Malnutrition, Poverty and Intellectual Development," *Scientific American* 247 (February 1996): 38–43.

85. Shore, *Ahead of the Curve.*

86. S. J. Heymann and A. Earle, "The Work-Family Balance: What Hurdles Are Parents Leaving Welfare Likely to Confront?" *Insights* (Association for Public Policy Analysis and Management): 313–321 (1998); Heymann and Earle, *Parents' Ability*, 502–4.

87. Bureau of Labor Statistics, *Employment Status of the Population by Sex, Marital Status, and Age of Own Children under 18, 1999–2000 Annual Averages.* See: www.bls.gov/news.release/famee.to5.htm.

88. E. Galinsky and J. Swanberg, "Employed Mothers and Fathers in the United States: Understanding How Work and Family Life Fit Together," in *Organizational Change and Gender Equity,* edited by L. Haas, P. Hwang, and G. Russell (California: Sage, 2000), 15–28; J. T. Bond, E. Galinsky, and J. Swanberg,

The 1997 National Study of the Changing Workforce (New York: Families and Work Institute, 1998).

89. P. Loprest, *How Families That Left Welfare Are Doing: A National Picture,* series B, no. B-1 (Washington, D.C.: Urban Institute, 1999).

90. Bureau of Labor Statistics, "Employment Situation, Table A-10. Persons not in the labor force and multiple jobholders by sex, not seasonally adjusted" (Washington, D.C.: Department of Labor, 2002). See: www.bls.gov/news. release/empsit.t10.htm.

91. S. J. Heymann, S. Toomey, and F. Furstenberg, "Working Parents: What Factors Are Involved in Their Ability to Take Time Off from Work When Their Children Are Sick?" *Archives of Pediatric & Adolescent Medicine* 153 (1999): 870–74.

92. Heymann and Earle, "Work-Family Balance," 313–21.

93. Heymann, Toomey, and Furstenberg, "Working Parents," 870–74.

94. Heymann and Earle, "Work-family Balance," 313–21.

95. Heymann, Toomey, and Furstenberg, "Working Parents," 870–74.

96. D. Burlingham and A. Freud, *Infants Without Families* (London: Allen and Univin, 1944).

97. Presentation by Robert Pynos at Columbia University, 8 December 2001.

98. Presentation by Peter Fonagy at Columbia University, 8 December 2001.

99. J. Bruner, *Acts of Meaning* (Cambridge: Harvard University Press, 1990), 49–50.

100. J. Bruner, *The Culture of Education* (Cambridge: Harvard University Press, 1996), 98–99.

101. B. Shore, *Culture in Mind: Cognition, Culture, and the Problem of Meaning* (New York: Oxford University Press, 1996), 58–59.

102. *Zero to Three: Key Findings from a Nationwide Survey among Parents of Zero-to-Three-Year-Olds* (Washington, D.C.: National Center for Infants, Toddlers, and Families, April 1997).

103. Author's interview with Lillian Katz, 1998.

104. Author's interview with T. Berry Brazelton, 1998.

105. Public Agenda, *First Things First: What Americans Expect from the Public Schools* (New York: Author, 1994).

106. These assumptions come from Family Support America website.

107. National Institute for Literacy. See: www.novel.nifl.gov/nifl/faqs.html #literacy__rates.

108. Statement by Robert Muller, deputy assistant secretary for vocational and adult education, on the Fiscal Year 2002 Request for Vocational and Adult Edu-

cation Programs, before the U.S. House of Representatives Subcommittee on Labor, Health and Human Services, and Education Appropriations, 26 April 2001.

109. U.S. Department of Education, *Even Start: Evidence from the Past and a Look at the Future,* undated. See: www.ed.gov/pubs/EvenStart/highlights.html.

110. K. A. Johnson, *No Place Like Home: Home Visiting Policies and Programs* (New York: Commonwealth Fund, 2001).

111. Ibid. Of the forty-two states that responded, thirty-seven reported state-based home visiting programs. An additional three states have state-level quality improvement or technical assistance projects that support a range of locally based home visiting programs.

112. Ibid.

113. Ibid.

114. Johnson, *No Place Like Home.*

115. Cited in *Future of Children,* spring/summer 1999 issue.

116. D. Olds, "The Prenatal/Early Infancy Project: Fifteen Years Later," in *Primary Prevention Works,* edited by G. W. Albee and T. P. Gullotta (London: Sage Publications, 1997), 43.

117. Presentation by David Olds, conference call transcript. Children Now Conference Call no. 5, Home Visiting, 12 November 1999. See: www.childrennow.org/health/conference-call-5.html.

118. D. S. Gomby, P. L. Culross, and R. E. Behrman, "Home Visiting: Recent Program Evaluations—Analysis and Recommendations," *The Future of Children* 9, no. 1 (1999):4–26. This issue found that "results are mixed and, where positive, often modest in magnitude. Studies have revealed some benefits in parenting practices, attitudes, and knowledge, but the benefits for children in the areas of health, development, and abuse and neglect rates that are supposed to derive from these changes have been more elusive. Only one program model revealed marked benefits in maternal life course. When benefits were achieved in any area, they were often concentrated among particular subgroups of families, but there was little consistency in these subgroups across program models." The findings of the special issue were summarized in a presentation by Deanna Gomby, conference call transcript. Children Now Conference Call no. 5, Home Visiting, 12 November 1999. See: www.childrennow.org/health/conference-call-5.html.

119. State of Vermont Agency of Human Services, *The Social Well-Being of Vermonters 2000: A Report on Outcomes for Vermont's Citizens,* 2000 (Waterbury, Vt.: Author, 2000).

120. D. A. Dara and K. A. Harding, "Healthy Families America: Using Research to Enhance Practice," *The Future of Children* 9, no. 1: 152–76 (1999).

2. Infants and Toddlers

1. "Caring for Infants and Toddlers: Executive Summary." *The Future of Children* 11, no. 1 (2001): 3.

2. Shore, *Culture in Mind*, introduction.

3. Remarks by Donald Cohen, White House Conference on Early Childhood Development and Learning, Washington, D.C., 17 April 1997.

4. M. R. Grumet, *Bitter Milk: Women and Teaching* (Amherst: University of Massachusetts Press, 1988), 98–99.

5. B. Rogoff, *Apprenticeship in Thinking: Cognitive Development in Social Context* (New York: Oxford University Press, 1990), 3.

6. J. D. Bransford, A. L. Brown, and R. R. Cocking, eds. *How People Learn: Brain, Mind, Experience, and School* (Washington, D.C.: National Academy Press, 1999), 71–73.

7. Ibid.

8. Shonkoff and Phillips, *From Neurons to Neighborhoods*, 30–31.

9. Ibid., 32.

10. Ibid., 258–59.

11. M. Gunnar, *Studying Stress Physiology in Internationally Adopted Children*, presented at the International Conference on Adoption Research, Minneapolis, Minnesota, 10–14 August 1999. See: http://fsos.che.umn.edu/mtarp/Papers.htm.

12. Shonkoff and Phillips, *From Neurons to Neighborhoods*, 258–59.

13. American Academy of Pediatrics, "Scope of Health Care Benefits for Newborns, Infants, Children, Adolescents, and Young Adults Through Age 21 Years," *Pediatrics* 100 (1997):6.

14. U.S. Census Bureau, "Children Without Health Insurance for the Entire Year by Age, Race, and Ethnicity: 1999 and 2000," *Current Population Survey*, March 2000 and 2001, table 4. See: www.census.gov/hhes/hlthins/hlthin00/dtable4.html.

15. R. Wertheimer, *Working Poor Families with Children* (Washington, D.C.: Child Trends, 1999).

16. Johnson and Rosenbaum, *Making Medicaid and SCHIP Work*; D. W.

Liska, N. J. Brennan, and B. K. Bruen, *State-Level Databook on Health Care Access and Financing*, 3rd ed. (Urban Institute, 1998). See also M. E. Lewin and S. Altman, eds., *America's Health Care Safety Net: Intact but Endangered* (Washington, D.C.: National Academy Press, 2000), and T. Selden, J. Banthin, and J. Cohen, "Medicaid's Problem Children: Eligible but Not Enrolled," *Health Affairs* 17, no. 3 (1998): 192–200.

17. U.S. Bureau of the Census, March 1993, 1994, and 1995 Current Population Surveys.

18. E. R. Brown et al., "Access to Health Insurance and Health Care for Children in Immigrant Families," in *Children of Immigrants: Health, Adjustment, and Public Assistance*, edited by D. J. Hernandez (Washington, D.C.: National Academy Press, 1999).

19. American Federation of State, County and Municipal Employees, SCHIP *Update: Some States Could Have More Money for Outreach*, issue brief, July 2001. See: www.afscme.org/publications/issueb/ib0107b.htm.

20. E. H. James Duke, *Statement on Fiscal Year 2002 President's Budget Request for the Health Resources and Services Administration* (Washington, D.C.: U.S. Department of Health and Human Services, 2001). See: www.hhs.gov/budget/testify/b20010508a.html.

21. American Academy of Pediatrics, *The Medical Home*. Policy statement, *Pediatrics* 90(5): 774 (November 1992).

22. U.S. Public Health Service, *Report of the Surgeon General's Conference on Children's Mental Health: A National Action Agenda* (Washington, D.C.: U.S. Department of Health and Human Services, 2000), 3.

23. U.S. Department of Health and Human Service, *Mental Health: A Report of the Surgeon General* (Rockville, Md.: U.S. Department of Health and Human Services, Substance Abuse and Mental Health Services Administration, Center for Mental Health Services, National Institutes of Health, National Institute of Mental Health, 1999).

24. G. Dawson, S. Ashman, and L. Carver, "The Role of Early Experience in Shaping Behavioral and Brain Development and Its Implications for Social Policy." *Development and Psychopathology* 12 (2000): 695–712; D. Hessl et al., "A Longitudinal Study of Children of Depressed Mothers: Psychobiological Findings Related to Stress," in *Advancing Research on Developmental Plasticity: Integrating the Behavioral Science and the Neuroscience of Mental Health*, edited by D. M. Hann, L. C. Huffman, K. K. Lederhendler, and D. Meinecke (Bethesda, Md.: National Institute of Mental Health, 1998).

25. Experiments by Murray and Trevarthen (1985) reported by Rogoff, *Apprenticeship in Thinking*, 75.

26. Grumet, *Bitter Milk*, 99.

27. D. J. Siegel, *The Developing Mind: Toward a Neurobiology of Interpersonal Experience* (New York and London: Guilford Press, 1999).

28. Siegel, *The Developing Mind*, 259.

29. Siegel, *The Developing Mind*, 68.

30. Zero to Three Task Force on Infrastructure, *Infants, Families and Communities: Strengthening Supports for Healthy Development* (Washington, D.C.: Author, May, 1999), 10.

31. J. Mehler et al., "A Precursor of Language Acquisition in Young Infants," *Cognition* 29 (1988): 143–78.

32. P. K. Kuhl, "The Development of Speech and Language," in *Mechanistic Relationships Between Development and Learning*, edited by T. J. Carew, R. Menzel, and C. J. Shatz (New York: Wiley, 1998), 53–73.

33. P. Bloom, "Overview: Controversies in Language Acquisition," in *Language Acquisition: Core Readings*, edited by P. Bloom (Cambridge, Mass.: MIT Press, 1993), 6–8.

34. E. M. Markman, "Constraints Children Place on Word Meanings," in *Language Acquisition: Core Readings*, edited by P. Bloom (Cambridge, Mass.: MIT Press, 1993), 154.

35. D. A. Phillips, *Written Testimony: Committee on Education and the Workforce, U.S. House of Representatives*, 31 July 2001, 6.

36. S. Pinker, *Words and Rules* (New York: Basic Books, 1999).

37. U.S. Department of Health and Human Service, *Mental Health*, 126.

38. D. A. Baldwin, "Infant Contributions to the Achievement of Joint Reference," in *Language Acquisition: Core Readings*, edited by P. Bloom (Cambridge, Mass.: MIT Press, 1993), 129–153.

39. K. Sylvester, "Caring for Our Youngest: Public Attitudes in the United States." Cited in Executive Summary, *Caring for Infants and Toddlers, The Future of Children* 11, no. 1 (2001): 3.

40. S. Farkas, A. Duffett, and J. Johnson, *Necessary Compromises: How Parents, Employers and Children's Advocates View Child Care Today* (New York: Public Agenda, 2000).

41. National Partnership for Women and Families, *Family Matters: A National Survey of Women and Men*, February 1998. See: www.nationalpartnership.org/survey/survey1.htm.

42. National Women's Law Center. To be eligible, employees must have worked for a covered employer for at least twelve months, and must have worked at least 1,250 hours over the previous twelve months. According to the National Women's Law Center, if the FMLA were expanded to cover employers with twenty-five or more employees, it would cover about 71 percent of the workforce.

43. U.S. Department of Labor, *Balancing the Needs of Families and Employers: The Family and Medical Leave Surveys 2000 Update* (Washington, D.C.: Author, 2001). See www.familyleavesurvey.homestead.com/FMLAStats.html.

44. Shonkoff and Phillips, *From Neurons to Neighborhoods*, 8–10.

45. National Women's Law Center, "There Is No Conflict Between Helping Working Families Meet Their Child Care Needs and Supporting 'Stay-at-Home' Parents," See: www.nwlc.org/details.cfm?id=49&section=childcare.

46. J. Ehrle, G. Adams, and K. Tout, *Who's Caring for Our Youngest Children? Child Care Patterns of Infants and Toddlers* (Washington, D.C.: Urban Institute, 2001).

47. J. Capizzano and G. Adams, *The Hours that Children Under Five Spend in Child Care: Variation Across States* (Washington, D.C.: Urban Institute, 2000).

48. Cost, Quality, and Child Outcomes Study Team, *Cost, Quality, and Child Outcomes in Child Care Centers* (Denver: University of Colorado, 1995).

49. Phillips, *Written Testimony*, 2.

50. M. Lamb, "Nonparental Child Care: Context, Quality, Correlates, and Consequences," *Handbook of Child Psychology*, vol. 4: *Child Psychology in Practice*, edited by W. Damon, I. E. Sigel, and K. A. Renninger (New York: John Wiley, 1998), 104.

51. NICHD Early Child Care Research Network, "Child Outcomes When Child Care Center Classes Meet Recommended Standards of Quality," *American Journal of Public Health* 89, no. 7 (1999): 1072–77.

52. C. Howes, "Children's Experiences in Center-Based Child Care as a Function of Teacher Background and Adult:Child Ratio," *Merrill-Palmer Quarterly* 43 (1997): 404–25.

53. M. R. Burchinal, J. E. Roberts, L. A. Nabors, and D. M. Bryant, "Quality of Center Child Care and Infant Cognitive and Language Development," *Child Development* 67 (1996): 606–20.

54. Howes, "Children's Experiences."

55. D. L. Vandell and B. Wolfe, *Child Care Quality: Does It Matter and Does It Need to Be Improved?* (Madison, Wisc.: University of Wisconsin Institute for Research on Poverty, 2000), 17.

56. National Association for the Education of Young Children, *Position Statement on Licensing and Public Regulation of Early Childhood Programs*, 1997, 5.

57. Cited in U.S. Office of Personnel Management, *Determining the Quality of Child Care*. See: www1.opm.gov/wrkfam/html/cchb502.html.

58. Vandell and Wolfe, *Child Care Quality: Does It Matter and Does It Need to Be Improved?*, 38.

59. R. Shore, *Our Basic Dream: Keeping Faith with America's Working Families and Their Children* (New York: Foundation for Child Development, 2000).

60. U.S. Consumer Product Safety Commission, *CPSC Staff Study of Safety Hazards in Child Care Settings* (Washington, D.C.: Author, 1999). See: www.cpsc.gov/library/ccstudy.html.

61. J. Capizzano and G. Adams, *The Number of Child Care Arrangements Used by Children Under Five: Variation Across States* (Washington, D.C.: Urban Institute, 2000).

62. Ehrle, Adams, and Tout, *Who's Caring*, 21.

63. E. M. Delaney, "The Administrator's Role in Making Inclusion Work," *Young Children* 565 (September 2001): 66–70.

64. A. Carr and M. J. Hanson, *Positive Outcomes for Children with Disabilities and Other Special Needs* (Rohnert Park, Calif.: California Institute on Human Services, 2001), 2.

65. E. Gilman and A. Collins, *Better Strategies for Babies: Strengthening the Caregivers and Families of Infants and Toddlers* (New York: National Center for Children in Poverty, 2000).

66. Brown-Lyons, Robertson, and Layzer, *Kith and Kin—Informal Child Care*, 21–23.

67. NICHD Early Child Care Research Network, "Characteristics of Infant Child Care: Factors Contributing to Positive Caregiving." *Early Childhood Research Quarterly* 11, no. 3, 269–306.

68. Center for the Child Care Workforce, *Current Data on Child Care Salaries and Benefits in the United States* (Washington, D.C.: Author, 2001).

69. T. Porter, *Neighborhood Child Care: Family, Friends, and Neighbors Talk About Caring for Other People's Children* (New York: Bank Street College of Education, 1998).

70. A. Collins and B. Carlson, *Child Care by Kith and Kin: Supporting Family, Friends, and Neighbors Caring for Children* (New York: National Center for Children in Poverty, 1998), 12.

71. Council of Economic Advisors, *The Economics of Child Care* (Washington, D.C.: Author, 1997).

72. J. Capizzano, G. Adams, and F. Sonenstein, *Child Care Arrangements for Children Under Five: Variation Across States* (Washington, D.C.: Urban Institute, 2000).

73. Porter, *Neighborhood Child Care*, 3.

74. Ehrle, Adams, and Tout, *Who's Caring*, 16.

75. Brown-Lyons, Robertson, and Layzer, *Kith and Kin—Informal Child Care*, 11.

76. Brown-Lyons, Robertson, and Layzer, *Kith and Kin—Informal Child Care*, 10.

77. Collins and Carlson, *Kith and Kin*, 6.

78. Collins and Carlson, *Kith and Kin*, 7.

79. Porter, *Neighborhood Child Care*.

80. Collins and Carlson, *Kith and Kin*, 13.

81. I. Sawhill, "Investing in Children." *Brookings Children's Roundtable* 1 (April 1999): 3. For a table summarizing findings on the share of low-income families' income spent on child care in various states, see J. Bernstein, C. Brocht, and M. Spade-Aguilar, *How Much Is Enough: Basic Family Budgets for Working Families* (Washington, D.C.: Economic Policy Institute, 2000). See also L. Stoney and M. Greenberg, "The Financing of Child Care: Current and Emerging Trends," *The Future of Children* 6, no. 2 (1996): 2–6.

82. L. Giannarelli and J. Barsimantov, *Child Care Expenses of America's Families* (Washington, D.C.: Urban Institute, 2000).

83. Bernstein, Brocht, and Aguilar, *How Much Is Enough*, 2000.

84. M. H. Greenberg, *Spend or Transfer, Federal or State? Considerations in Using TANF and TANF-Related Dollars for Child Care* (Washington, D.C.: Center for Law and Social Policy, 1998).

85. Sawhill, "Investing in Children."

86. L. Giannarelli and J. Barsimantov, *Child Care Expenses of America's Families* (Washington, D.C.: Urban Institute, 2000).

87. R. Schumacher and M. Greenberg, *Child Care After Leaving Welfare: Early Evidence from State Studies* (Washington, D.C.: Center for Law and Social Policy, 1999), 4.

88. Author's interview with Mark Greenberg, 22 March 2000.

89. R. Powell and M. Cahill, *Nowhere to Turn: New York City's Failure to Inform Parents on Public Assistance About Their Child Care Rights* (New York: NOW Legal Defense and Education Fund, 2000).

90. Schumacher and Greenberg, *Child Care After Leaving Welfare*.

91. M. Zaslow, K. Trout, S. Smith, and K. Moore, "Implications of the 1996 Welfare Legislation for Children: A Research Perspective" *Social Policy Report* 12, no. 3 (1998): 1–35.

92. J. M. Love et al., *Building Their Futures: How Early Head Start Programs Are Enhancing the Lives of Infants and Toddlers in Low-Income Families* (Princeton, N.J.: Mathematica, 2001).

93. R. Lally et al., "Caring for Infants and Toddlers in Groups: Developmentally Appropriate Practice," *Zero to Three*, 1995.

94. U.S. Consumer Product Safety Commission, CPSC *Staff Study of Safety Hazards in Child Care Settings* (Washington, D.C.: Author, 1999). See: www.cpsc.gov/library/ccstudy.html.

95. U.S. Consumer Product Safety Commission, *Safety Hazards in Child Care Settings* (Washington, D.C.: Author, 1997).

96. T. F. Tonniges, "Promoting Optimal Health in Child Care Settings," *Healthy Child Care America* 1, no. 3 (1997), 1–5.

97. Remarks by Eleanor Maccoby, "Roundtable: Infant Care and Child Development," The University of Texas at Dallas, March 1997.

3. The Preschool Years

1. OECD, OECD Country Note: *Early Childhood Education and Care Policy in the United States of America* (Paris: Author, February 2000), 47.

2. K. Schulman, H. Blank, and D. Ewen, *Seeds of Success: State Prekindergarten Initiatives 1998–1999* (Washington, D.C.: Children's Defense Fund, September 1999), 4.

3. Author's interview with Donna Bryant, 23 December 2000.

4. Anne W. Mitchell suggested this parallel in an interview conducted 9 January 2001.

5. National Center for Education Statistics, "Enrollment in Preprimary Education," *Condition of Education 2001*. (Washington, D.C.: Author, 2001), 6.

6. Ibid.

7. Presentation at a meeting on state early childhood initiatives convened by the Pew Charitable Trusts, 9 August 2001.

8. L. C. Huffman et al., *Off to a Good Start: Research on the Risk Factors for Early School Problems and Selected Federal Policies Affecting Children's Social and Emotional Development and Their Readiness for School* (Washington, D.C.: The Child Mental Health Foundations and Agencies Network, 2000).

9. A. W. Mitchell, cited in Hechinger Institute on Education and the Media, *A Journalist's Primer on Covering Prekindergarten Education* (New York: Teachers College, Columbia University, 1999). There were a few exceptions, notably New York, California, and Texas.

10. Cauthen, Knitzer, and Ripple, *Map and Track*.

11. Schulman, Blank, and Ewen, *Seeds of Success*, 1.

12. Cauthen, Knitzer, and Ripple, *Map and Track*.

13. D. Hinkle, *School Involvement in Early Childhood* (Washington, D.C.: U.S. Department of Education Office of Educational Research and Improvement, July 2000), 1.

14. Ibid.

15. Schulman, Blank, and Ewen, *Seeds of Success*.

16. Cauthen, Knitzer, and Ripple, *Map and Track*.

17. Carnegie Task Force on Learning in the Primary Grades, *Years of Promise: A Comprehensive Learning Plan for America's Children* (New York: Carnegie Corporation of New York, 1996).

18. Council of Chief State School Officers, *Early Childhood and Family Education* (Washington, D.C.: Author, 1999), 7.

19. Research and Policy Committee of the Committee for Economic Development, *Preschool for All: Investing in a Productive and Just Society* (New York: Author, 2002).

20. Press Release, Bell Labs Innovations in the News: Lucent Foundation's $1M Grant Supporting 13 Preschool Programs, 24 January 2000.

21. School Readiness Working Group, *Final Report to the Joint Committee to Develop a Master Plan for Education—Kindergarten Through University* (Sacramento: California Children and Families Commission, 2002).

22. A. Raden, *Universal Prekindergarten in Georgia: A Study of Georgia's Lottery-Funded Pre-K Program* (New York: Foundation for Child Development, 1999).

23. Ibid.

24. Schulman, Blank, and Ewen, *Seeds of Success*, 61.

25. J. J. Gallagher, J. R. Clayton, and S. E. Heinemeier, *Education for Four-Year-Olds: State Initiatives*, Executive Summary (Chapel Hill: University of North Carolina, FPG Child Development Center, National Center for Early Development and Learning, 2001), 3.

26. R. Shore, *Rethinking the Brain: New Insights into Early Development* (New York: Families and Work Institute, 1997). This report summarizes research re-

ported at a meeting of neuroscientists, behavioral scientists, educators, and human service providers that took place in Chicago, June 1996.

27. D. Edwards, "Public Factors That Contribute to School Readiness," *Early Childhood Research & Practice* 1, no. 2 (fall 1999); E. M. Lewit and L. Schuurmann Baker, "School Readiness," *Future of Children* 5, no. 2 (1995): 128–39.

28. M. S. Burns, P. Griffin, and C. E. Snow, eds., *Starting Out Right: A Guide to Promoting Children's Reading Success* (Washington, D.C.: National Academy Press, 1999), 5.

29. N. Baydar, J. Brooks-Gunn, and F. F. Furstenberg, 1993, cited in G. J. Whitehurst and J. E. Fischel, *Reading and Language Impairments in Conditions of Poverty* (Stony Brook: State University of New York at Stony Brook, 1999), 7.

30. F. E. Lentz, "Effective Reading Interventions in the Regular Classroom," in *Alternative Educational Delivery Systems: Enhancing Instructional Options for All Students,* edited by J. L. Graden, J. E. Zins, and M. J. Curtis (Washington, D. C.: National Association of School Psychologists, 1988).

31. Ewing Marion Kauffman Foundation, *Financing Child Care in the United States: An Illustrative Catalog of Current Strategies* (Kansas City: Author, 1999).

32. E. Boyer, *Ready to Learn: A Mandate for the Nation* (Princeton, N.J.: Princeton University Press, 1991).

33. Goal 1 Technical Planning Group, *Reconsidering Children's Early Development and Learning: Toward Common Views and Vocabulary* (Washington, D.C.: National Education Goals Panel, 1995).

34. R. Shore, *Ready Schools* (Washington, D.C.: The National Education Goals Panel, 1999).

35. National Bureau of Economic Research (1999), *Reducing Accidents Is Key to Lower Child Mortality,* www.nber.org/digest/dec99/glied.html, accessed 1 June 2001.

36. Federal Interagency Forum on Child and Family Statistics (1998), *America's Children: Key National Indicators Of Well-Being,* available at www.childstats.org; see also A. C. Kubisch, "On the Term Community: An Informal Contribution," in *Children and Their Families In Big Cities: Strategies for Service Reform,* edited by A. J. Kahn and S. B. Kamerman (New York: Columbia University School of Social Work, 1996).

37. Council of Chief State School Officers, *Early Childhood and Family Education,* 9.

38. A. L. den Ouden et al., "The Relation Between Neonatal Thyroxine Levels and Neurodevelopmental Outcome at Age 5 and 9 Years in a National Cohort

of Very Preterm and/or Very Low Birth Weight Infants," *Pediatric Residency* 39 (1996):142–45, cited in Huffman et al., *Off to a Good Start,* 62.

39. Huffman et al., *Off to a Good Start,* 11.

40. L. J. Platt and M. C. Cabezas, *Early Childhood Dental Caries* (Los Angeles: UCLA Center for Healthier Children, Families and Communities, 2000), 3.

41. J. Kozol, *Savage Inequalities: Children in America's Schools* (New York: Crown Publishers, 1991).

42. Platt and Cabezas, *Dental Caries,* 6.

43. J. L. Brown and E. Pollitt, "Malnutrition, Poverty and Intellectual Development" *Scientific American* (February 1996): 26–31; Center on Hunger, Poverty and Nutrition Policy, *Statement on the Link Between Nutrition and Cognitive Development in Children* (Medford, Mass.: Tufts University School of Nutrition Science and Policy, 1998); S. H. Venner, A. F. Sullivan, and D. Seavey, *Paradox of Our Times: Hunger in a Strong Economy* (Medford, Mass.: Center on Hunger and Poverty at Tufts University, 2000).

44. This is a major finding of Huffman et al., *Off to a Good Start.*

45. Huffman et al., *Off to a Good Start,* 11.

46. Ibid.

47. L. Baving, M. Laucht, and M. H. Schmidt, "Atypical Frontal Brain Activation in ADHD: preschool and Elementary School Boys and Girls," *Journal of American Academy of Child and Adolescent Psychiatry* 38, no. 11 (November 1999): 1363–71.

48. S. Neuwirth, *Attention Deficit Hyperactivity Disorder* (1994; reprint, Washington, D.C.: National Institute of Mental Health, 1996).

49. Office of the Surgeon General, *Mental Health: A Report of the Surgeon General* (Washington, D.C.: Author, 2000), 145–50.

50. M. Schleifer et al., "Hyperactivity in Preschoolers and the Effect of Methylphenidate," *American Journal of Orthopsychiatry* 45, no. 1 (January 1975): 38–50; B. L. Handen, H. M. Feldman, A. Lurier, and P. J. Murray, "Efficacy of Methylphenidate among Preschool Children with Developmental Disabilities and ADHD," *Journal of the American Academy of Child and Adolescent Psychiatry* 38, no.7 (July 1999): 805–12.

51. NIMH, *Attention Deficit Hyperactivity Disorder (ADHD)–Questions and Answers,* www.nimh.nih.gov/publicat/adhdqa.cfm, accessed on 3 January 2001.

52. J. T. Coyle, "Psychotropic Drug Use in Very Young Children," *JAMA* (23 February 2000): 1059–60.

53. *Mental Health: A Report of the Surgeon General.*

54. National Institute of Mental Health, *Developing, Testing and Implementing Innovative Interventions for* ADHD. RFA MH-00–005. 21 January 2000.

55. National Dropout Prevention Center website. According to NDPC, a growing body of research is confirming the benefits of prevention and early intervention. In fact, one of the most significant recent findings on dropouts is that early identification is vital to effective prevention. NDPC reports, "Social and task-related behavioral problems that develop into school adjustment problems can be identified at the beginning of the elementary grades. The dropout problem is not one that can be addressed exclusively at the middle or high school levels; by then it is too late for some students."

56. S. L. Kagan, E. Moore, and S. Bredekamp, eds., *Reconsidering Children's Early Development and Learning: Toward Common Views and Vocabulary* (Washington, D.C.: National Education Goals Panel, 1995), 4.

57. Kagan, Moore, and Bredekamp, eds., *Children's Early Development*, 28.

58. National Research Council, *Strategic Education Research Plan*, 1999.

59. National Research Council, *Strategic Education Research Plan*, 1999: 30–31.

60. National Research Council, *Preventing Reading Difficulties in Young Children*, 1998.

61. N. M. Astone and S. S. McLanahan, "Family Structure and High School Completion: The Role of Parental Practices," *American Sociological Review* 56, no. 3 (1991): 309–20; J. D. Finn, "Withdrawing from School," *Review of Educational Research* 59 (1989): 117–42.

62. D. R. Entwisle and L. A.Hayduk, *Early Schooling* (Baltimore, Md.: Johns Hopkins Press, 1982).

63. D. R. Entwisle and K. L. Alexander, "Early Schooling as a 'Critical Period' Phenomenon," in *Sociology of Education and Socialization*, edited by K. Namboodiri and R. G. Corwin (Greenwich, Conn.: JAI Press, 1989), 27–55; D. R. Entwisle and K. L. Alexander, "Entry into Schools: The Beginning School Transition and Educational Stratification in the United States," in *Annual Review of Sociology* 19 (Palo Alto, Calif.: Annual Reviews, 1993), 401–23.

64. J. West, K. Denton, and E. Germino-Hausken, *America's Kindergartners*.

65. R. S. New, "What Should Children Learn: Making Choices and Taking Chances," *Early Childhood Research and Practice* 1, no. 2 (fall 1999): 11.

66. G. Saluja, C. Scott-Little, and R. M. Clifford. "Readiness for School: A Survey of State Policies and Definitions," *Early Childhood Research and Practice* 2, no. 2 (fall 2000): 4.

67. For the National Association of School Psychologists position statement on early childhood assessment, see: www.nasponline.org/information/pospaper__eca.html.

68. L. Shapard, S. L. Kagan, and Emily Wurtz, eds., *Principles and Recommendations for Early Childhood Assessments* (Washington, D.C.: National Education Goals Panel, 1998).

69. E. Boyer, *Ready to Learn: A Mandate for the Nation* (Princeton, N.J.: Princeton University Press, 1991).

70. Communication from Donna Bryant, Study of kindergarten readiness in three states, 2000.

71. Kindergarten transitions, "NCEDL Spotlights [Online]," 1 (July 1998). www.fpg.unc.edu/~ncedl/PAGES/spotlt.htm.

72. Frank Porter Graham-University of North Carolina Smart Start Evaluation Team, *Kindergartners' Skills in Smart Start Counties in 1995: A Baseline from Which to Measure Change* (Chapel Hill: Author, 1997). See: www.fpg.unc.edu/~smartstart/KTC-REPweb.htm.

73. E. Zigler, "The Wrong Read on Head Start," *New York Times,* 23 December 2000.

74. Clark et al., cited in *America's Kindergartners: Findings from the Early Childhood Longitudinal Study, Kindergarten Class of 1998–99, Fall 1998,* edited by J. West, K. Denton, and E. Germino-Hausken (Washington, D.C.: U.S. Department of Education, NCES, 2000), 44.

75. Tramontana et al., 1988, cited in *America's Kindergartners,* edited by West, Denton, and Germino-Hausken.

76. Huffman et al., *Off to a Good Start,* 13.

77. Shore, *Ready Schools,* 5.

78. Shore, *Ready Schools,* 9.

79. Huffman et al., *Off to a Good Start,* 11–12.

80. M. E. Kraft-Sayre and R. C. Pianta, *Enhancing the Transition to Kindergarten: Linking Children, Families, and Schools* (Charlottesville, Va.: National Center for Early Development and Learning at the University of Virginia, 2000).

81. Carnegie Task Force, *Years of Promise,* 104–7.

82. Cited in Grumet, *Bitter Milk,* 140.

83. D. August and K. Hakuta, eds., *Improving Schooling for Language-Minority Children* (Washington, D.C.: National Academy Press, 1997).

84. J. Chall, *Learning to Read: The Great Debate* (New York: McGraw-Hill, 1967).

85. Burns, Griffin, and Snow, eds., *Starting Out Right,* 9.

86. Whitehurst and Fischel, *Reading and Language Impairments,* 5.

87. West, Denton, and Germino-Hausken, *America's Kindergartners,* 16.

88. This passage was selected by the president of the National Academy of Sciences, Bruce Alberts, and his wife Betty Alberts, to convey the magic of reading in his introduction to *Starting Out Right.* From L. Bemelmans, *Madeline* (New York: The Viking Press, 1939).

89. Whitehurst and Fischel, *Reading and Language Impairments,* 27.

90. Burns, Griffin, and Snow, eds., *Starting Out Right.*

91. Tramontana et al., *America's Kindergartners, 35.* Other studies show that although cognitive measures are more effective predictors of reading vocabulary, perceptual measures are better predictors of reading comprehension (Wallbrown et al., *America's Kindergartners,* 25).

92. Carnegie Task Force, *Years of Promise,* 105.

93. Emelie Parker, Fairfax County, Va., quoted in *Starting Out Right,* 134.

94. National Association for the Eeucation of Young Children. *Responding to Linguistic and Cultural Diversity: Recommendations for Effective Early Childhood Education.* (Washington, D.C.: Author, 1995.)

95. K. Alexander and D. Entwistle, "Achievement in the First Two Years of School: Patterns and Processes," *Monographs of the Society for Research in Child Development,* 218, 53, no. 2 (1998).

96. West, Denton, and Germino-Hausken, *America's Kindergartners,* 22.

97. Whitehurst and Fischel, *Reading and Language Impairments,* 23.

98. Whitehurst and Fischel, *Reading and Language Impairments,* 26.

99. August and Hakuta, eds., *Improving Schooling,* 59.

100. August and Hakuta, eds., *Improving Schooling.*

101. M. S. Burns, P. Griffin, and C. E. Snow, eds., *Preventing Reading Difficulties.*

102. S. J. Campos, "The Carpinteria Preschool Program: A Long-Term Effects Study," in *Meeting the Challenge of Linguistic and Cultural Diversity in Early Childhood Education,* edited by E. Garcia and B. McLaughlin (New York: Teacher's College, 1995).

103. August and Hakuta, eds., *Improving Schooling.*

104. D. Legarreta, "The Effects of Program Models on Language Acquisition by Spanish-Speaking Children," TESOL *Quarterly* 13, no. 4 (1979):521–34; J. Ramirez et al., *Final Report: Longitudinal Study of Structured English Immersion Strategy, Early-Exit and Late-Exit Transitional Bilingual Education Programs for Language Minority Students* (San Mateo, Calif.: Aguirre International, 1991).

105. August and Hakuta, eds., *Improving Schooling*, 179.

106. Burns, Griffin, and Snow, eds., *Starting Out Right*, 131–32.

107. Burns, Griffin, and Snow, eds., *Starting Out Right*, 133.

108. Vartan Gregorian, quoted in Burns, Griffin, and Snow, eds., *Starting Out Right*, vii.

109. Grumet, *Bitter Milk*, 149.

110. Carnegie Task Force, *Years of Promise*, 64.

111. Burns, Griffin, and Snow, eds., *Starting Out Right*, 44.

112. Grumet, *Bitter Milk*, 142.

113. Steve Barnett, cited in Hechinger Institute, 1999, 4.

114. Ibid.

115. Hinkle, *School Involvement*, 1, cites work by Entwisle, 1995.

116. Ibid.

117. A. J. Reynolds, J. A. Temple, D. L. Robertson, and E. A. Mann, "Long-term Effects of an Early Childhood Intervention on Educational Achievement and Juvenile Arrest: A 15-Year Follow-up of Low-Income Children in Public Schools," *JAMA* 285 (2001): 2339–46.

118. Groginsky, Robinson, and Smith, *State Initiatives*, 23–25.

119. Groginsky, Robinson, and Smith, *State Initiatives*, 29; *Georgia Pre-K Program Study: Prekindergarten Longitudinal Study 1997–98 School Year, Report 2, Summary of Findings* (Atlanta, Ga.: Georgia State University, Applied Research Center, 1999).

120. Schulman, Blank, and Ewen, *Seeds of Success*, 175–77 (appendix A).

121. Interview with Donna Bryant, 23 December 2000.

122. NAEYC position statement, in S. B. Neumann, C. Copple, and S. Bredecamp, *Learning to Read and Write: Developmentally Appropriate Practices for Young Children* (Washington, D.C.: National Association for the Education of Young Children, 2000), 5.

123. D. Edwards, "Public Factors That Contribute to School Readiness," *Early Childhood Research & Practice* 1, no. 2 (fall 1999).

124. NAS, *Eager to Learn*, 12–14.

125. Schulman, Blank, and Ewen, *Seeds of Success*, 85–88.

126. Whitebrook and Phillips, *Child Care Employment*.

127. Cohn, 48.

128. Whitebrook and Phillips, *Child Care Employment*.

129. M. Whitebrook, L. Sakai, E. Gerber, and C. Howes, *Then & Now: Changes in Child Care Staffing, 1994–2000* (Washington, D.C.: Center for the

Child Care Workforce and Institute of Industrial Relations, University of California at Berkeley, 2001).

130. Current Data on Child Care Salaries and Benefits in the United States. March 2000. Center for the Child Care Workforce, 7.

131. Whitebrook and Phillips, *Child Care Employment.*

4. Common Ground, Higher Ground

1. R. Marshall, introduction to *Back to Shared Prosperity*, edited by R. Marshall (Armonk, N.Y.: M. E. Sharpe, 2000).

2. Annie E. Casey Foundation, *The Right Start: Conditions of Babies and Their Families across the Nation and in America's Largest Cities* (Baltimore: Author, 2001).

3. Ibid.

4. Charles Bruner provided this analysis by the Child and Family Policy Center of Kids Count data for the city of Chicago. See C. Bruner and S. Scott, *The Effects of Concentrated Child Poverty on Child Welfare Policy and Practice—Implications from Chicago Kids Count Data and Interviews with Foster Children* (Des Moines, Iowa: Child and Family Policy Center, National Center for Service Integration, 1994).

5. J. L. Aber, M. A. Gephart, J. Brooks-Bunn, and J. P. Connell, "Development in Context: Implications for Studying Neighborhood Effects," in *Neighborhood Poverty: Context and Consequences for Children* (New York: Russell Sage Foundation, 1997).

6. Furstenberg, *The Effects of Welfare Reform on the Family.*

7. R. J. Sampson, S. W. Raudenbush, and F. Earls, "Neighborhoods and Violent Crime: A Multilevel Study of Collective Efficacy." *Science Magazine* 277 (15 August 1997): 5328.

8. See statements by Michael H. Levine, quoted in Dombro et al., *Community Mobilization: Strategies to Support Young Children and Their Families* (New York: Families and Work Institute, 1996), 2.

9. L. Schorr, *Common Purpose: Strengthening Families and Neighborhoods to Rebuild America* (New York: Anchor Books/Doubleday, 1997).

10. A. L. Dombro et al., *Community Mobilization*, 8.

11. Cited by L. Schorr, *Common Purpose*, introduction.

12. Quoted in C. Dahle, "Social Justice—Ernesto Cortes, Jr," *Fast Company* 30, no. 294 (December 1999).

13. C. Weiss, "Nothing as Practical as a Good Theory: Exploring Theory-Based Evaluation for Comprehensive Community Initiatives for Children and Families," in *New Approaches to Evaluating Community Initiatives,* edited by J. Connell, A. Kubisch, L. Schorr, and C. Weiss (New York: The Aspen Institute, 1995); C. Coulton and R. Hollister, "Measuring Comprehensive Community Initiative Outcomes Using Data Available for Small Areas," in *New Approaches to Evaluating Community Initiative,* vol. 2: *Theory, Measurement and Analysis,* edited by K. Fulbright-Anderson, A. Kubisch, and J. Connell (Washington, D.C.: The Aspen Institute, 1998).

14. P. Dreier, "Community Empowerment Strategies: The Limits and Potential of Community Organizing in Urban Neighborhoods," *Cityscape: A Journal of Policy Development and Research* 2, no. 2 (1996): 120–50, 127. See: www.huduser.org/periodicals/citiscpe/vol2num2/dreier.pdf.

15. Author's interview with Jeff Kirsch, 31 January 2002.

16. Schrayer and Associations, Inc., *Organizing Parents: Strategies for the Children's Community* (Washington, D.C.: The Children's Partnership, 1999).

17. C. Bruner and L. Parachini, *Building Community: Exploring New Relationships Across Service Systems Reform, Community Organizing, and Community Economic Development* (Washington, D.C.: Together We Can, 1998).

18. W. A. Morrill, "Overview of Service Delivery to Children," in R. E. Behrnian, ed., *The Future of Children: School-linked Services* 2 (1992):32–43.

19. Personal communication from Charles Bruner, July 2001; F. Farrow, S. Watson, and L. Schorr, *A Framework for Improving Outcomes for Children and Families: Family Resource Coalition Report,* 3 and 4 (Chicago, Ill.: Family Resource Coalition, 1993–94).

20. R. Halpern, *Tying Family Development and Community Development Closer Together* (Baltimore, Md.: Annie E. Casey Foundation, 1998).

21. *Building Their Futures: How Early Head Start Programs Are Enhancing the Lives of Infants and Toddlers in Low-Income Families,* vol. 1: Technical Report June 2001. See: www.acf.dhhs.gov/programs/core/ongoing__research/ehs/ehs__intro.html.

22. D. Tyack, "Choice Options," *The American Prospect* 10, no. 42 (1 January–1 February 1999): 19.

23. Committee for Economic Development, *Putting Learning First: Governing and Managing the Schools of High Achievement* (New York: Author, 1994), 6.

24. National Black Child Development Institute, *Safeguards: Guidelines for Establishing Child Development Programs for 4-Year-Olds in Public Schools* (Wash-

ington, D.C.: Author), cited in M. Finn-Stevenson and E. Zigler, *Schools of the 21st Century: Linking Child Care and Education* (Boulder, Colo.: Westview Press, 1999), 68–70.

25. Finn-Stevenson and Zigler, *Schools of the 21st Century.*

26. Shore, *Ahead of the Curve,* ix.

27. R. Rapoport and L. Bailyn, *Relinking Life and Work: Toward a Better Future* (New York: Ford Foundation, 1996).

28. E. Galinsky and J. T. Bond, *The 1998 Business Work-Life Study* (New York: Families and Work Institute, 1998), xi-xii.

29. Reported in J. Cohn, "Child's Play," *The American Prospect* 11, no. 15 (19 June–3 July 2000): 48.

30. Shore, *Ahead of the Curve,* 24.

31. M. Blood and M. Ludtke, *Business Leaders as Legislative Advocates for Children* (New York: Foundation for Child Development, 1999).

32. Sazer O'Donnell and Galinsky, *Seven Lessons.*

33. L. Grundy, L. Bell, and N. Firestein, *Labor's Role* in *Addressing the Child Care Crisis* (New York: Foundation for Child Development, 1999), 13.

34. R. A. Cnaan and G. Yancey, *Sacred Places at Risk: New Evidence on How Endangered Older Churches and Synagogues Serve Communities* (Philadelphia: University of Pennsylvania Center for Research on Religion and Urban Civil Society, 1997).

35. For further information, see: www.pfc.org/question.shtml.

36. D. Murphey, *The Social Well-Being of Vermonters 2000: A Report on Outcomes for Vermont's Citizens* (Waterbury: Vermont Agency of Human Services, 2000); C. D. Hogan, *Vermont Communities Count: Using Results to Strengthen Services for Families and Children* (Baltimore, Md.: The Annie E. Casey Foundation, 2000).

37. Carnegie Task Force on Learning in the Primary Grades, *Years of Promise: A Comprehensive Learning Strategy for America's Children* (New York, Carnegie Corporation of New York, 1996).

38. S. L. Kagan and N. E. Cohen, *Not By Chance: Final Report of the Quality 2000 Initiative* (New Haven: Yale University Bush Center in Child Development and Social Policy, 1997).

39. This research is summarized in Annie E. Casey Foundation, *Kids Count* (Baltimore: Author, 2000), introduction.

40. C. Bruner, *Where's the Beef? Getting Bold About What 'Comprehensive' Means* (Des Moines, Ia.: Child and Family Policy Center, October 1995).

5. The Agenda for Change

1. Shonkoff and Phillips, *From Neurons to Neighborhoods*, 384.

2. M. K. Meyers et al., *Public Policies*.

3. A. C. Kubisch, "On the Term Community: An Informal Contribution," in *Children and Their Families in Big Cities: Strategies for Service Reform*, edited by A. J. Kahn and S. B. Kamerman (New York: Columbia University School of Social Work, 1996).

4. B. H. Singer and C. D. Ryff, eds., *New Horizons In Health: An Integrative Approach* (Washington, D.C.: National Academy Press, 2001).

5. National Women's Law Center, *Be All That We Can Be: Lessons from the Military for Improving Our Nation's Child Care System* (Washington, D.C.: Author, 2000); M.-A. Lucas, "The Military Child Care Connection," *Future of Children* 11, no. 1 (spring/summer 2001):129–33.

6. D. A. Phillips, *Written Testimony to the Committee on Education and the Workforce*, U.S. House of Representatives, 31 July 2001, 2. Phillips stated that striking differences can be discerned by age two.

7. West, Denton, and Germino-Hausken, *America's Kindergartners*.

8. Shonkoff and Phillips, *From Neurons to Neighborhoods*, 388.

9. U.S. Department of Health and Human Services, *Racial and Ethnic Disparities in Infant Mortality* (Washington, D.C.: HHS Office of Minority Health, 2001).

10. National Center for Education in Maternal and Child Health, *Knowledge Path: Infant Mortality* (June 2000). See: www.ncemch.org/RefDes/infmort KP.html.

11. Singer and Ryff, *New Horizons in Health*.

12. Forste, J. Weiss, and E. Lippincott, "The Decision to Breast Feed in the United States: Does Race Matter?" *Pediatrics* 108, no. 2 (2001): 291–96.

13. P. L. Culross, D. S. Gomby, and R. E. Behrman, "Home Visiting: Recent Program Evaluations—Analysis and Recommendations," *Future of Children* 9, no. 1 (spring/summer 1999).

14. K. Johnson, *No Place Like Home: State Home Visiting Policies and Programs* (New York: Commonwealth Fund, 2001).

15. Council of Chief State School Officers, *Early Childhood and Family Education*, 14.

16. Shonkoff and Phillips, *From Neurons to Neighborhoods*, 396.

17. S. Farkas, A. Duffett, and J. Johnson, *Necessary Compromises: How Parents,*

Employers and Children's Advocates View Child Care Today (New York: Public Agenda, 2000).

18. Shonkoff and Phillips, *From Neurons to Neighborhoods*, 392.

19. Shore, *Our Basic Dream*, 53.

20. D. Friedman, "Employer Supports for Parents with Young Children," *Future of Children* 11, no. 1 (spring/summer 2001): 63–78.

21. American Academy of Pediatrics, "Scope of Health Care Benefits for Newborns, Infants, Children, Adolescents, and Young Adults Through Age 21 Years." *Pediatrics* 100 (December 1997): 6.

22. American Academy of Pediatrics, *An Analysis of the Costs to Provide Health Care Coverage to Children and Adolescents*, 1998. Available at www.aap.org/advocacy/towers/cstover.htm.

23. U.S. Department of Health and Human Services, *Healthy People 2010: Understanding and Improving Health*, 2nd ed. (Washington, D.C.: Author, 2000).

24. The American Academy of Pediatrics has developed an "Every Child Deserves a Medical Home" training program which is available free of charge to any individual or organization. See: www.aap.org/advocacy/medhome/cirfree-materials.htm.

25. Zero to Three, *New Visions for the Developmental Assessment of Infants and Young Children* (Washington, D.C.: Author, 1996); Zero to Three, *Infants, Families and Communities: Strengthening Supports for Healthy Development: A Report to the David and Lucile Packard Foundation*. (Washington, D.C.: Author, 1999).

26. J. Knitzer, *Building Services and Systems to Support the Healthy Emotional Development of Young Children—An Action Guide for Policymakers* (New York: National Center for Children in Poverty, 2002).

27. Physicians for Human Rights, *Hunger at Home: A Study of Food Insecurity and Hunger among Legal Immigrants in the United States* (Boston: Author, 2000).

28. Recent findings of the NICHD study are summarized in C. M. Todd, *The NICHD Child-Care Study Results: What Do They Mean for Parents, Child-Care Professionals, Employers and Decision Makers?* (National Network for Child Care, 2001). See: http://www.nncc.org/Research/NICHD.ECIresponse.html.

29. Mitchell and Shore, *Next Steps*. See also A. W. Mitchell, *The Role of States and the Federal Government in Promoting Prekindergaren and Kindergarten* (New York: Foundation for Child Development, 2001).

30. See: Zero to Three, *Heart Start: The Emotional Foundations of School Readiness* (Washington, D.C.: Author, 1994); National Education Goals Panel Goal 1 Technical Planning Group, *Reconsidering Children's Early Development and*

Learning: Toward Common Views and Vocabulary (Washington, D.C.: National Education Goals Panel, 1995); Huffman, Mehlinger, and Kerivan, *Off to a Good Start*.

31. International Reading Association and National Association for the Education of Young Children, Overview of *Learning to Read and Write: Developmentally Appropriate Practices for Young Children: A Joint Position of the IRA and NAEYC*, adopted May 1998. See: www.naeyc.org/resources/position__statements/psread-o.htm.

32. August and Hakuta, *Improving Schooling for Language-Minority Children*.

33. Vandell and Wolfe, *Child Care Quality: Does It Matter and Does It Need to Be Improved?*; D. Phillips and G. Adams, *"Child Care and Our Youngest Children," Future of Children* 11, no. 1 (spring/summer 2001):35–51.

34. Shonkoff and Phillips, *From Neurons to Neighborhoods*, 393.

35. Reynolds et al., "Long-term Effects of an Early Childhood Intervention on Educational Achievement and Juvenile Arrest."

36. Council of Chief State School Officers, *Early Childhood and Family Education*, 11.

37. R. Shore, *Ready Schools* (Washington, D.C.: National Education Goals Panel, 1998).

38. Kagan and Cohen, *Not By Chance*.

39. Council of Chief State School Officers, *Early Childhood and Family Education*, 5.

40. National Association for the Education of Young Children, *Position Statement on Licensing and Public Regulation of Early Childhood Programs*, 1997, 5.

41. K. Sylvester, *Listening to Families* (New York: Carnegie Corporation of New York, 2001); Dufett, Johnson, and Farkas, *Kids These Days*.

42. "Public Agenda," survey for the Ad Council and Ronald McDonald House Charities, 1998. See: www.publicagenda.org/issues/angles__graph.cfm?issue__type=family&id=408&graph=rf7.gif.

ACKNOWLEDGMENTS

This book builds on decades of work by Carnegie Corporation of New York to gather, convey, and act on knowledge about how children learn and what they need for healthy development. These efforts involved many more people—researchers, practitioners, and policymakers—than can be acknowledged here. Many of these individuals took part in task forces that produced the two major Carnegie reports on young children that preceded this one: *Starting Points: Meeting the Needs of Our Youngest Children* (1994) and *Years of Promise: A Comprehensive Learning Plan for America's Children* (1996). These reports helped to shape a decade of policy and practice in the early childhood field.

What Kids Need was also informed by the work and perspectives of many authorities in the early childhood field. Many thanks to the colleagues who reviewed the manuscript in its entirety and offered invaluable suggestions: Sharon Lynn Kagan, Joan Lombardi, Kathryn Taaffe McLearn, and Deborah A. Phillips. Individual chapters were reviewed by Rebecca Barrera, Charles Bruner, Ellen Galinsky, Evelyn Moore, Julius B. Richmond, Jack Shonkoff, Kathleen Sylvester, Susan Zelman, and Edward Zigler. Many of their insights are reflected in the pages that follow. However, any errors or omissions are mine alone.

Strands of conversation with other colleagues and advisors thread through this book. Among them are Gina Adams, T. Berry Brazelton, Donna Bryant, Mark Greenberg, Scott Groginsky, Madeleine Grumet, Jane Knitzer, John Love, Anne Mitchell, David Olds, Marjorie Petruska, and Ruby Takanishi.

These individuals represent some of today's best thinking about early child-hood and education. Nevertheless, the manuscript informed by their collective wisdom might have remained in a filing cabinet on Madison Avenue if not for the decision by Carnegie Corporation's officers to sustain a project that could easily have been put aside during a change in the foundation's administration and direction. I want to thank President Vartan Gregorian for his conviction that the Corporation's work in early childhood needed to reach a wide audience. The foreword he contributed to this volume applies to young children the question he has explored throughout a distinguished career in academia and philanthropy: what does it mean to be an educated person?

I am grateful to Susan King, Carnegie's vice president for public affairs. It was her initiative that resulted in publication of *What Kids Need* by Beacon Press. Other Carnegie Corporation officers and staff, including Daniel Fallon, Neil R. Grabois, Andrés Henríquez, and Eleanor Lerman, have offered consistent counsel and encouragement and made substantive contributions to the project. Sara Wolpert was a steady, patient support over many years. Maggie Vargas and Valerie Vitale were extremely helpful as well.

I also want to acknowledge former Carnegie Corporation officers and staff who originated and sustained the line of work that culminated in *What Kids Need*. During his tenure as president of Carnegie Corporation, David A. Hamburg articulated a vision of a nation committed to children's healthy development and oversaw grantmaking initiatives geared to realizing that vision. Along with Barbara D. Finberg, Vivien Stewart, Avery Russell, Susan V. Smith, and senior consultant Judith E. Jones, he was instrumental in launching this project. I want to acknowledge, in particular, all that I have learned from my long association and friendship with Michael Levine, former Carnegie senior program officer. The idea of reporting on a decade of progress in the early childhood field was his, and our continuing conversation about this project in particular and the early childhood field in general is reflected in every chapter of this book.

Many thanks to our friends at Beacon Press. Deb Chasman saw that a book could be carved out of the massive report that landed on her desk and did some chipping away of her own. The task of recasting the report as a book was entrusted primarily to editor Patricia Mulcahy, who did so with unusual delicacy and respect for the material. Managing editor David Coen and copyeditor Doug Colglazier were remarkably patient and helpful. Thanks, too, to Julie Hassel.

Alesh Bradac, Nidhi Chaudhary, and Peter Novobatzky provided careful assistance with research.

Acknowledgments [263]

What Kids Need benefited from daily interactions with two experts on the subject, Daniel Greenwald and Alex Schwartz. It reflects conversation, over many years, with Barbara Shore, Bradd Shore, and Ken Shore. My mother, Florence K. Shore, read and commented on every chapter. The mother of five, owner of a small business, and a founder in her spare time of a cooperative nursery school, a community mental health center, and a newspaper that campaigned for greater public investment in education, she inspired all of her children to think inventively and compassionately about what kids need.

Finally, my greatest debt is to Adria Schwartz. This book is dedicated to her.

Rima Shore

INDEX